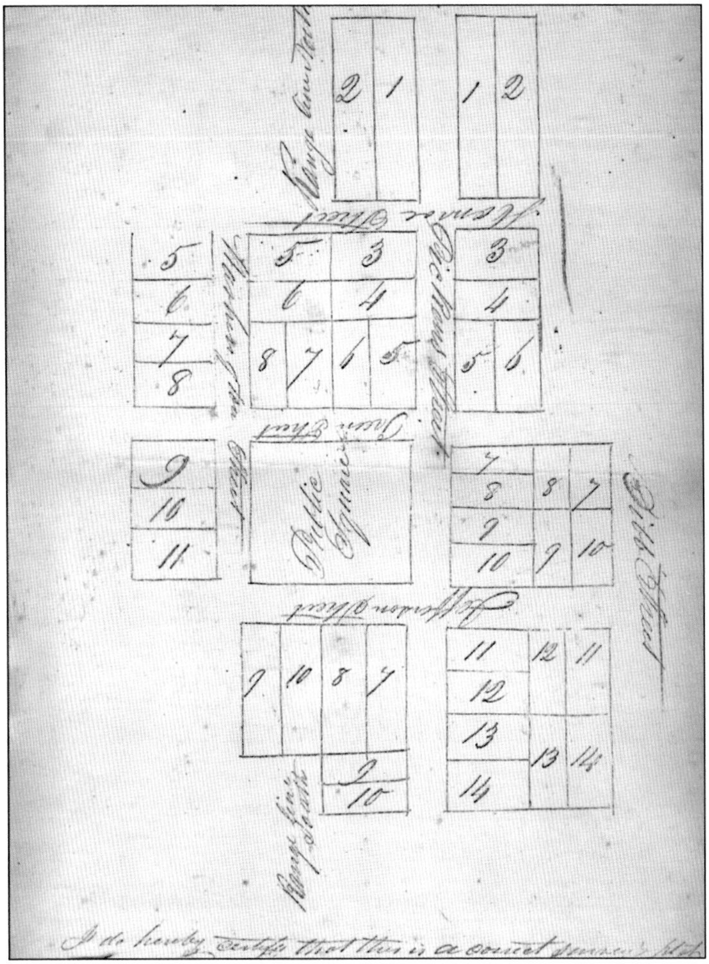

This is the earliest map of the city of Marion. It is dated 1824 and is recorded in Deed Book A, page 251, in the probate office in the Perry County Courthouse. Marion began as Muckle's Ridge, but when it was chosen as the county seat in 1822, several of the citizens, including Joseph Evans, Anderson West, Dr. Alexander, William Moore, and George Weissinger, met to discuss an appropriate name for the new county seat. After much discussion over various names, Marion was chosen in honor of Gen. Francis Marion, the "Swamp Fox" of the American Revolution. Anderson West had previously sold lots in the new town. Some time after this, a survey was made of the town and filed in the appropriate county record book. The street names are still in place today. Also note that a range line runs through the town. (Courtesy of the Perry County Historical and Preservation Society.)

ON THE COVER: Pictured is a scene from 1880 at Judson Female Institute, founded in 1838 by the Baptists of Marion as a school for young women. The Alabama Legislature authorized the school to award degrees in 1841. In 1843, the owners deeded the school to the Alabama Baptist State Convention. It has operated under the auspices of that body ever since. In 1904, it became Judson College by act of the state legislature. It continues to be a school for young women in 2010. In the cover scene, Dr. Luther Rice Gwaltney, president, is seen talking with Mrs. J. M. Peterson, a governess at the school. Dr. Gwaltney had come to Judson in 1876 as president and remained as such until 1882, when he accepted the presidency of Shorter College in Georgia. The others in the photograph are faculty and students. (Courtesy of the Judson College Archives.)

IMAGES
of America

PERRY COUNTY

Eleanor C. Drake

ARCADIA
PUBLISHING

ISBN 978-0-7385-8662-5

Published by Arcadia Publishing
Charleston, South Carolina

Printed in the United States of America

Library of Congress Control Number: 2010927327

For all general information, please contact Arcadia Publishing:
Telephone 843-853-2070
Fax 843-853-0044
E-mail sales@arcadiapublishing.com
For customer service and orders:
Toll-Free 1-888-313-2665

Visit us on the Internet at www.arcadiapublishing.com

Over the years, my husband, Walton, has supported me in all my "projects," and it is to him that I wish to dedicate this book.

Contents

ACKNOWLEDGMENTS

My sincere thanks go to all who have helped with this work—groups as well as individuals. It would not have been possible without the support of the Perry County Historical and Preservation Society (PCHPS) and Paul Reitzer, the curator of its museum. Likewise, the Judson College Archives (JCA), Samford University (SU), Lincoln Museum (LM), Alabama Women's Hall of Fame (AWHOF), Alabama Military Hall of Honor (AMHOH), and the Marion Military Institute Foundation (MMIFA) have provided much material. We are still getting calls with the offer of pictures from individuals. Again, my sincere thanks go to all who have contributed to this book in any way. A special thanks goes to those who made the effort to see that our history was preserved for future generations. To Bill Mathews, a fellow laborer in work and in local historical research, I cannot say thank you enough. Without you, there would be no book. Even though neither of us are natives of Perry County, we have come to love the place and people—past and present. To the board members of the Perry County Historical Society, thank you for your support and interest over the past few months.

INTRODUCTION

As you explore Perry County today, you may find fossils of sea creatures and other marine life from the time when part of the area was covered by ocean. This sea coverage led to the formation of the area in the southern part of the county called the Black Belt, known for it rich black soil. Even as early as 1844, these fossils were noted in Samuel A. Townes's *History of Marion, Alabama*. The northern part of the county is hilly and has a sandy loam soil.

The first inhabitants of the area were the Native Americans. Remains believed to be 500 to 700 years old have been found north of Marion in the Heiberger area. Even though the area belonged to the Creeks, the Choctaws squatted here. Quite a few of the names of creeks and rivers are of Choctaw origin. Much of Perry County served as hunting grounds for them. Arrowheads can still be found in the open fields of the area. The Choctaws had a large town near the Cahaba River and another at Cahaba Old Town. By the Treaty of Fort Jackson on August 9, 1814, the Creeks ceded a large portion of their land to the United States. Present-day Perry County was a part of this land, and the treaty opened the area to settlement.

The first settlers in the Marion area came about 1816. These early settlers included the Naves, Brocks, Durdens, Olivers, Reids, Means, and Wests. A son-in-law of Nathan Reid, Michael McElroy or Muckle, settled in the area that became known as Muckle's Ridge and later as Marion. Murrell, a young son of Thomas Oliver, was purported to have been kidnapped by Native Americans. Evidently he was returned to his parents, for his name appears on quite a number of land records in the late 19th century. Cotton was grown in this early period, causing cotton gins to be in operation by 1817. In 1818, the Wood brothers—Robert, Henry, and James—settled near what would become Uniontown.

Alabama Territory was created in 1817, and it became a state on December 14, 1819. The day before statehood, the Alabama Legislature created six new counties, including Perry County. The county was named in honor of Commodore Oliver Hazard Perry, a naval hero of the War of 1812. Though county lines changed several times over the next 50 years, no noticeable changes have been made since 1867. The county seat was originally located at Perry Ridge, but in 1822, it was moved to Muckle's Ridge. Town lots were sold, and soon afterward, its name was changed to Marion in honor of Gen. Francis Marion of Revolutionary War fame. There have been three courthouses since 1822, all on the same lot, with the last one built in 1856.

Over the next 10 to 15 years, Marion began to evolve from a frontier town to one of peaceful surroundings with churches, businesses (many started by settlers from northeastern states), schools, and other trappings that made for a quiet, cultured life. Settlers and businessmen of the period were not only from southern states but also from Connecticut and Vermont, as well as direct from Scotland and Ireland. Siloam Baptist Church was organized in 1822, and Methodists and Presbyterians had a presence in Marion by 1832. After the auction of town lots in 1822, town commissioners specified that 4 acres of land north of Lafayette Street be used for churches and the adjacent 4 acres be used as a graveyard. The local churches first met here, and they later purchased lots in other parts of town upon which to erect their buildings.

To the south, settlers began moving into the Woodville area, where the Wood brothers were residing. Records show Henry Wood living on the post road from Cahaba to the Falls of the Cahaba—present-day Centreville. Evidently the settlers were unable to get the post office named Woodville, so the surrounding area became known as Uniontown and was incorporated as such in 1836. Before 1844, Dr. C. W. Woodruff stated that the "decomposition of vegetables or animal matter, induced by moisture and heat" in the southern part of the county made the area unhealthy for human habitation. Once it was determined that this was not the case, settlers began to arrive. When it was discovered that the Black Belt soil was just right for growing cotton, there was a great influx of settlers from Virginia and the Carolinas.

As cotton became king, schools were organized, plantation homes were built, slave ownership increased, the wealth of the citizenry increased, and the standard of living grew. In fact, when Alabama's state capital was moved from Tuscaloosa to Montgomery, Marion was one of the towns considered for the capital.

In 1836, Marion citizens established the Marion Female Seminary, which closed its doors in 1915. In 1838, Judson Female Institute was organized by Baptist leaders in Marion. These leaders deeded the school to the Alabama Baptist State Convention in 1843. After several fires and other setbacks, Judson College is alive and well in Marion. Howard College, a school for men, was established by Baptists in 1841. It moved to East Lake (Birmingham) in 1887 and today is known as Samford University. Marion Military Institute replaced it in the existing facilities. The institute operates in Marion today as the state's only two-year military school. In the 1840s, Uniontown had a "School House and Free Church" using the same building. The county had various academies for boys and girls during the 19th century. For a while, the William R. King Female College operated in Uniontown.

In 1867, the American Missionary Association, an auxiliary of the Congregationalist Church, joined local blacks in operating a school in Marion. It had a primary and normal school for the children and young people of the area. In 1874, Alabama assumed responsibility for the normal department of the school, which had been named Lincoln Normal School. After an 1887 fire destroyed the normal school building, it was moved to Montgomery and became the state normal school. It is known today as Alabama State University. The primary school continued operation. When Mary Elizabeth Phillips came to Lincoln as principal in 1896, the school continued to grow. When she died in 1927, there were 596 students from kindergarten through the 12th grade and 26 teachers. The campus was spacious, and the school had a 40-acre farm. After Phillips's death, Phillips Memorial Auditorium was erected. This is the only remaining building on the Lincoln campus. The school operated until 1972, when integration brought about the merger of county schools.

Perry County was early embroiled in the Civil War, since one of its native sons, Andrew Barry Moore, was governor of the state from 1858 to 1862. He authorized the seizure of federal forts along the coast and the federal arsenal at Mount Vernon. Another Marion citizen, William Maclin Brooks, served as president of the Alabama Secession Convention. Governor Moore approached his friend Mary Lockett about the need for a flag for the Confederate states. At that time, Nicola Marschall, a Prussian artist and musician, was teaching at the Marion Female Seminary. Mary Lockett asked Marschall to design a flag for the Confederacy. The flag, known as the Stars and Bars, was sewn in the front parlor of the Lockett home by ladies of the town, who also provided the material for the flag. Marschall is also credited with designing the Confederate uniform. Perry County furnished many soldiers for the South. In 1863, the Confederacy established the Breckenridge Division Hospital in the buildings of Howard College. Officers commanding the hospital in Marion were Dr. William Augustus Evans and Dr. James McCown Greene. Soldiers who died were buried to the rear of the college buildings, and in 1871, the Ladies' Memorial Association of Marion had the bodies moved and re-interred at St. Wilfrid's Cemetery. Union troops were stationed in Marion and Uniontown after the war.

For many years, even after the Civil War, cotton was king in Perry County. Gins dotted the countryside in the smaller communities of the county as well as in Marion. By the beginning of the 20th century, Uniontown had a cotton mill with its mill village, stores, a school, and churches along with supporting industries such as cotton oil mills, cotton seed industries, a rope mill, warehouses, and other businesses. The cotton mill left Uniontown in 1954. Today, cattle and catfish have replaced cotton.

As the activities for equal rights become more prevalent in the 1960s, Perry County citizens became more involved. In 1965, Jimmy Lee Jackson was shot in Marion by James B. Fowler, an Alabama state trooper assigned to Marion to help keep order during this troubled time. Jackson died as a result of the shot. This incident provided the basis for the Selma to Montgomery March. It had been scheduled to begin in Marion, but the starting point was changed to Selma. Perry County was also the site of two weddings that brought it closer to the civil rights movement. Jean Childs of Marion married Andrew Young at the Congregationalist church, and Coretta Scott married Martin Luther King Jr. at her home church in North Perry County.

One

The Western Frontier

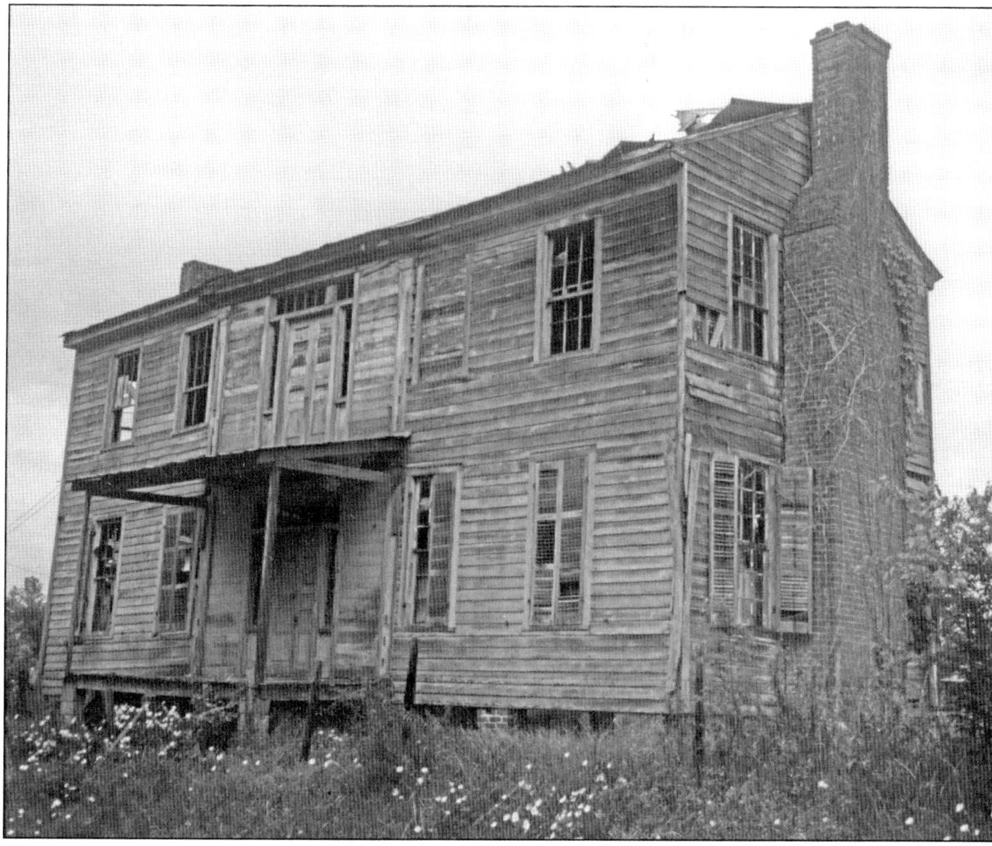

This stagecoach stop once offered hospitality to visitors on the road from Cahaba to Marion and Greensboro. As early as 1825, the owner of the property was granted a license to sell liquor. This old inn was located south of Marion on Perry County Road 45, across from Gus Mitchell's old store. The building, abandoned and dilapidated, collapsed around 1975. (MMIFA.)

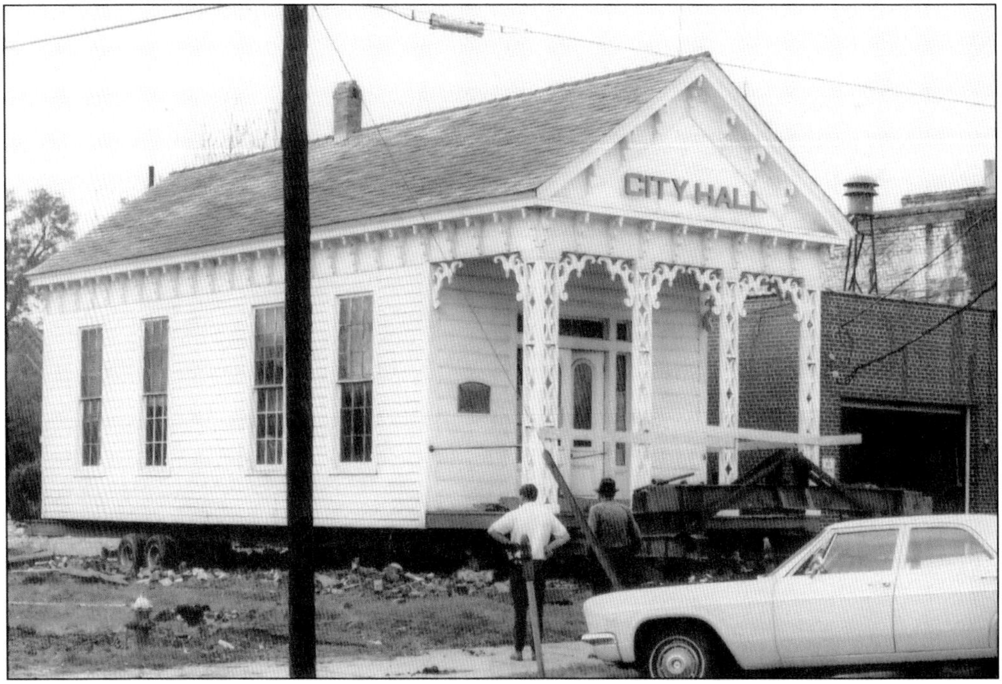

This building was originally built on the town square by John Lockhart to serve as his law office. It was the first building owned by a Young Men's Christian Association in the South. It served many purposes until it was purchased by the City of Marion in 1928 for use as a city hall. In 1968, it was moved to the campus of Marion Military Institute. (AMHOH.)

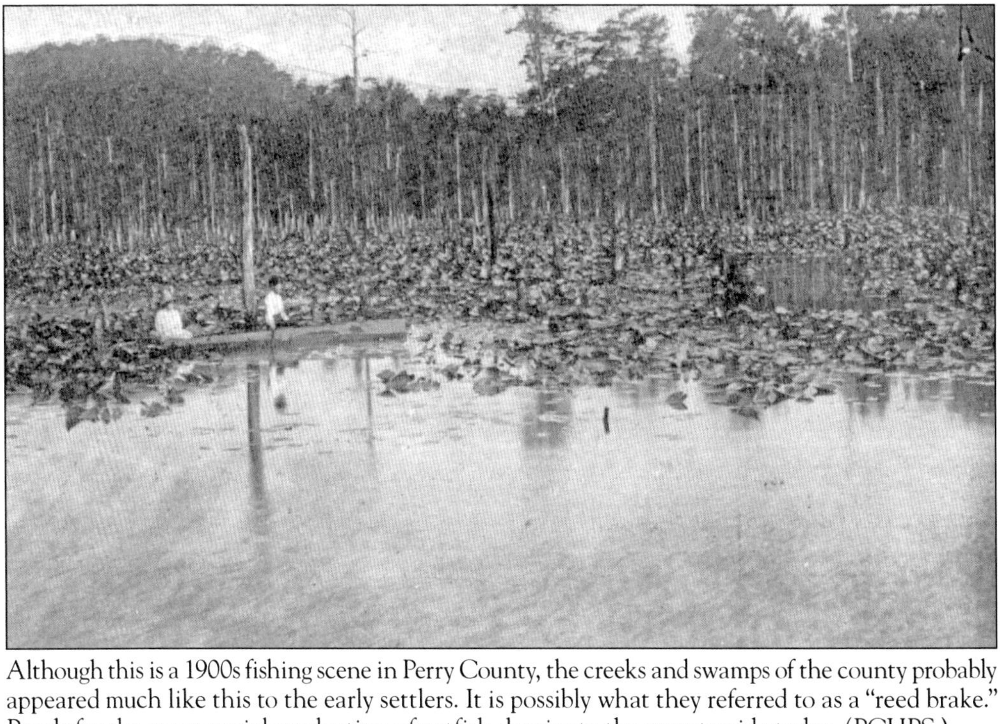

Although this is a 1900s fishing scene in Perry County, the creeks and swamps of the county probably appeared much like this to the early settlers. It is possibly what they referred to as a "reed brake." Ponds for the commercial production of catfish dominate the countryside today. (PCHPS.)

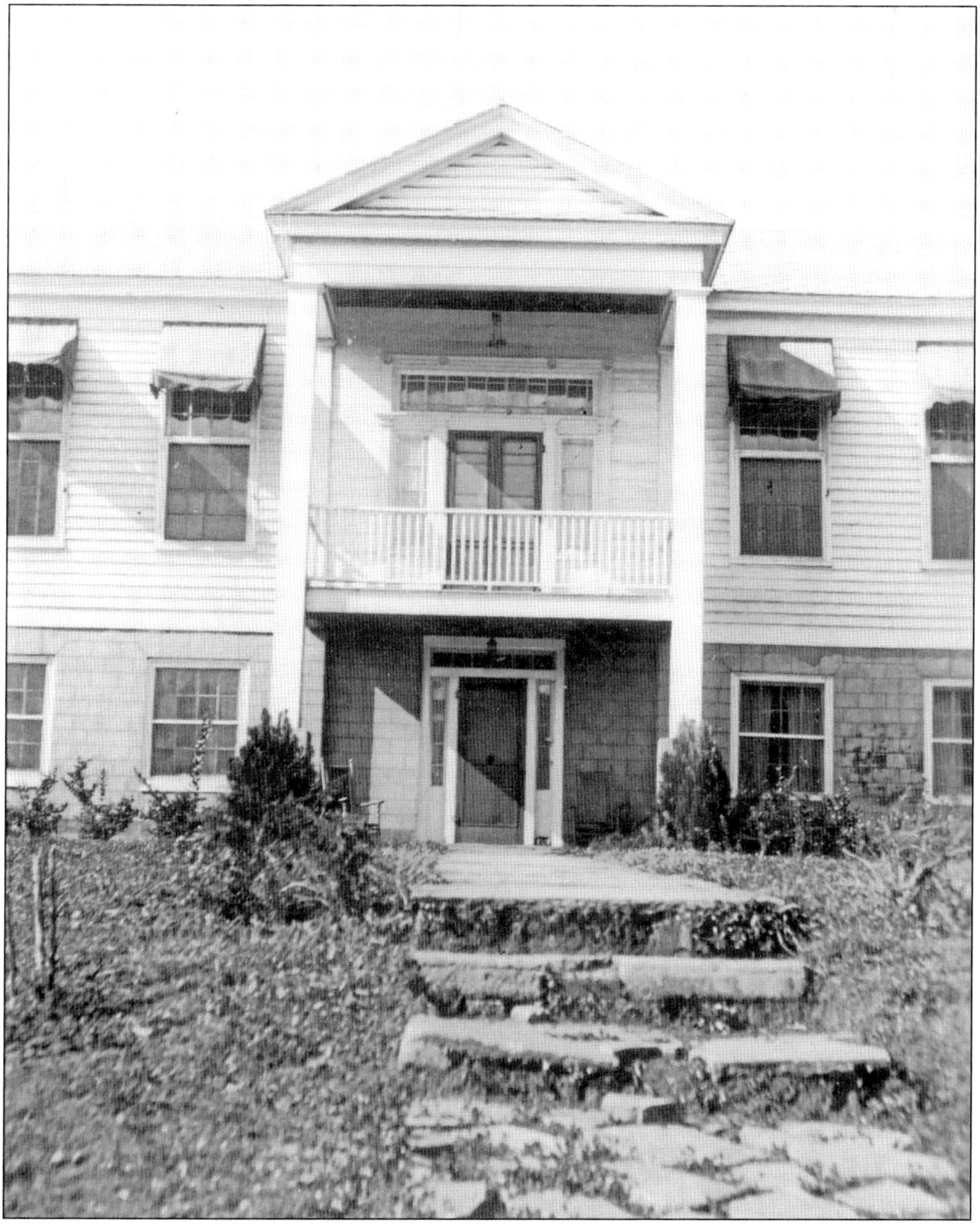

About 1834, this transitional Federal–Greek Revival house was erected on Green Street in Marion. It is L-shaped and has a semi-raised basement of gray stone or brick walls that are 18 inches thick. The basement is entered by a few downward steps. The second floor is of weatherboarding. Originally, the second floor was reached by a pair of stairs that led to a veranda. The formal reception rooms were on the second floor, while the formal dining area was on the ground floor. It was the residence of the Henry Clinton Lea family for quite a number of years. Lea was a lawyer and legislator and was a founder and served on the board of trustees of Marion Female Seminary, Judson Female Institute, and Howard College. His family included his mother and younger sisters, Margaret and Antoinette. Margaret Lea married Gen. Sam Houston in the right reception room on the second floor on May 9, 1840. (Courtesy of Carolyn Sandlin.)

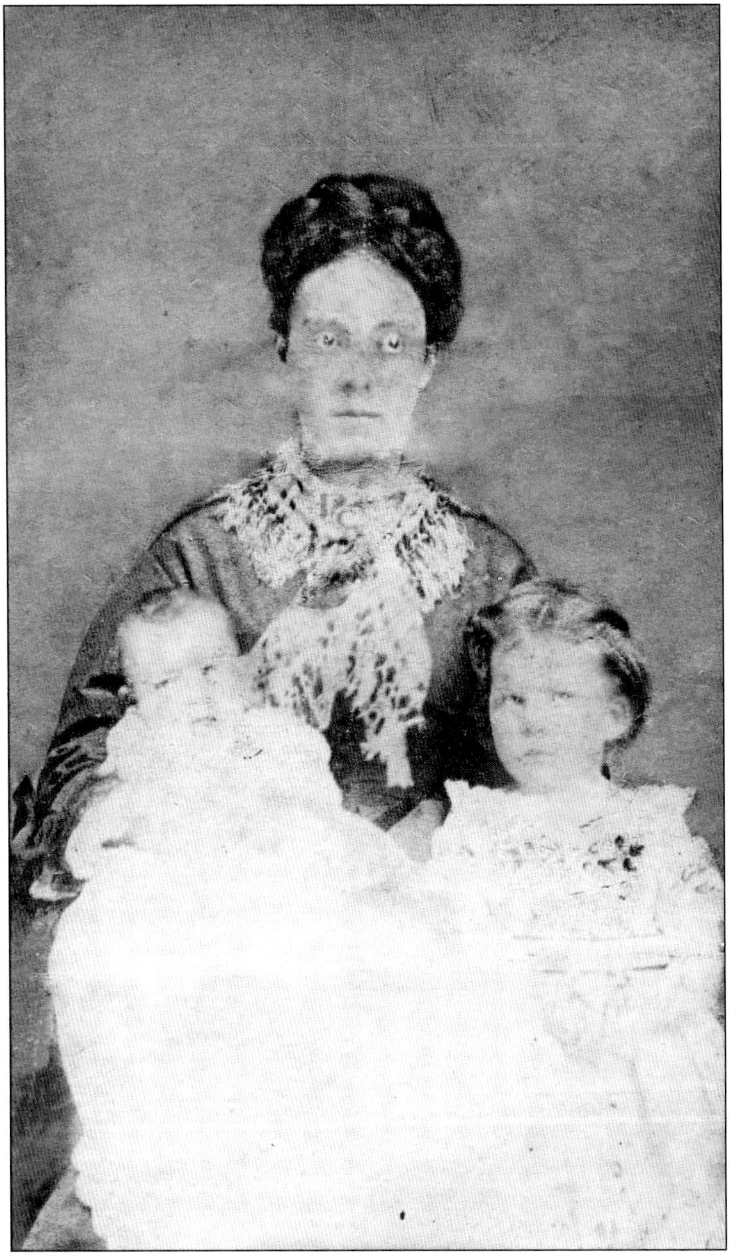

The photograph above shows Nancy Moffett Lea and her two youngest daughters, Margaret (right) and Antoinette. Her husband, Temple, died before 1840. Their home was near the Cahaba River. They were active members of the Concord Baptist Church and then Siloam Baptist Church in Marion. Nancy and Temple Lea were both at the organizational meeting of the Alabama Baptist State Convention in 1822. To her father, Temple, Margaret owed her early education and religious training, and to her mother, Nancy, she owed her training in the social graces. Margaret had met General Houston at the home of her sister, Antoinette, in Mobile, where Antoinette lived with her husband, William Bledsoe. According to the family, General Houston charmed Nancy Lea, but she could not condone a romance between Margaret and a man of such questionable character. Needless to say, Margaret prevailed, and the marriage took place. (Courtesy of Carolyn Sandlin.)

William "the Wagon Maker" Moore came to Perry County in 1819. The original 80 acres that he homesteaded has grown to thousands. Pictured is the first cotton gin, which dates from the 1830s. Homestead, operated by descendants of Moore, is one of Alabama's last active plantations. It is located approximately 7 miles west of Marion. (Courtesy of Charles Holmes.)

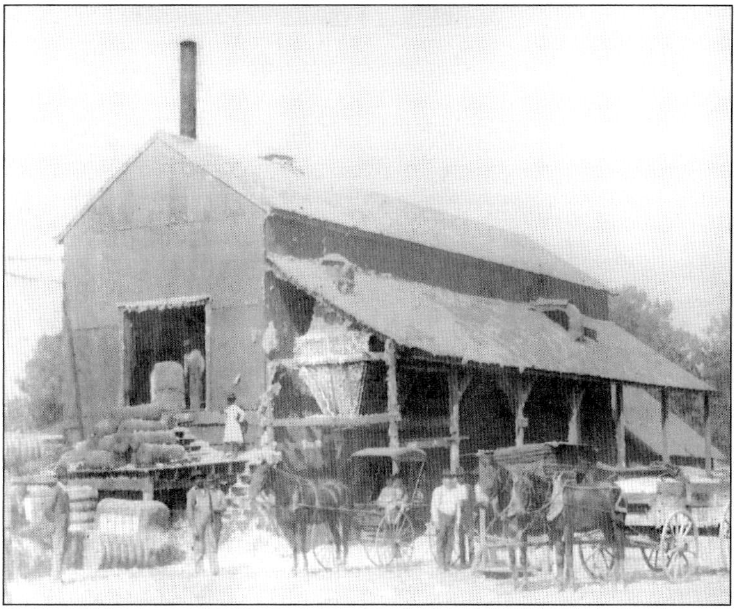

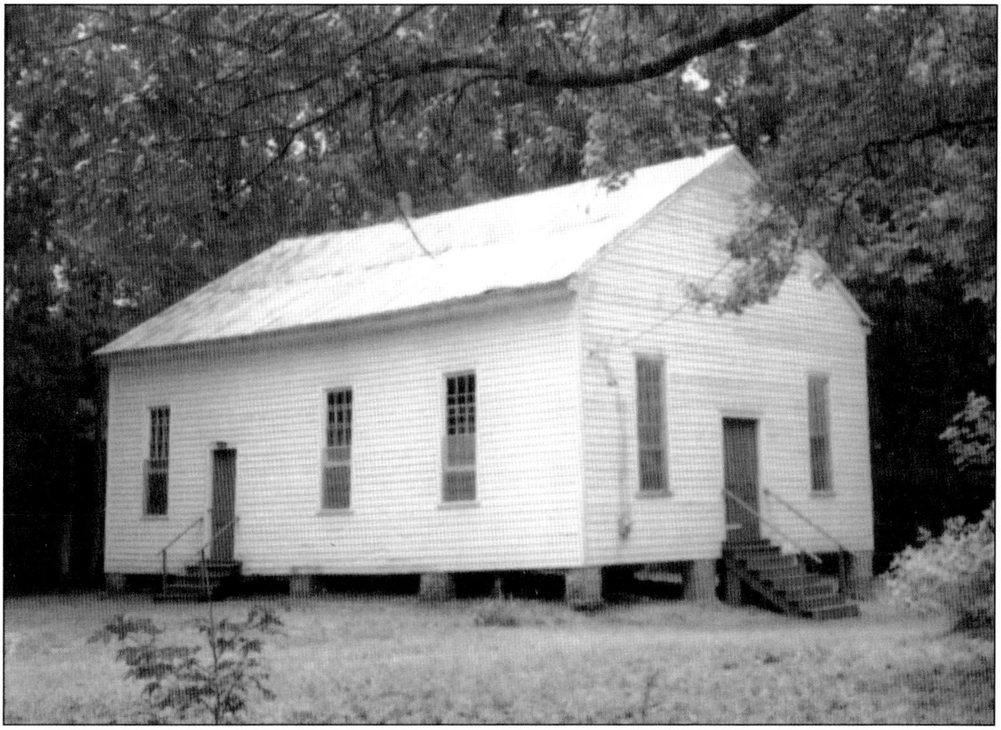

The cornerstone of Mount Zion Methodist Church is inscribed with the year 1822. Pioneer families of North Perry founded the church. Land for the church and cemetery was donated by the Griffin family. Stones in the cemetery bear the names of the early settlers of the area, such as Blackburn, Curb, Donavan, Terrell, Gayle, Moore, Ramsay, Richardson, Sanders, Wallace, and others. The church is no longer active. (PCHPS.)

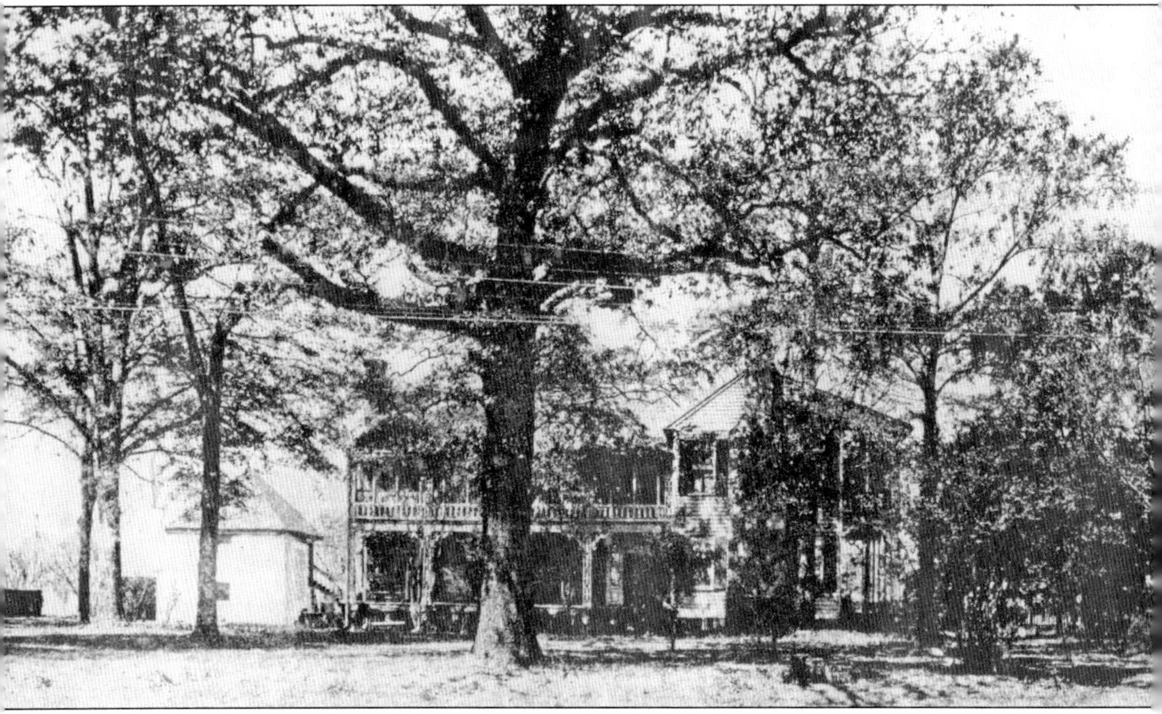

William Barron was a native of South Carolina who, with his brother John, came to Perry County in 1820. He was a merchant and was described as a man who had all the qualities needed to be successful in his field. He owned much of the land that constitutes the western part of Marion south of Lafayette Street. Barron built this home in 1827, prior to his marriage to Julia Tarrant. The housewarming, which was the most sumptuous entertainment offered to the citizens of Marion up to this time, was memorialized in W. L. Fagan's newspaper columns about early Marion. The first dance of the night was a stag dance by the male guests, since it was felt they needed to release their excess energy before dancing with the women. Barron was a wealthy man for his time and could afford to build a large home. It was the first clapboard house in Marion. It was the home of his widow, Julia Tarrant Barron, and their son, John Thomas, for many years after his death in 1832. (PCHPS.)

While searching for photographs, this one of an unidentified church in the county surfaced. It is presented here to show how various county churches looked for many years. The countryside was dotted with these small churches because of the distances that had to be traveled to attend church and the mode of available transportation. (PCHPS.)

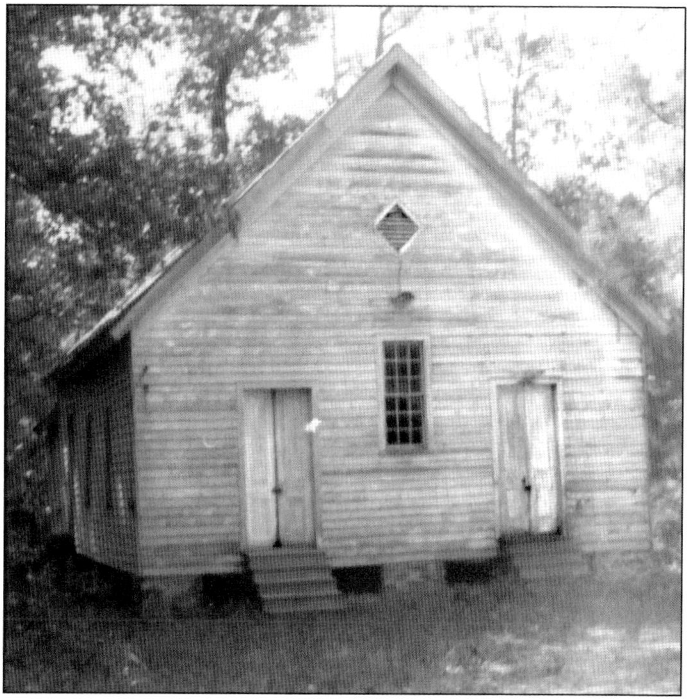

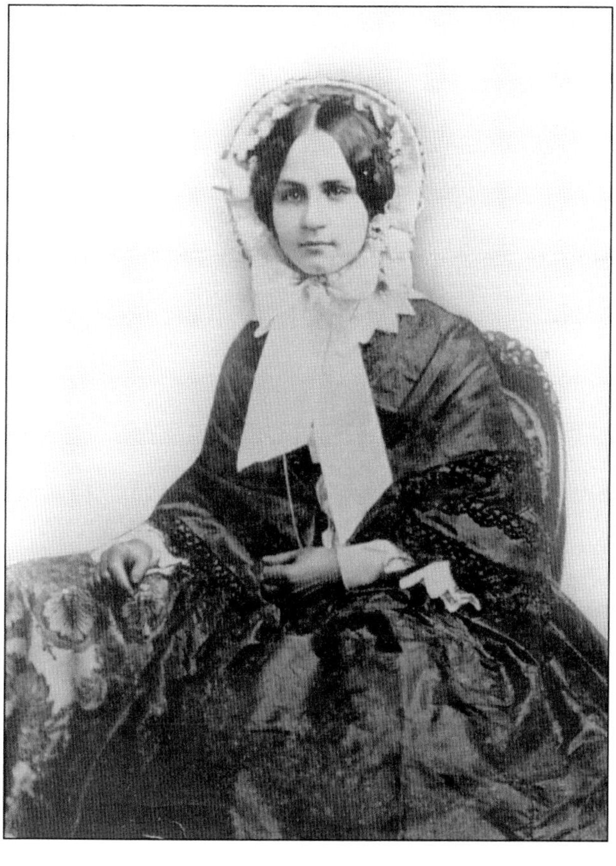

Margaret Lea is pictured about the time of her marriage to Gen. Sam Houston. She met him earlier at her sister's home in Mobile. He wanted their marriage to take place in Texas, but her mother insisted that, unless he came to Marion to marry Margaret, there would be no marriage. Peter Crawford, pastor of the Siloam Baptist Church, officiated at the ceremony. (Courtesy of Carolyn Sandlin.)

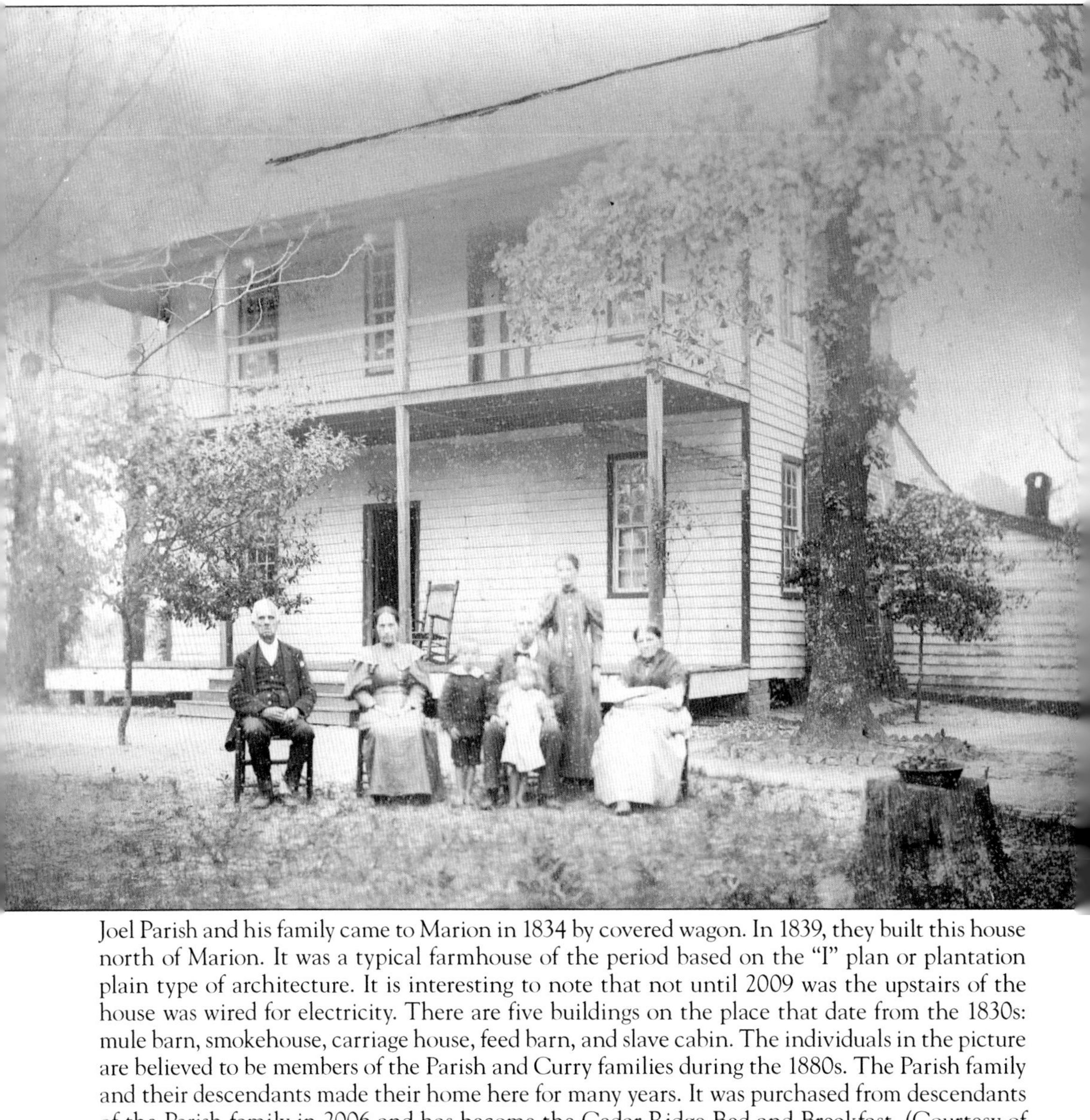

Joel Parish and his family came to Marion in 1834 by covered wagon. In 1839, they built this house north of Marion. It was a typical farmhouse of the period based on the "I" plan or plantation plain type of architecture. It is interesting to note that not until 2009 was the upstairs of the house was wired for electricity. There are five buildings on the place that date from the 1830s: mule barn, smokehouse, carriage house, feed barn, and slave cabin. The individuals in the picture are believed to be members of the Parish and Curry families during the 1880s. The Parish family and their descendants made their home here for many years. It was purchased from descendants of the Parish family in 2006 and has become the Cedar Ridge Bed and Breakfast. (Courtesy of Laurette Turner.)

Julia Tarrant Barron was born in 1806 in South Carolina. She married William Barron and moved to Marion. After William's death in 1832, she managed his large estate with excellent business acumen. A member of Siloam Baptist Church, she donated the land on which the church was built. She is credited as being one of the founders of Judson Female Institute. (JCA.)

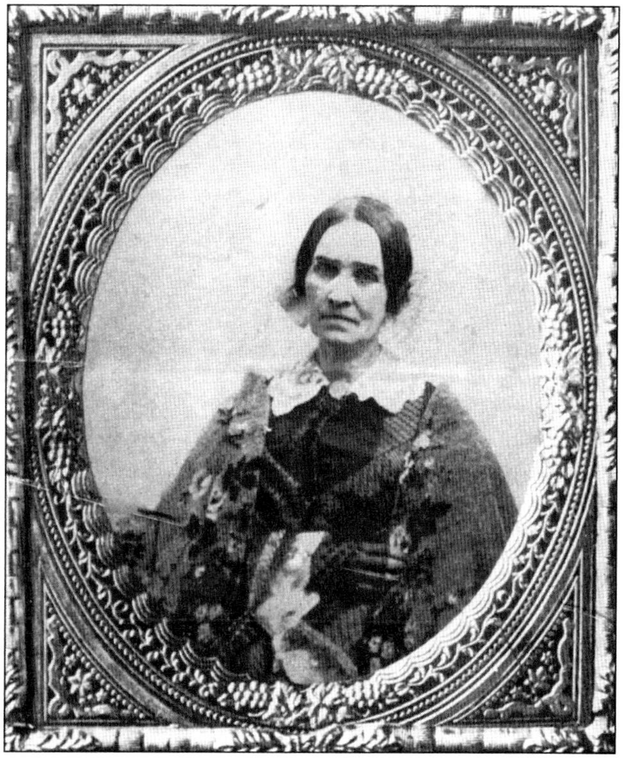

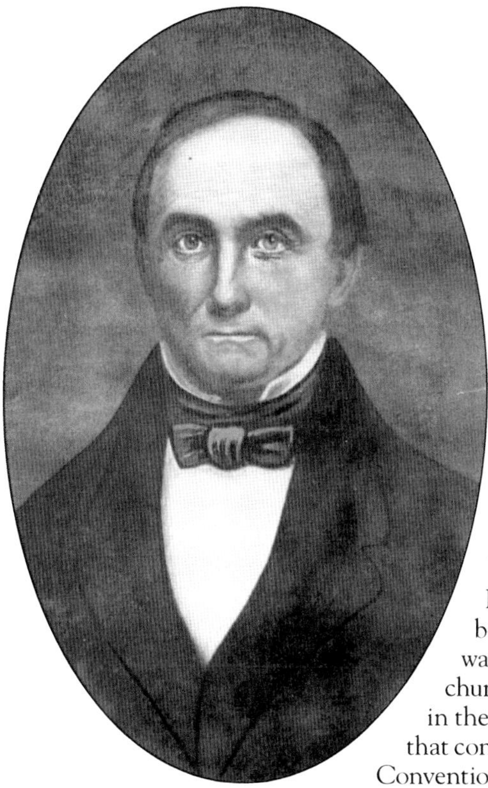

Edwin Davis King was born in Georgia and came to Perry County, Alabama, in 1816. Reported to have been one of the earliest millionaires in Alabama, he was a successful planter and became very influential in church and community affairs. He was especially active in the affairs of Siloam Baptist Church and represented that congregation at the founding of the Southern Baptist Convention in 1845. (JCA.)

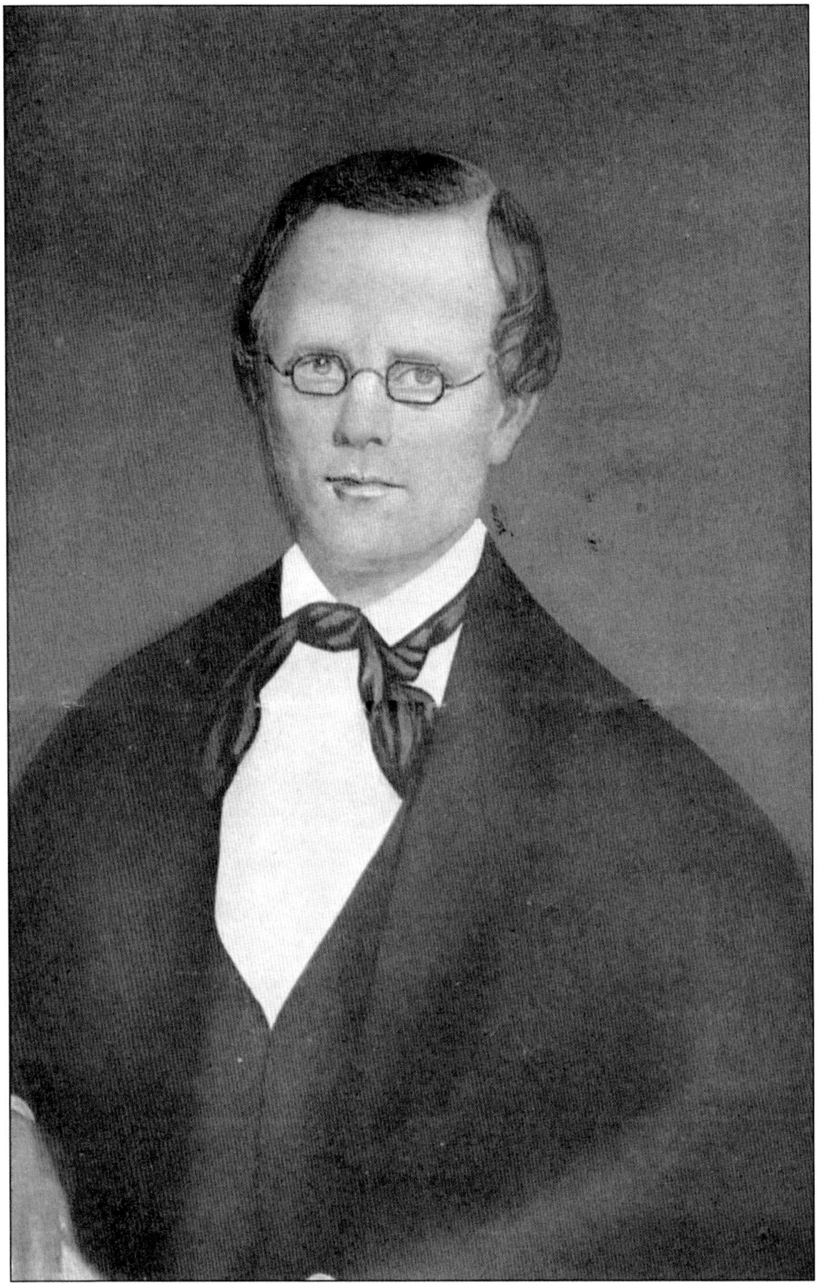

Milo P. Jewett, the third founder of Judson College, was a native of St. Johnsbury, Vermont. He and his wife, Jane Russell, were traveling in Alabama looking for a place to establish a girls' school when he met Edwin D. King, who invited them to visit Marion. He became president of Judson Female Institute, and though he was an excellent teacher, Jewett excelled in organizing, directing, and controlling the work of others. He was able to accomplish much with limited means. He traveled and wrote extensively to encourage attendance at Judson. It is said that under his leadership the school became the best known and most popular female seminary in the southwest. He remained there until 1855, and he was very involved in the life of the community and of the Siloam Baptist Church. (JCA.)

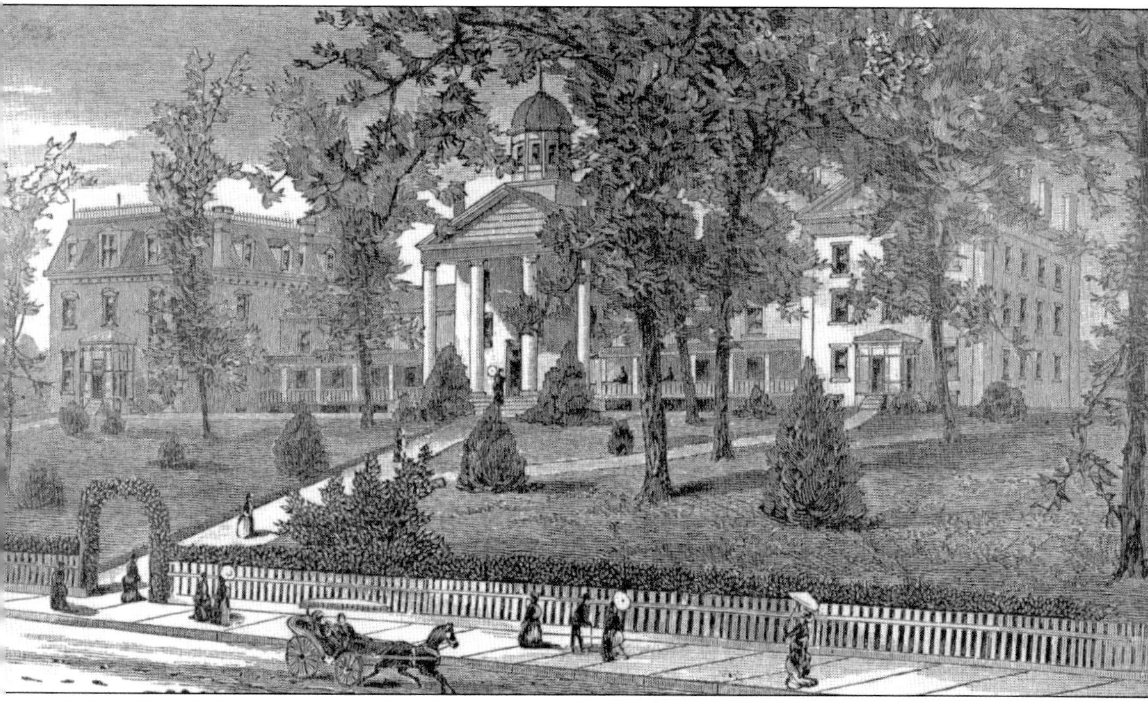

Judson Female Institute opened its doors for classes in 1838 with 14 students, and by 1844, there were 130. It was named for Ann Hasseltine Judson, a missionary to Burma. Students were accepted in primary, preparatory, irregular, junior, middle, senior, and resident graduate classes. This building was completed in 1841. The original building contained a steward's room, dining hall with storerooms, washroom, trunk room, parlor, library, schoolroom, principal's study, drawing and painting room, primary department, recitation room, music room, teachers' rooms, study hall, and dormitory rooms. Additions were made in 1853 and 1857 that almost doubled the boarding capacity of the school. On January 9, 1841, Judson received a charter from the state legislature that allowed them to issue diplomas, and in 1843, the owners deeded the property to the Alabama Baptist Convention. Today it remains the only women's college in Alabama and only one of five in the United States. (JCA.)

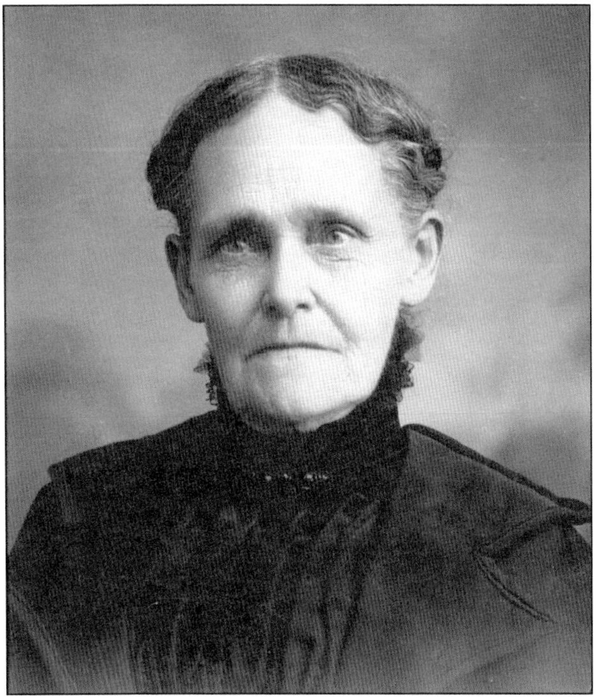

Eugenia Lockhart Bernhard, a native of Marion and the daughter of one of the first trustees, was in the very first class at Judson Female Institute. Over the years, she was present at the groundbreaking for the second Judson building in 1889 and for the Alumnae Auditorium in 1902. She was also a charter member of the Alumnae Society. (JCA.)

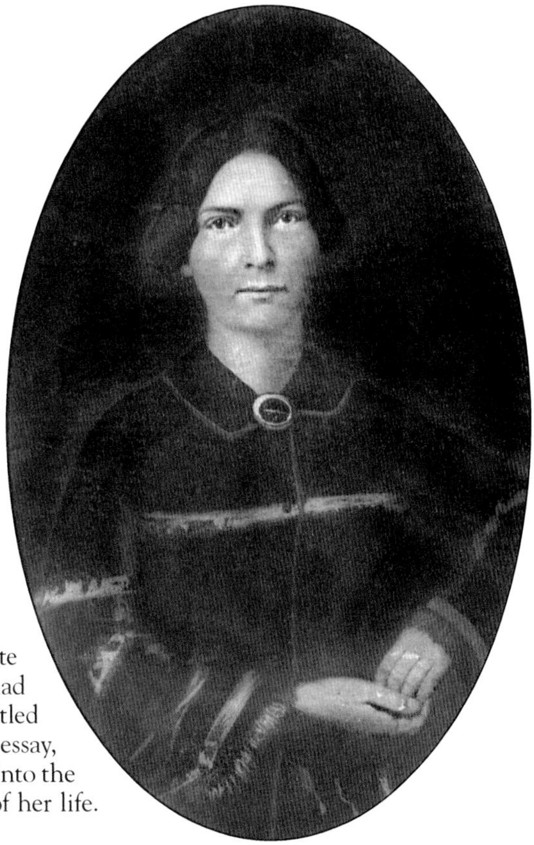

Caroline Frances Smith became the first graduate of the Judson Female Institute in 1841. She had entered in 1839. Her graduation essay was entitled "Elevated Aims Essential to Success." In the essay, she articulated her beliefs, which she formed into the living plan she followed for the remainder of her life. She married George Gilmer in 1843. (JCA.)

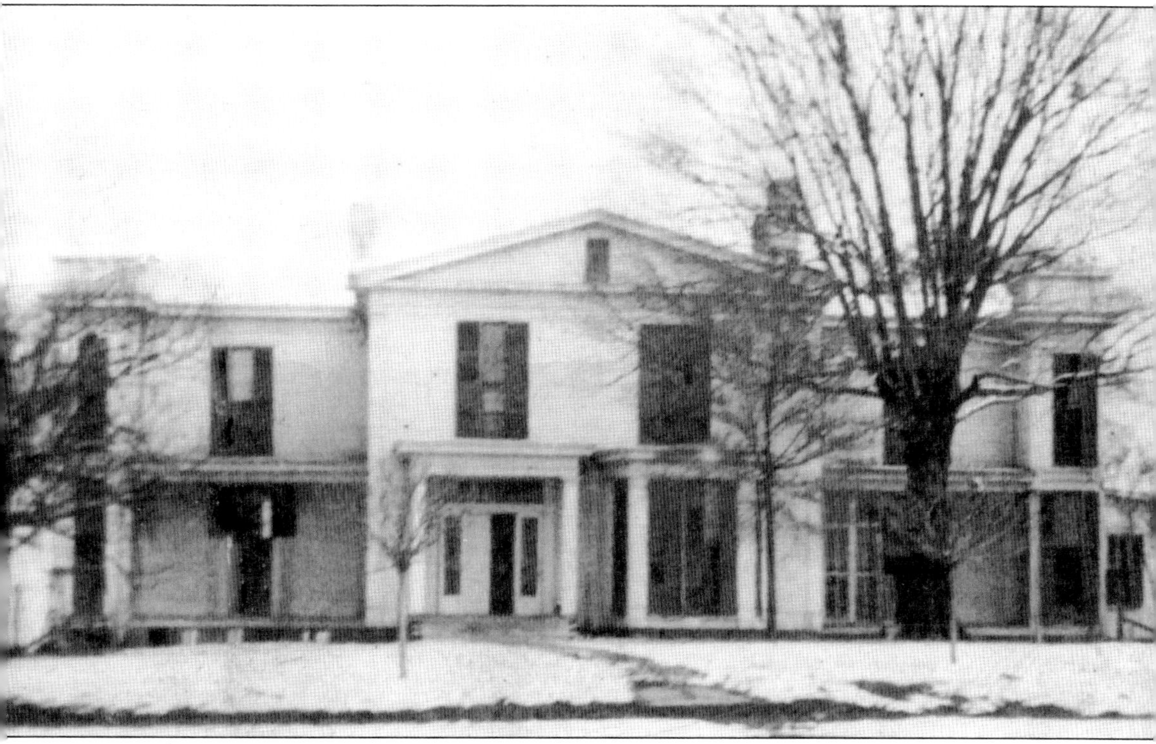

Westwood, on Alabama Highway 61 at the northern edge of Uniontown, was built between 1836 and 1840 by James Lewis Price. The house is Greek Revival with Italianate influences. Price, who was very involved in bringing the railroad to the area, later sold it to his son-in-law, Alexander Caldwell Davidson. Davidson purchased the house as a wedding gift for his wife, Maria Overton Price. The foundation timbers are 12 inches by 12 inches and put together with wooden pegs and square nails. Each wing has a recessed one-story porch with cast-iron trim. The dressing rooms in each corner are topped with square turrets. John Witherspoon Dubose, in *Chronicles of the Black Belt*, referred to Westwood as the "Mecca of Canebrake Society." A former owner, Louis Davidson, is quoted in *Stars Fell on Alabama* as saying, "There are only two places in the world where one may live a happy, civilized existence—Paris and Uniontown." It has remained in the possession of the family since its building. (Courtesy of Emma Glass Beasley.)

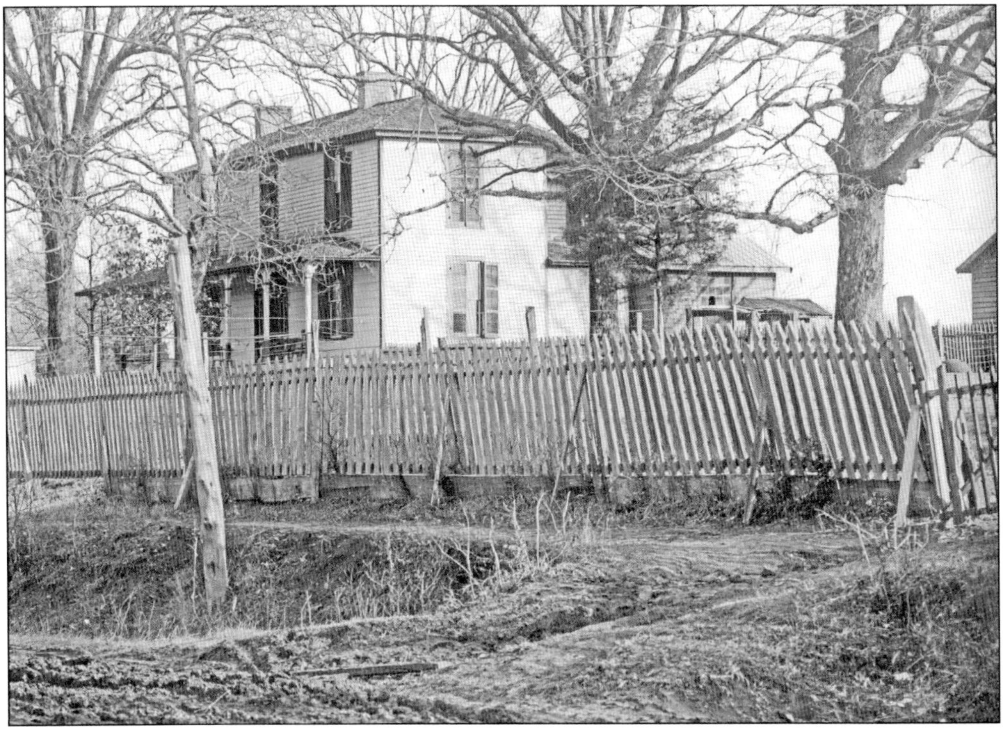

Napoleon Lockett built this house on Lafayette Street in the early 1840s. Gov. Andrew Moore asked Mary Lockett, Napoleon's wife, to help him obtain a design for a flag for the Confederacy. She asked Nicola Marschall, an artist, for help. Marschall designed the flag that is known as the "Stars and Bars." Ladies of the town provided the material, and the first Stars and Bars flag was sewn in the front parlor of this house. (JCA.)

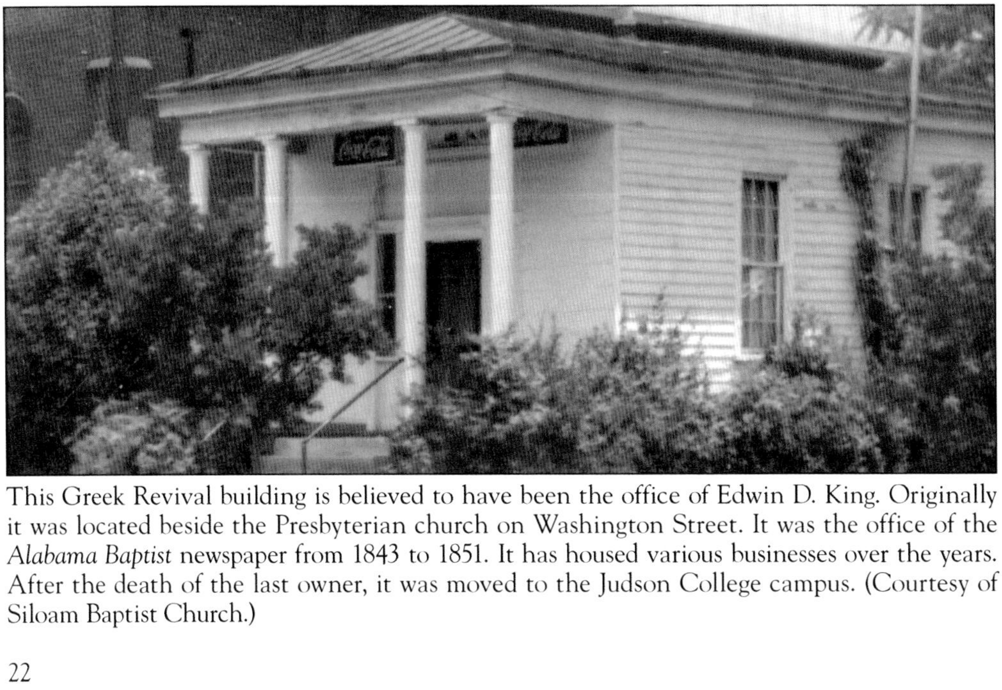

This Greek Revival building is believed to have been the office of Edwin D. King. Originally it was located beside the Presbyterian church on Washington Street. It was the office of the *Alabama Baptist* newspaper from 1843 to 1851. It has housed various businesses over the years. After the death of the last owner, it was moved to the Judson College campus. (Courtesy of Siloam Baptist Church.)

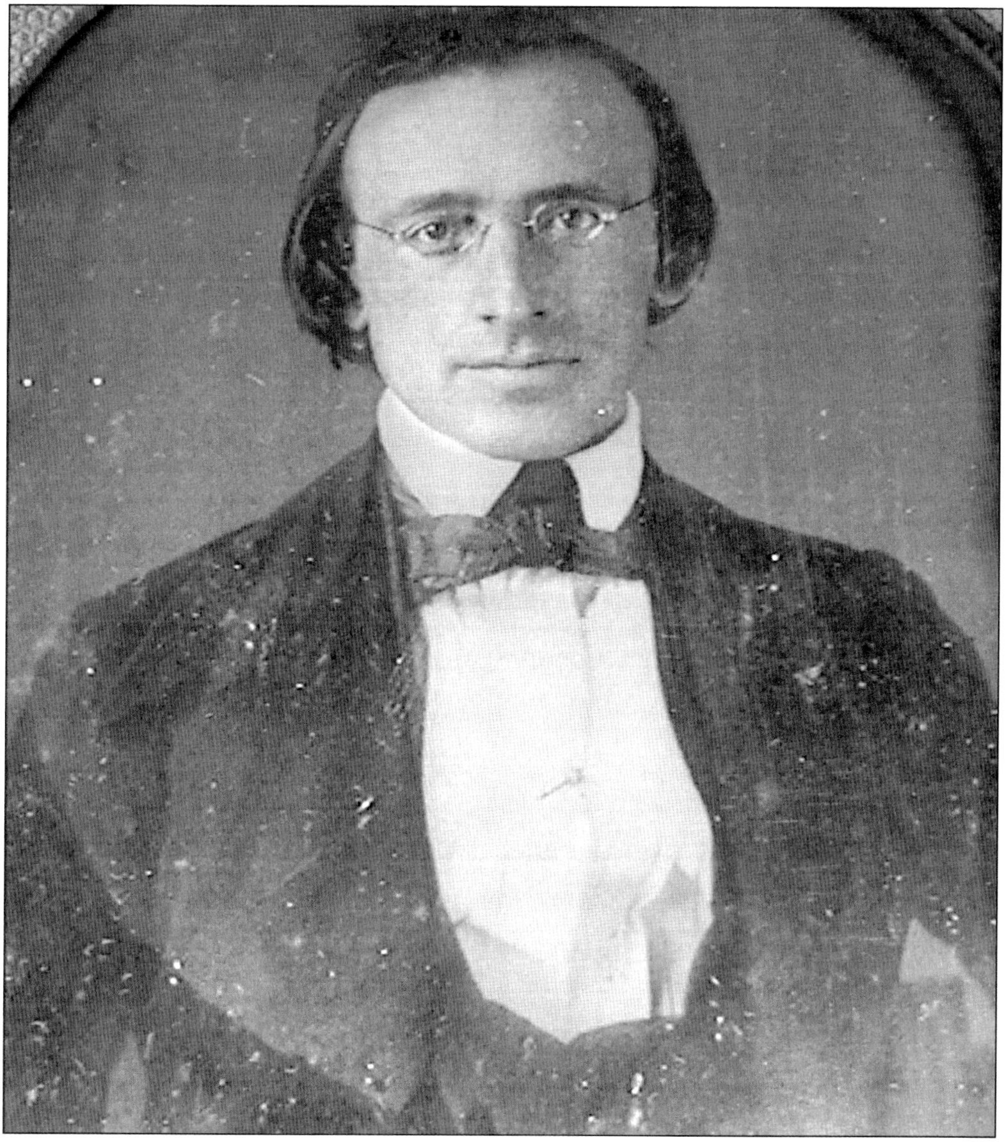

Samuel S. Sherman, a native of Vermont, was the first president of Howard College. After graduating from Middlebury College, he came to the University of Alabama as a tutor in foreign languages and as a librarian. When he came to Marion, he expected to find an established school but found that he was responsible for establishing it. The school began under his leadership in 1842 as the Howard English and Classical School of Marion. When Milo P. Jewett resigned from the Judson Female Institute in 1855, Samuel Sherman became the second president of that school. Realizing the inevitability of war, Sherman retired in 1859 and moved to Milwaukee, Wisconsin. During the War Between the States, he was permitted to give aid to southern prisoners—some from Marion—at Camp Douglas on Johnson Island. In 1866, the citizens of Marion invited Sherman back for a dinner in his honor and as a way to thank him for the services he provided the prisoners. (SU.)

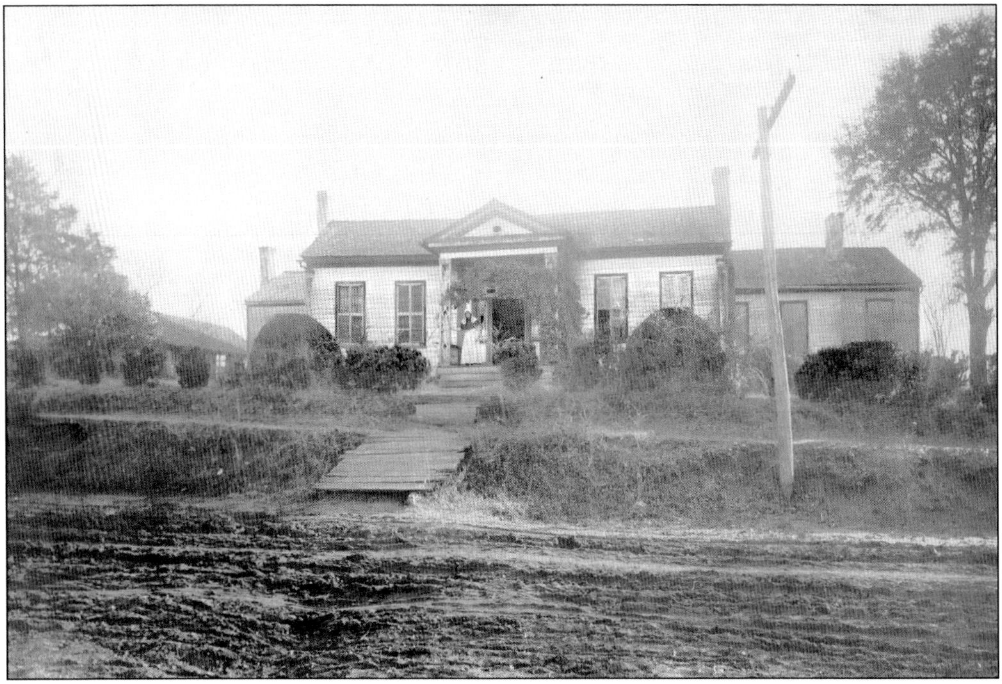

Vermont silversmiths Roswell and William Huntington and their families migrated to Marion in 1833. The family members were active citizens, buying and selling property, building homes, and running businesses. The Huntington family is credited with building this Greek Revival cottage and three other houses along Lafayette Street. William Huntington was actively engaged as a silversmith at the age of 81 in 1874. (JCA.)

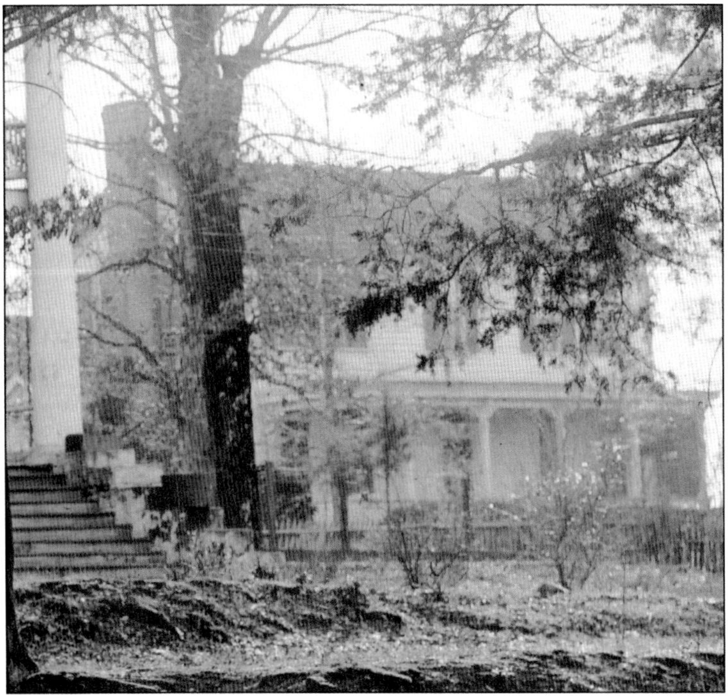

This is the second of four houses that the Huntington family built in Marion. The grounds leading up to the house were terraced, and traces of those terraces can be seen today. Amy Vary—a descendant of the Moore and Vary families, who were later owners of the home—left the house to her longtime employer, Judson College. The current owners call the house Belle Terrace. (JCA.)

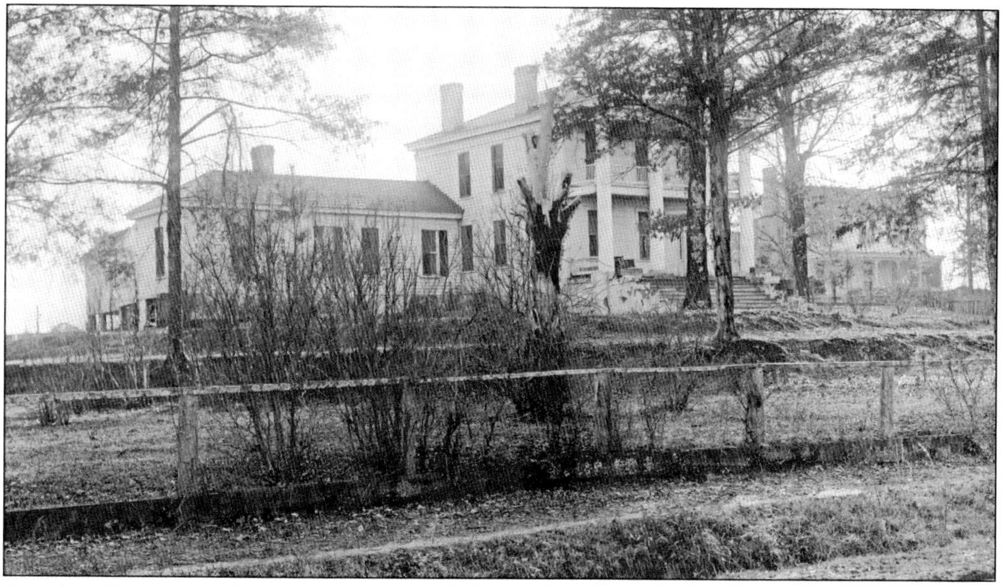

Another Huntington home was built in 1845 by John Huntington, son of Roswell. The most outstanding owner of this house was Gen. George Doherty Johnson, who purchased the house in 1855. The original carriage house and detached service kitchen remain intact. Today it is the Myrtle Hill Bed and Breakfast. (JCA.)

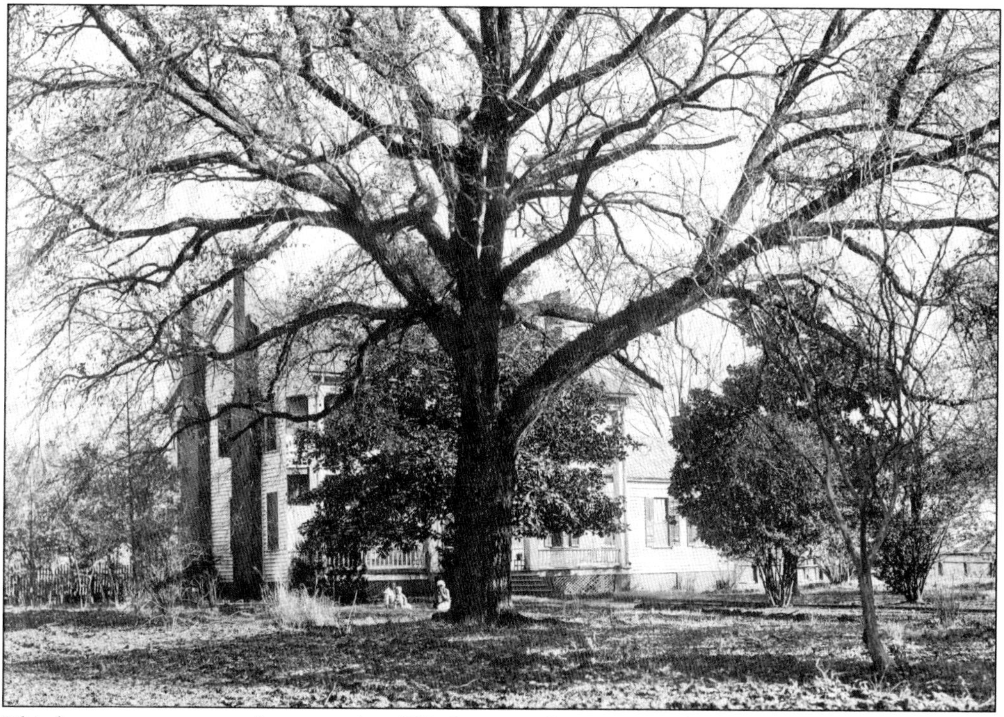

This house once sat on the east side of Washington Street across from the present Marion Bank and Trust Company. The information on the back of the pictures states that it was the Ann Smith–Huey house. Smith settled in Marion in 1822 and was a businesswoman. The lot later became the property of B. M. Huey, a former mayor. (JCA.)

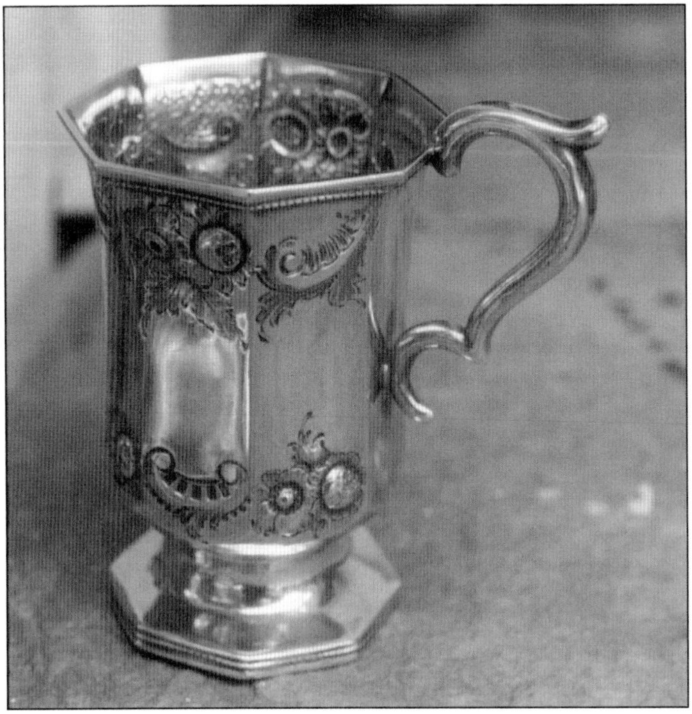

The Devotie coin silver cup was purchased at a yard sale in Atlanta. James Devotie was a pastor at Siloam Baptist from 1840 to 1855. He was very active in the Baptist affairs of the town, association, and state. The cup is engraved with the following: "Presented to Rev. J. H. Devotie by the colored members of the Siloam Baptist Church. Marion, Ala." (Courtesy of Siloam Baptist Church.)

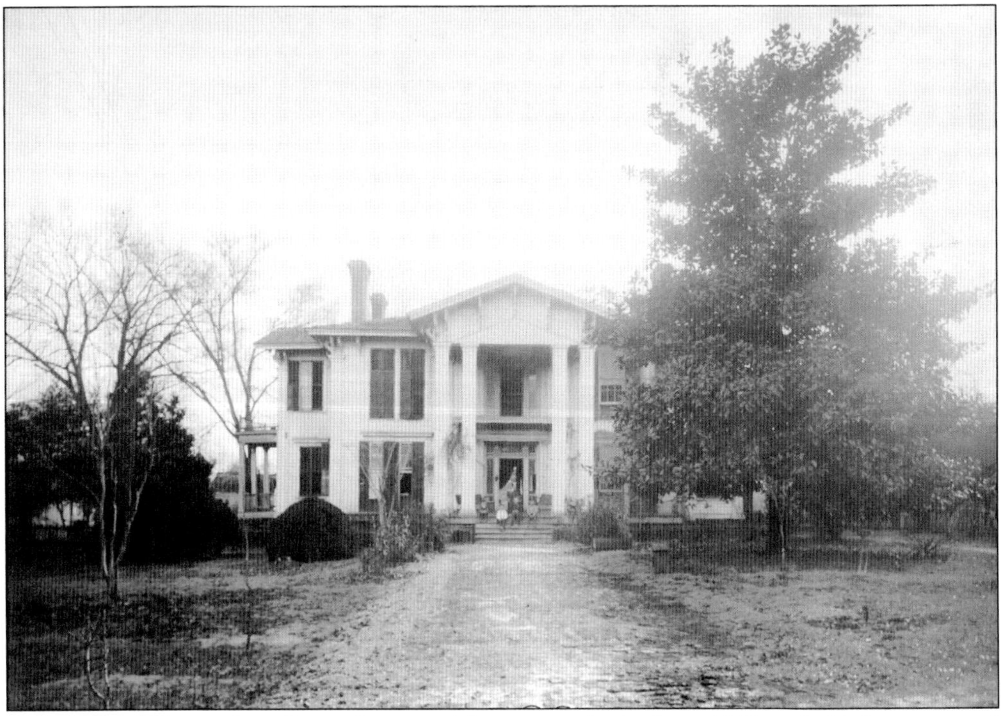

Magnolia Hill, located on Green Street in Marion, was built about 1847, probably by renowned lawyer James Phelan. The house contains 22 rooms; all rooms have access to a porch or balcony through windows with jib doors, and each of the main chambers has a separate service room. It was built with heavy Italianate influence. (JCA.)

The Alabama Historical Commission has noted that the front entrance to Magnolia Hill is one of the most elaborate in the state. The panes around the door are of Bohemian glass. Corinthian columns are used in the doorway. The door opens out to one of the largest magnolia trees in the area. (JCA.)

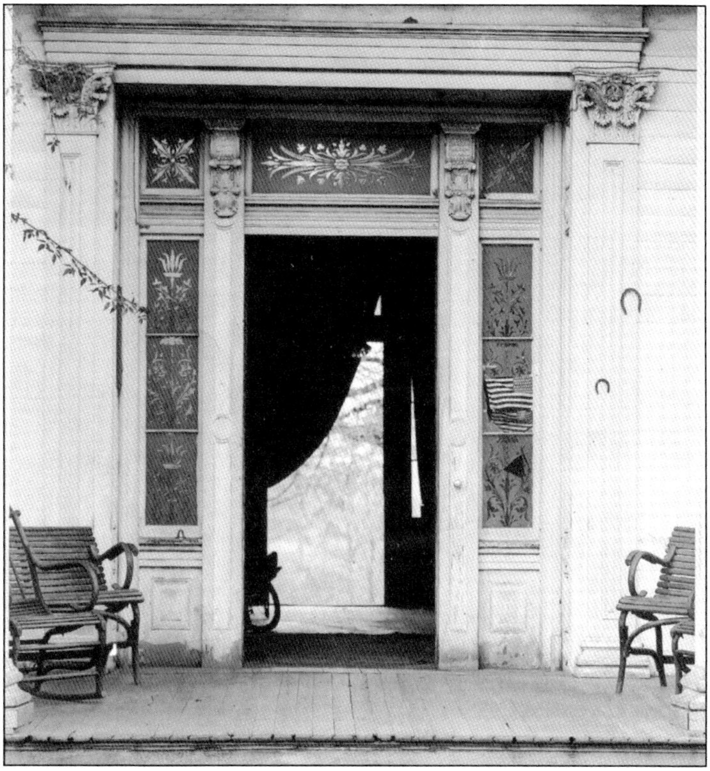

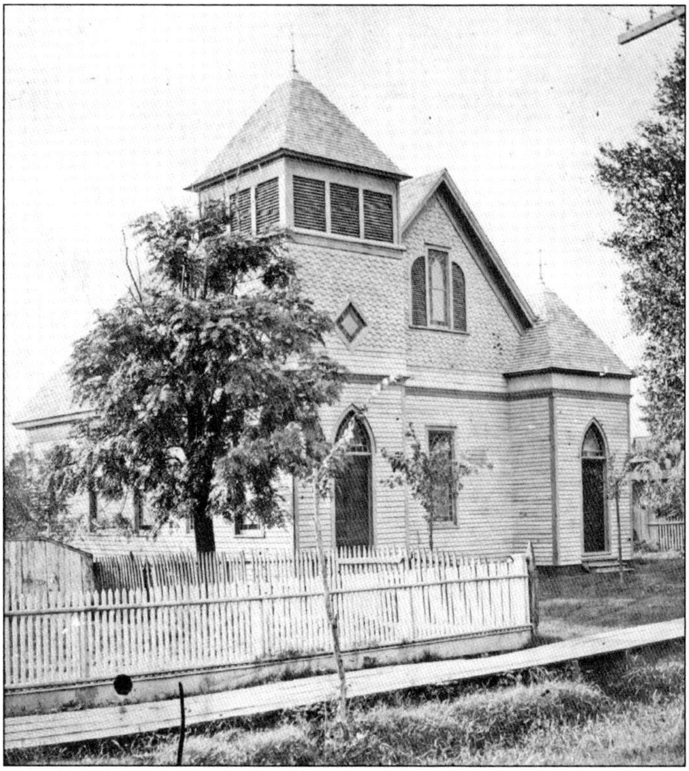

Baptists organized in Uniontown in 1838, according to their minutes. They were given a lot by Philip Weaver and bought an adjacent one in 1848. John V. Crosston erected a building at this time. This building was remodeled in 1896 and served until 1930, when a new one was erected. Pictured is the 1896-remodeled building. (Courtesy of the author.)

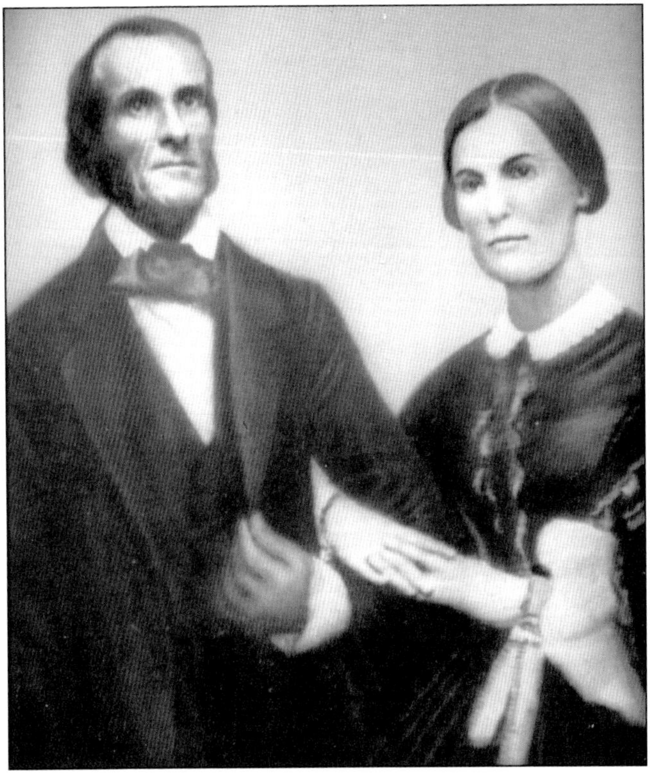

Lilburn L. and Jane Hudson Fox moved to Alabama before he became pastor of the Uniontown Baptist Church in 1848. He served that church for nearly 20 years. He led its first building program and in transferring its membership from the Bethel Baptist Association to the Cahaba Baptist Association. (Courtesy of the author.)

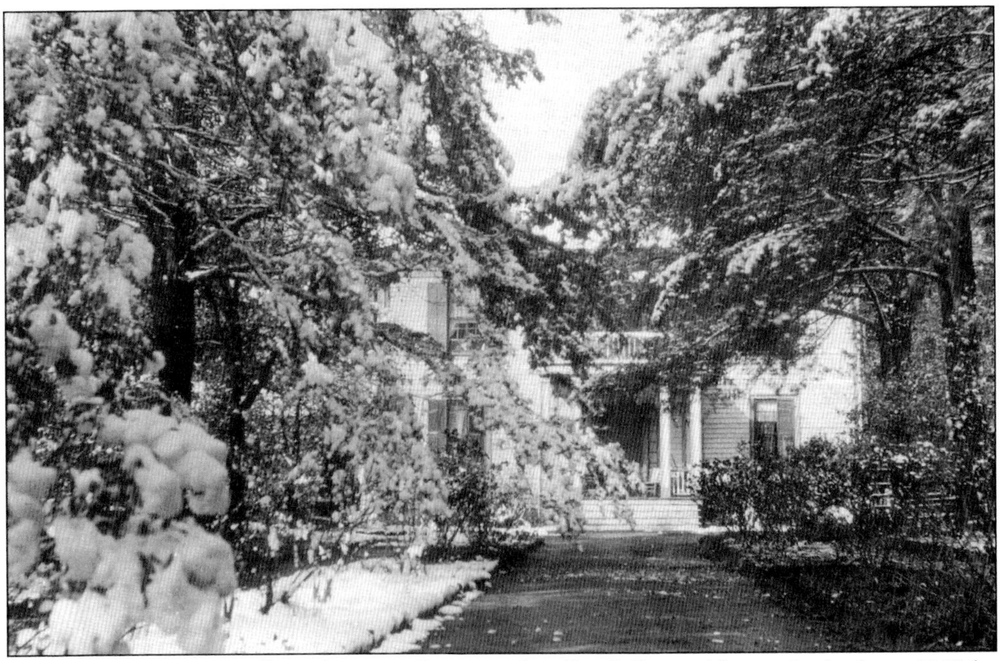

Facing but sitting just off Washington Street is this Greek Revival house built about 1848 by Larkin Young Tarrant for his sister-in-law, Mary Ann Tarrant. It is here that Dr. William Augustus Evans, superintendent of the Breckenridge Division Hospital, CSA, boarded. He stated in his correspondence that he had a nice place to live, but he was ready to go home. (JCA.)

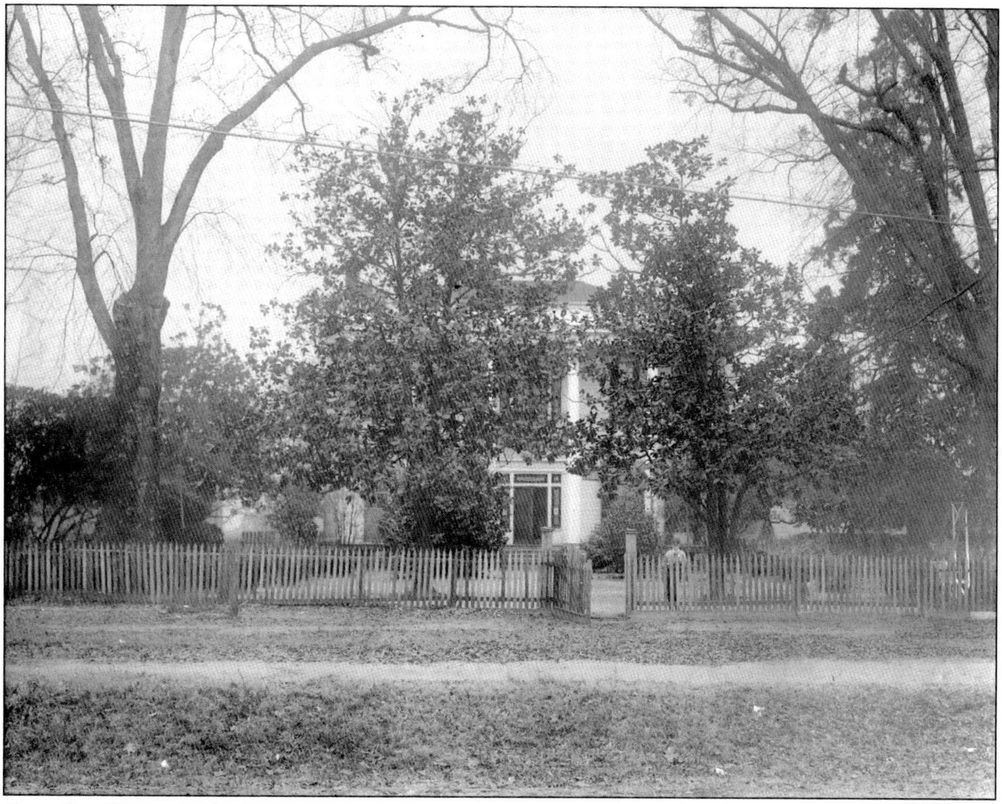

Camellia Place was built on Washington Street in Marion by Porter King in 1849. The classical Greek Revival house is believed to have been designed by Benjamin Parsons of Massachusetts. The original two-room kitchen is connected to the main house by a latticed breezeway. Underneath this room is the original coal cellar. (JCA.)

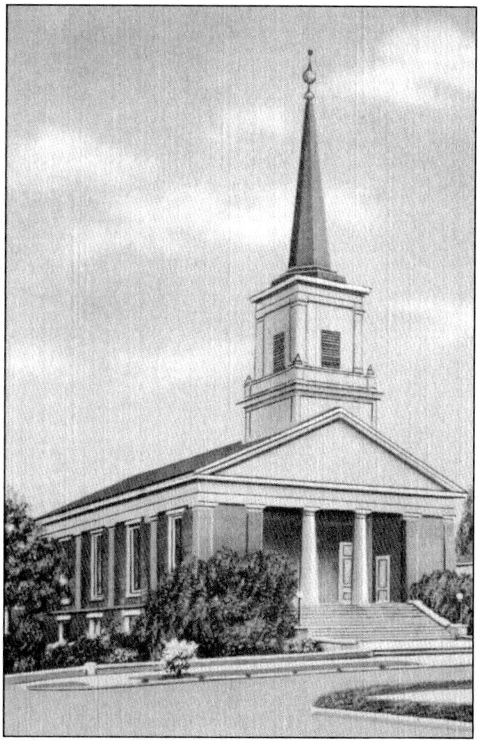

Siloam Baptist Church was organized in June 1822. It is believed that Charles Crow served as the first pastor of the church. This building was completed and dedicated in 1849. Over the years, it has been a leader in Baptist life in the city, the association, the state, and the Southern Baptist Convention. (JCA.)

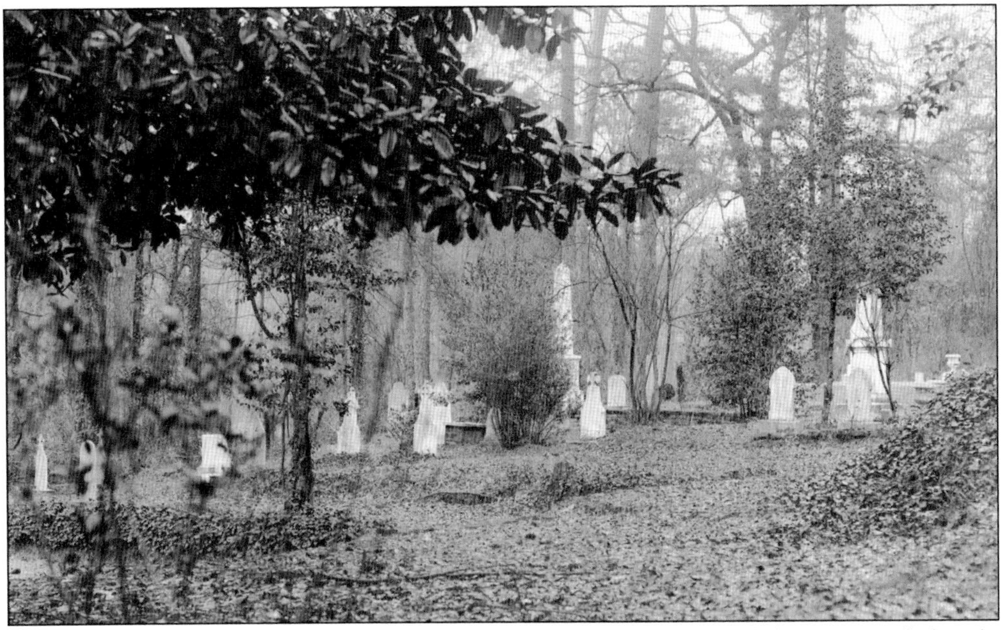

Beginning in 1849, Marion began burying many of its citizens behind the Episcopal church. Included among this number is William Maclin Brooks, a Marion lawyer who served as president of Alabama's Secession Convention in 1861. Also buried here are 77 soldiers who died in the Breckenridge Division Hospital, CSA, located in the South Barracks of Howard College, during the War Between the States. (JCA.)

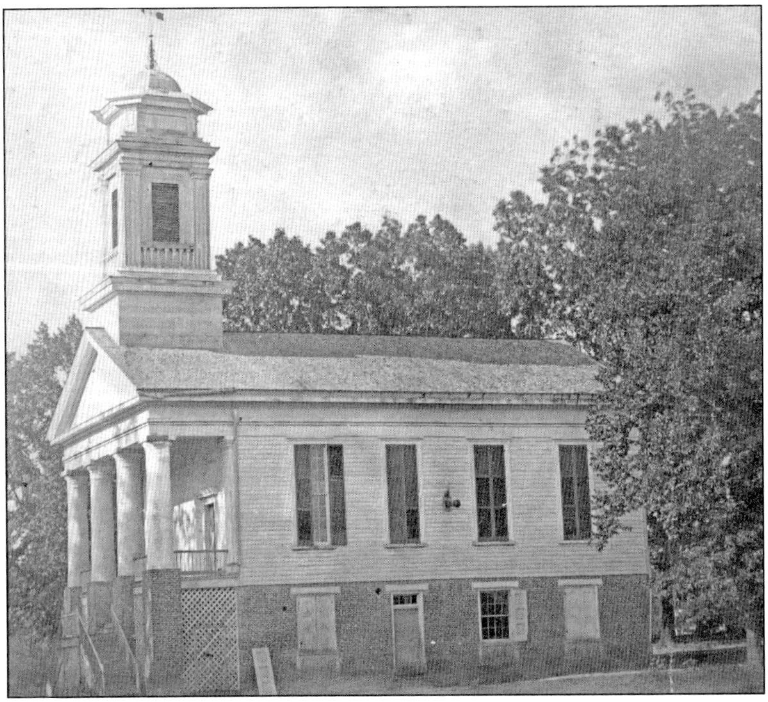

The first recording of the building of a Methodist church in Marion was in 1837. The church here is probably of a later date. Often it is recorded that the Methodists shared their building with the Masonic order. Records reveal that at one time the Methodists had a church about a block west of the present building. (SU.)

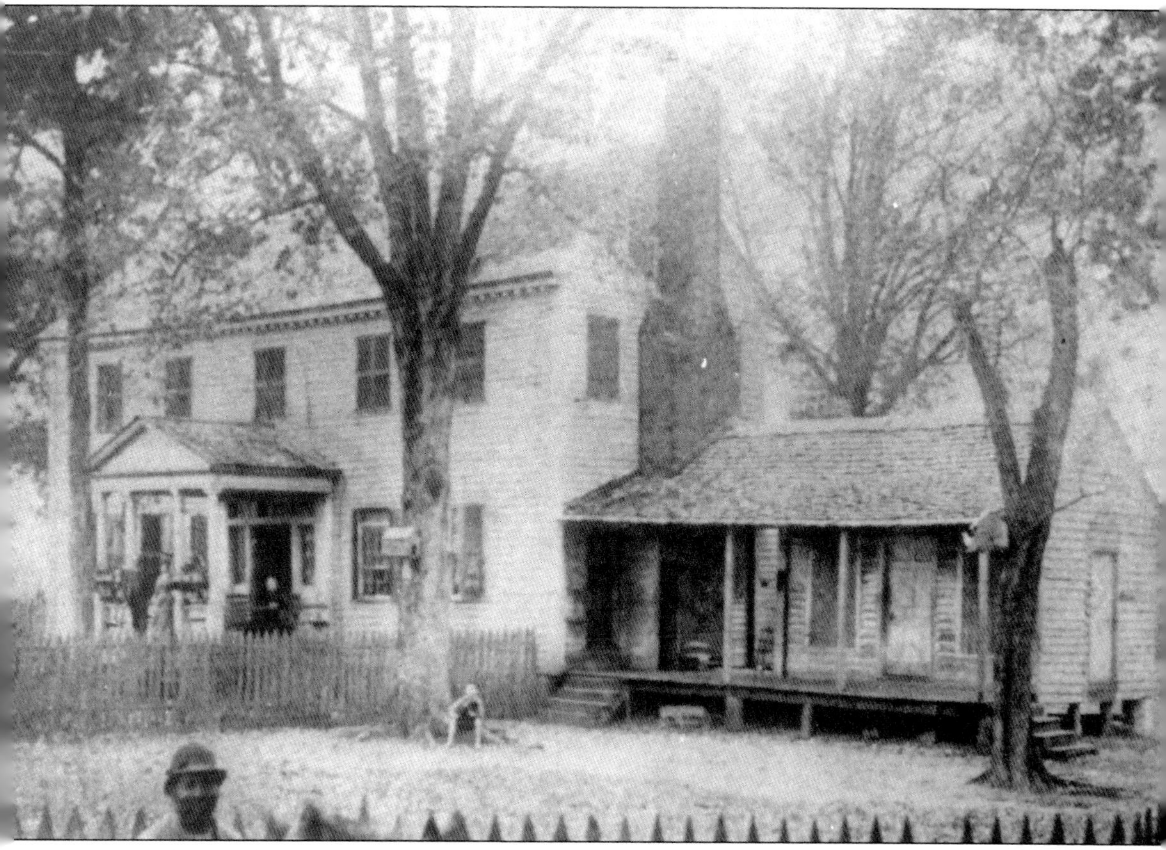

Weymouth T. Jordan used the farm and family journals of the Hugh Davis family in writing *Hugh Davis and His Alabama Plantation*. Hugh Davis was born in Mississippi and came to Marion in 1834. As a lawyer and the county solicitor, he was in a position to learn of land for sale in the area. By the mid-1850s, he owned 5,000 acres along the Cahaba River. Some believe the house was the original George Weissinger home. Jordan believes the house was built by Hugh Davis, stating that he was well able to afford to build it. It was described as a "comfortable, quite elaborate home." The family was active in the social and religious life of Hamburg. Davis died in 1862. His sons attempted to run the plantation, but due to circumstances arising from the War Between the States and the economy of the time, they were not successful. They began to sell land parcels, and the last acreage was sold about 1900. The home burned between 1907 and 1910. (Courtesy of Annie Ford Wheeler.)

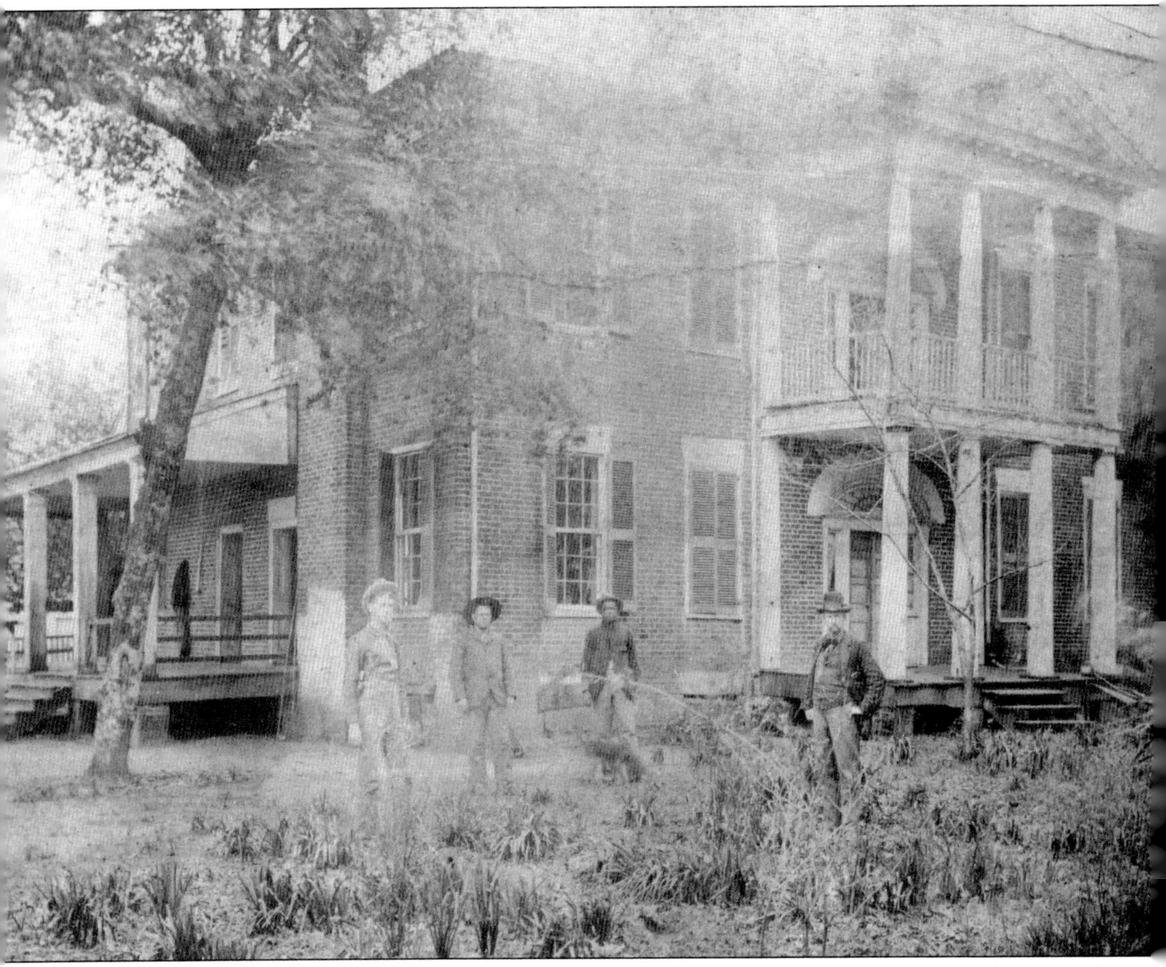

Joseph Crenshaw and his family were among the first families of Hamburg, coming to this area of Perry County in the 1820s. He was a native of Virginia. As early as 1829, his name began appearing in the county records, fulfilling assignments of responsibility with the construction of roads in his area. About 1835, Crenshaw and his wife, Susan, built this stately two-story brick home in old Hamburg. It was said that he was "numbered among those whose hospitality was dispensed with a lavish hand." Joseph Crenshaw died in 1840, and his son John Washington Crenshaw inherited the property. By the mid-1850s, he owned 1,860 acres. The house burned in June 1915. Pictured, from left to right, are Gerald Crenshaw; Gus Mitchell, a mulatto houseboy; an unidentified black servant; and John Lemuel Crenshaw. (Courtesy of Carrie Ramey.)

Two

Southern Gentility and War

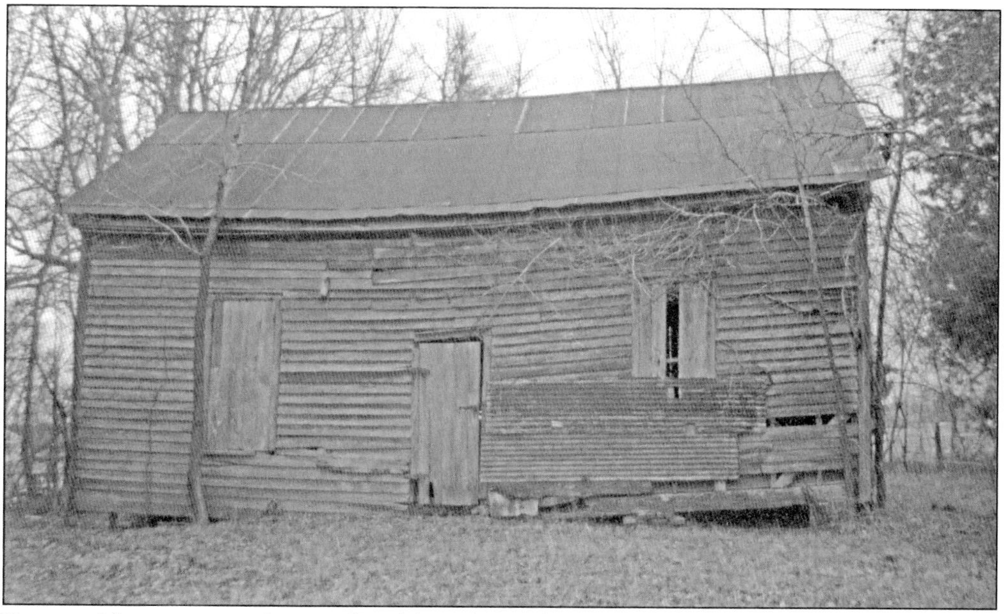

Protected by a screen of trees, the old Vaiden School is still in its original location. It was built in 1854 on land donated by T. M. Bondurant. I. B. Vaiden was schoolmaster for about 18 years, and the school became known by his name. The school continued to operate until the early 1900s. (PCHPS.)

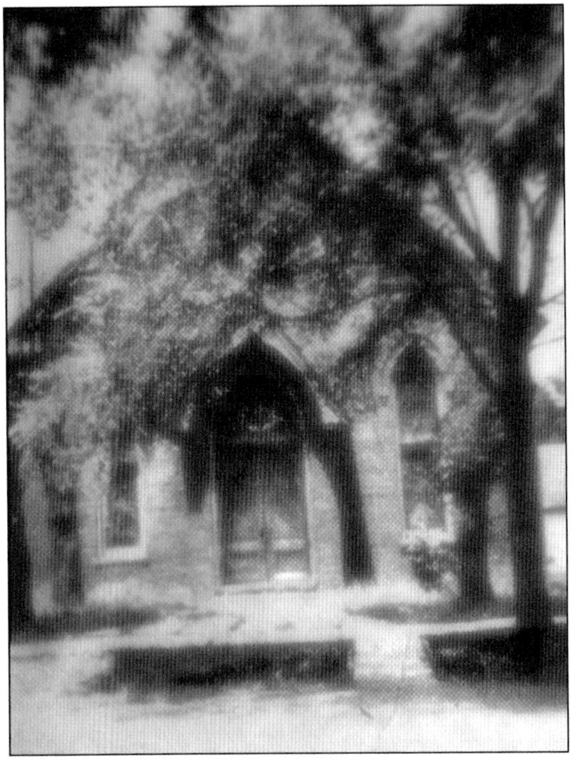

In 1854, the combined congregations of several small Presbyterian churches in the Uniontown area moved into this building on Green Street in Uniontown. Rev. W. H. McAuley was the first pastor. Of Gothic design, it served the members for 50 years. The church moved to its new building in 1915, and this building remained empty until it finally fell in of its own accord. (Courtesy of the author.)

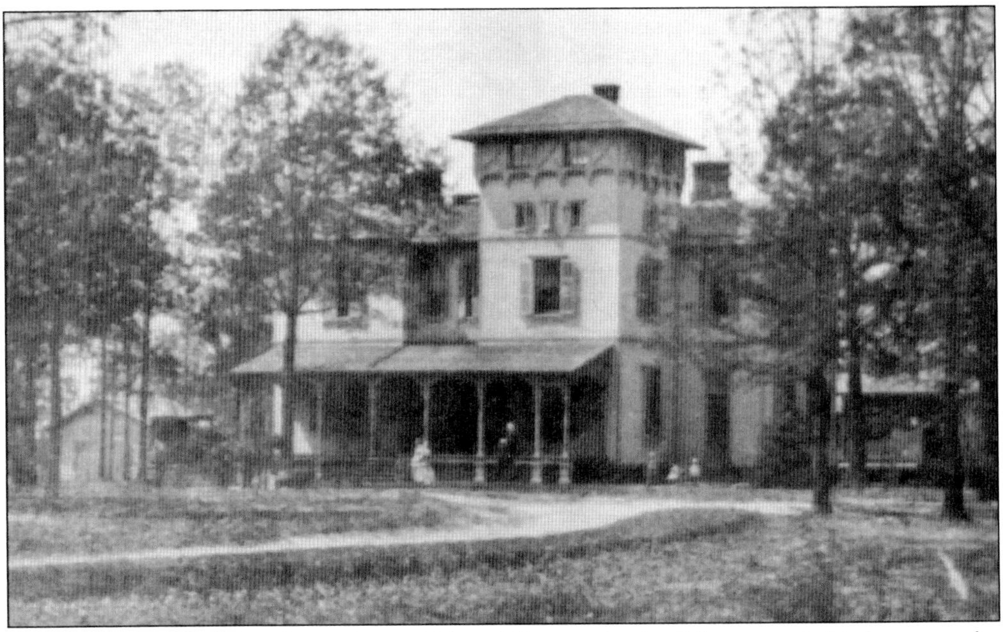

Leonidas N. Wathall, brother-in-law to Edward Kenworthy Carlisle, erected this house to the south of Carlisle Hall, with the two houses facing each other. Richard Upjohn designed both houses; this one was called Forest Hall. The designs are quite similar; however Wathall used wood instead of brick in the construction of his house. It burned during the early part of the 20th century. (SU.)

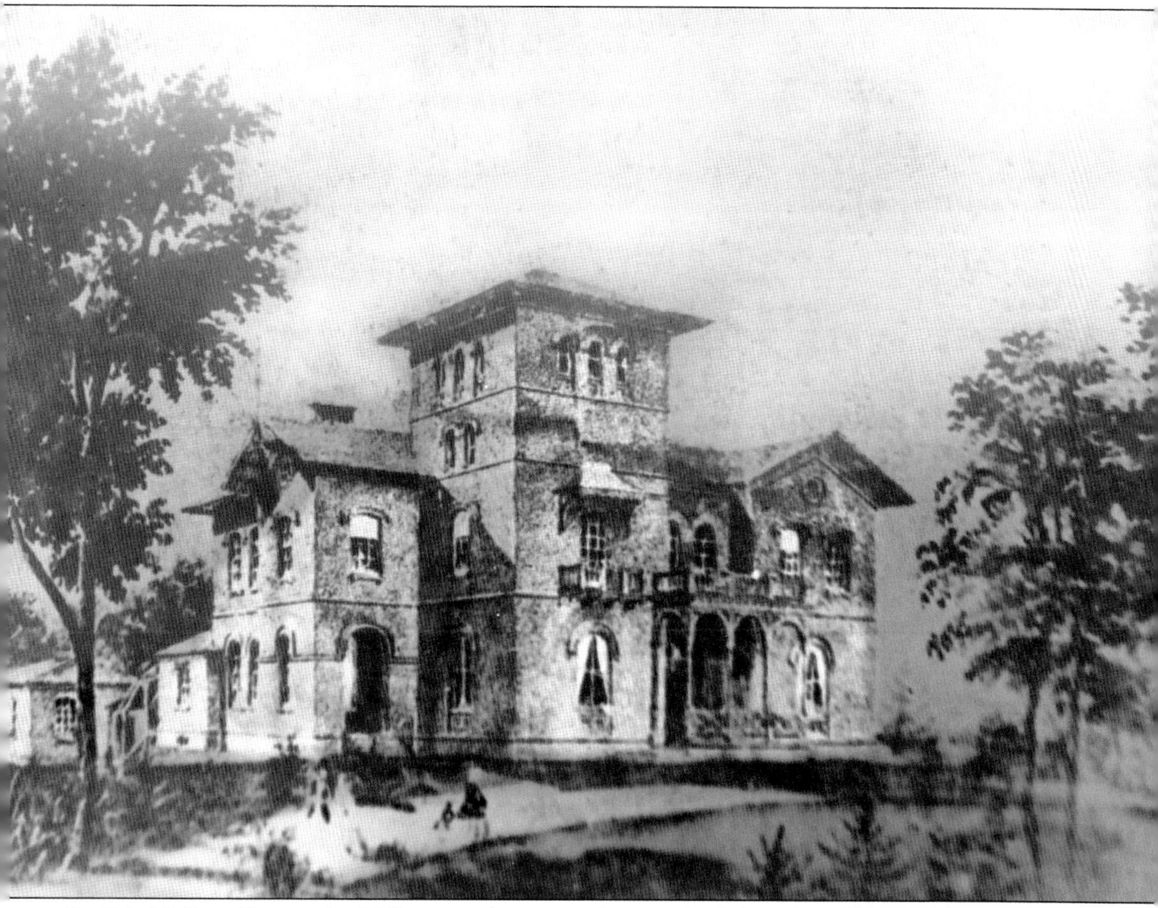

Carlisle Hall, or Kenworthy Hall, as it is known today, was built by Edward Kenworthy Carlisle between 1850 and 1860, when it was completed. Carlisle was a planter, cotton factor, and commission broker. As early as 1840, Carlisle had contacted Richard Upjohn, noted 19th-century architect, for a design for a large two-story dwelling. The house is one of the few Upjohn houses remaining in the South. The house was modeled after the Edward King house in Newport, Rhode Island. It is one of the best examples of the Italian villa style in Alabama. Its completed value was $80,000, which was extremely high for that time period. Remaining outbuildings include a kitchen connected to the house by a covered arcade, a carriage house, a brick cistern, and terraced landscape plans. Located on Highway 14 west of Marion, the house is on the National Register of Historic Places, as well as being classified a Historic Landmark. (PCHPS.)

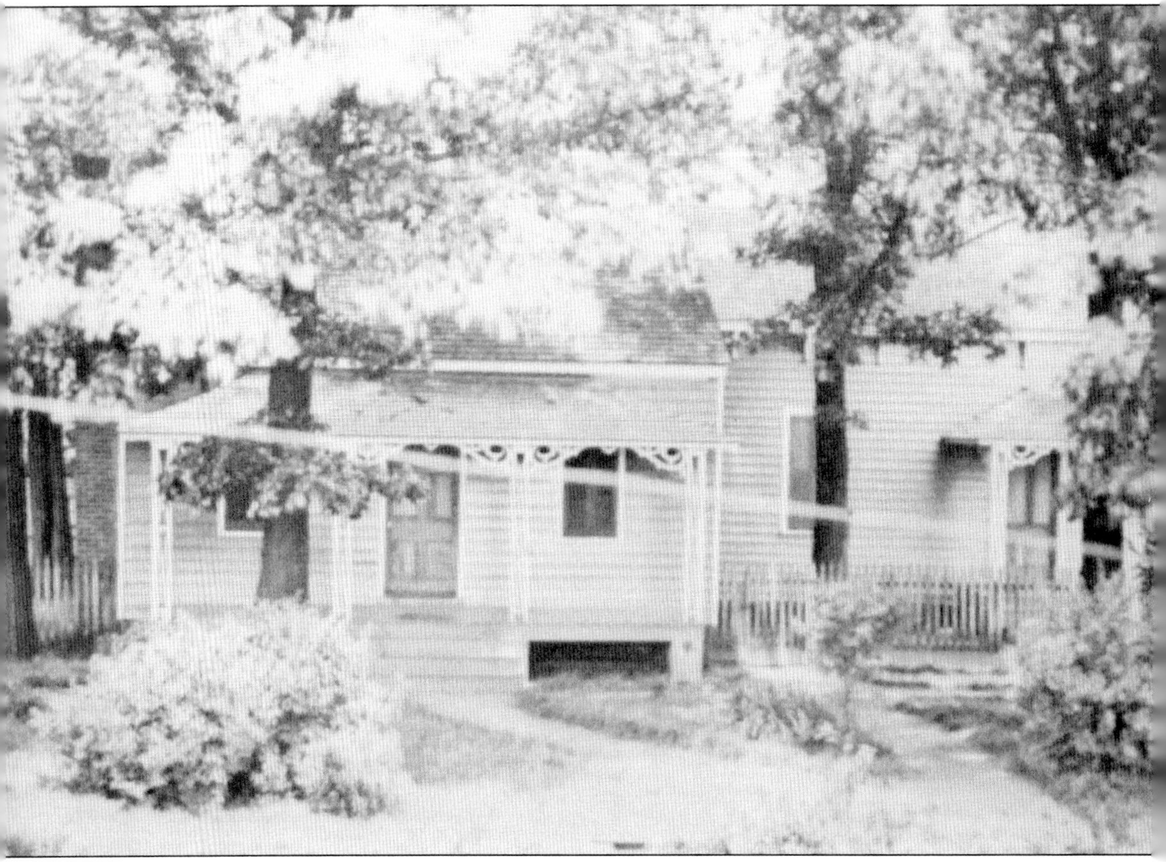

There is a note on this 1872 photograph that it was the home of Nicola Marschall. Marschall was born in Rhenish Prussia and came to the United States in 1849. There is a house a block from the Marion Female Seminary, where he taught, that older citizens allege to be Marschall's home. This house has been so altered over the years that it does not resemble this one. Marschall taught art and music at the seminary. It is said that he was unsurpassed for accuracy of drawing, boldness of conception, and richness of coloring. He was a very good performer on the guitar and violin and was also able to teach piano and harp. His name is listed as a communicant of St. Wilfrid's Episcopal Church in Marion. He served for a time in the Confederate army under Capt. John Moore and then as the chief draftsman in the 2nd Alabama Regiment of Engineers. He would travel during the summer, staying at various plantations and painting portraits of family members. (SU.)

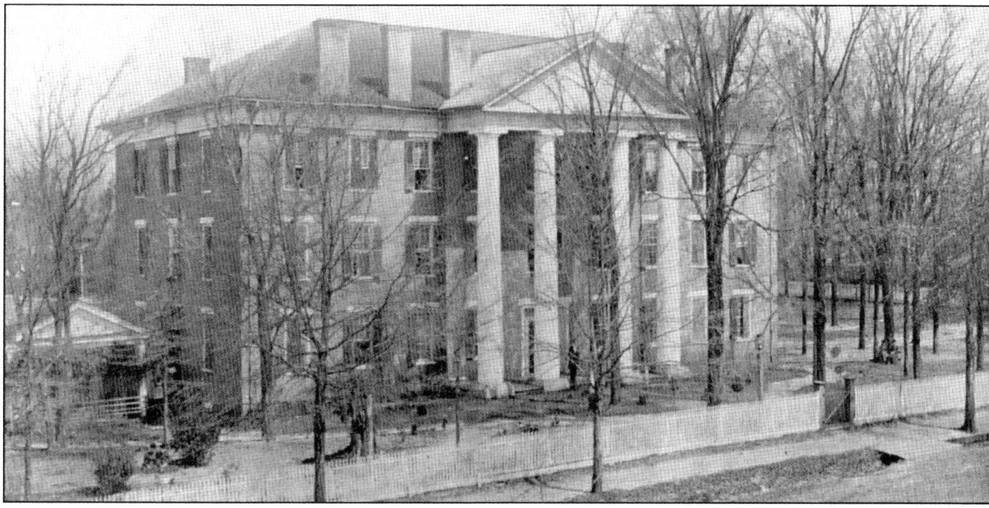

This 1850 building was home to the Marion Female Seminary, founded in 1836 as a nonsectarian school for young ladies. It was here that Nicola Marschall taught music and art. It operated as a girls' school until 1915. Although it was classified as being nonsectarian, the Presbyterians played a large role in operating the school. After that time, it served as the Perry County High School. During this time, the building was altered on the inside from a three-story building to one of two stories. Today it is owned by the Perry County Historical and Preservation Society. The first view is from the left, while the second one is from the right side of the building. The young ladies seem to be enjoying a game of tennis. If one looks carefully at the upper right side of the building today, one may see where windows were bricked over and new ones added when the building was altered to become two stories. (Both, PCHPS.)

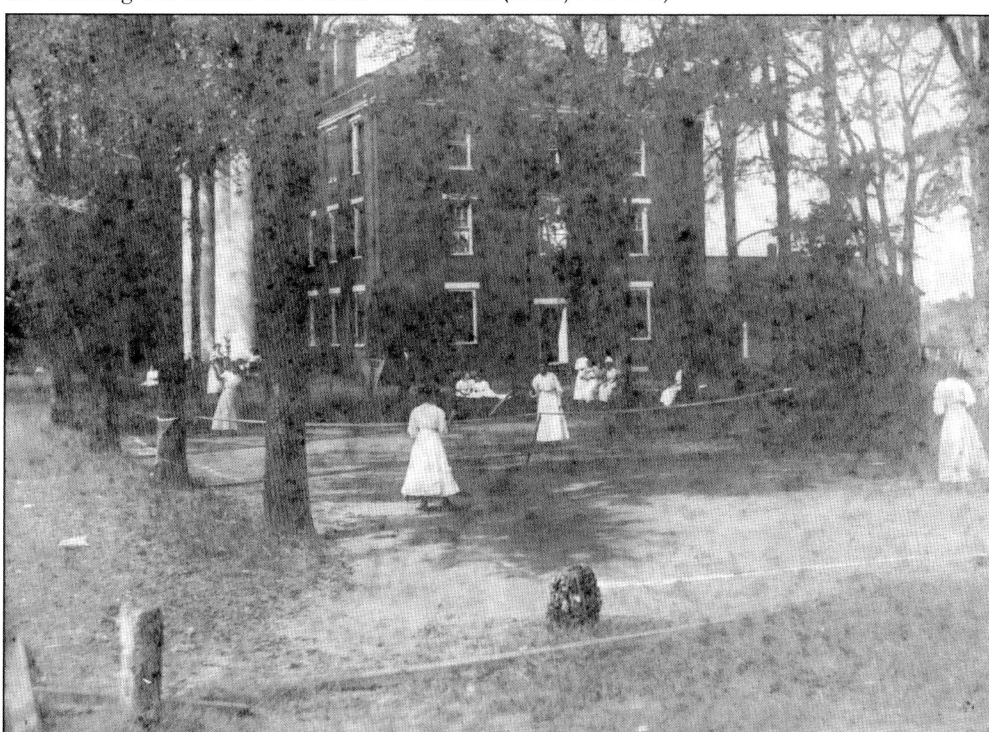

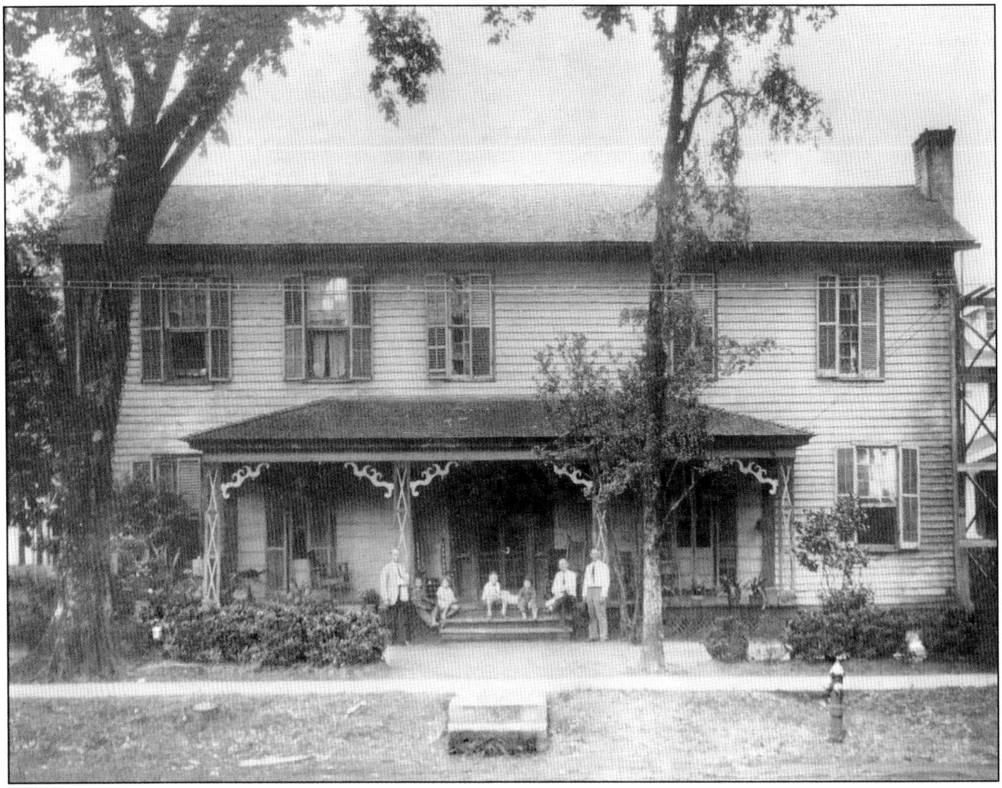

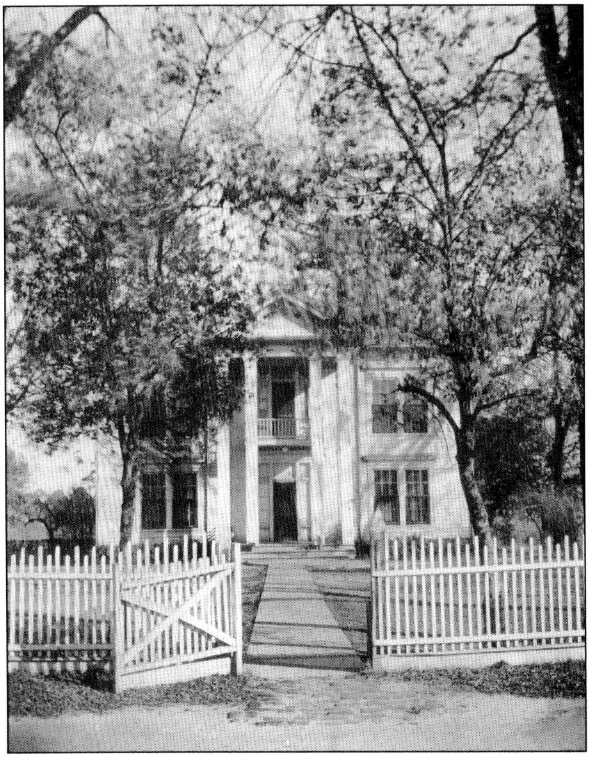

It is believed that the Temple Lea family once lived on this Lafayette Street lot. The Marshall family lived in this house during the early 1900s. Seen in front of the house, from left to right, are Ed Howell, Harry Solnick, "Possum" Howze, John Marshall, Perry Wilbourne, A. J. Marshall, and A. Perry Wilbourne. The house was torn down in 1924. (Courtesy of the author.)

Judge John Moore bought this house in 1851 from Samuel Fowlkes as a wedding gift for his bride, Emily Adelia Billingslea. It was remodeled and remained in the family for 50 years. In 1907, the house was sold to Judson College, and for some time, it housed the home economics department of the school. Today it is known as Elmcrest. (JCA.)

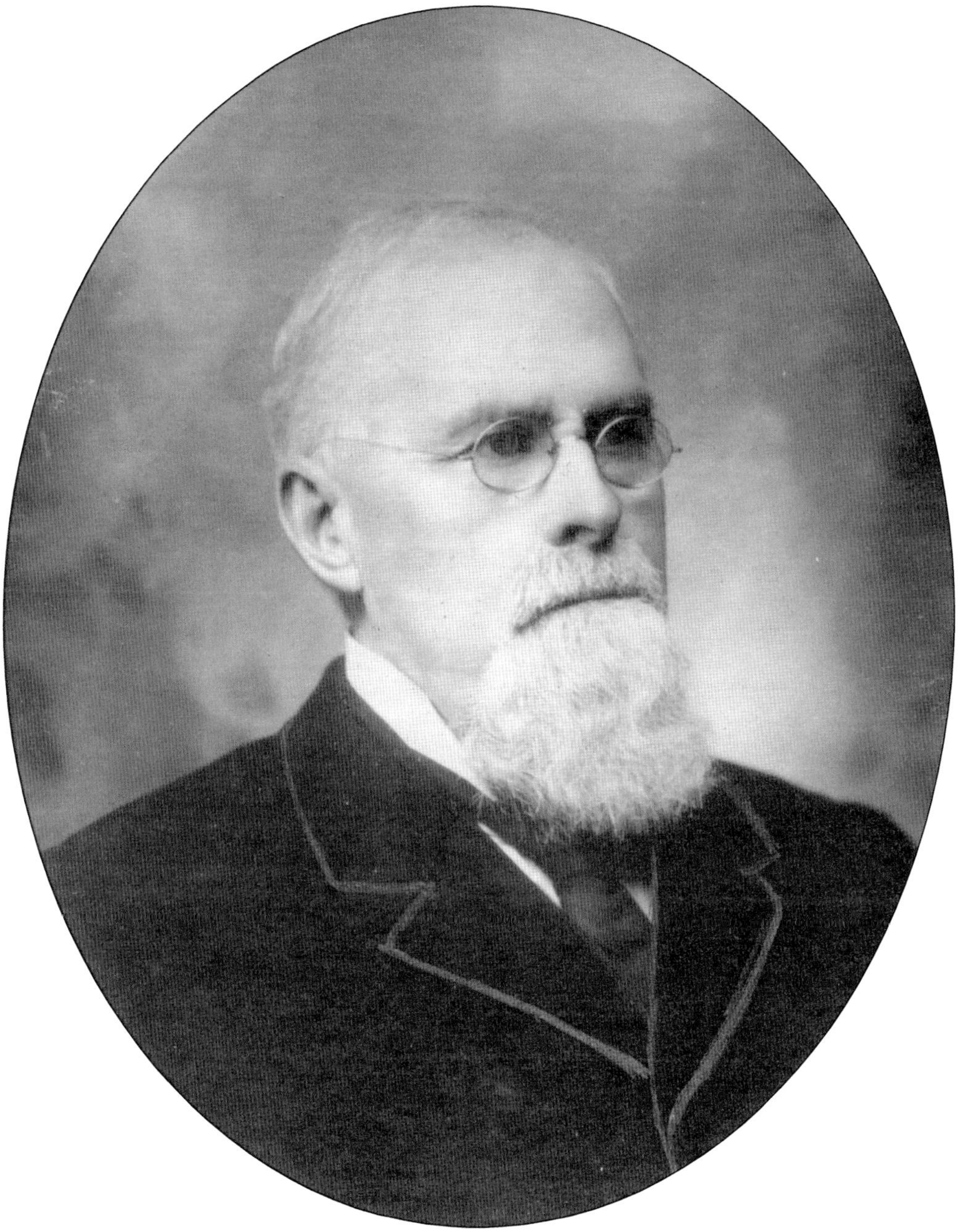

John Moore came to Marion in 1834 from North Carolina. He received his education at Howard College and the University of Alabama. He served in the Confederate army as a lieutenant in the 40th Alabama Infantry, only to be captured and imprisoned at Johnson's Island. After being exchanged, he returned home and was elected to the state legislature and later as judge of the first judicial circuit. He was removed from office in 1868, during Reconstruction. He practiced law for the next 12 years. In 1880, Moore was elected judge of the fourth judicial circuit. He also served on the board of trustees of Howard College and Judson College. Moore's son, John Trotwood, was teacher and poet. His writings were greatly influenced by his early years in the Black Belt. His later years were spent in Tennessee, during which he became a poet laureate of that state. (JCA.)

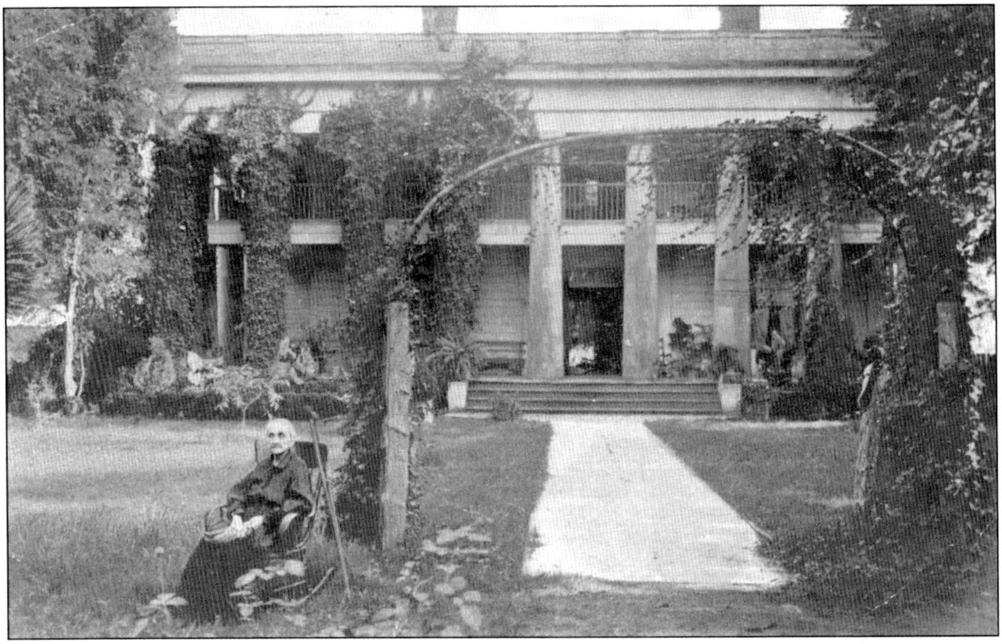

Pitts Folly, built in 1853 by Phillip Henry Pitts, is owned by descendants of the builder. Benjamin Parsons was the architect and builder. A casual remark about how foolish it was to build such a grand house in the middle of nowhere led to the house's name. Seated in the front yard is Patty Pitts Yarbrough, a descendant of the builder. (Courtesy of Emma Glass Beasley.)

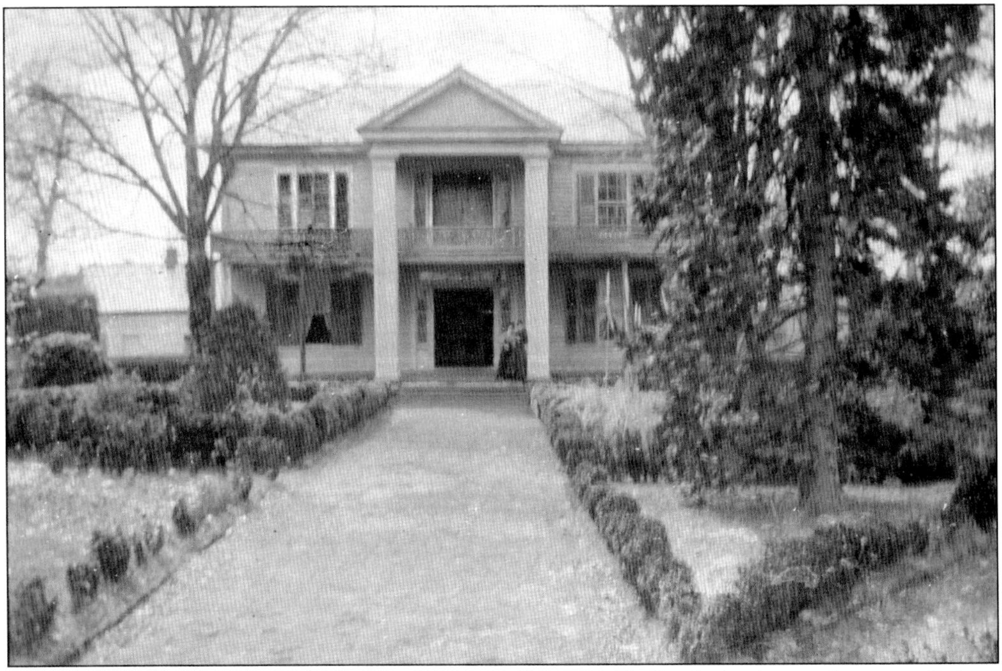

It is not clear whether it was the Jones or the Sewell family who built this house; however, Robert Tignal Jones first married a Jones and then Indiana Sewell. He died at the Battle of Seven Pines during the War Between the States. Later members of the Sewell family sold the house. A note on the back of the picture calls it the L. H. Sewell house. (JCA.)

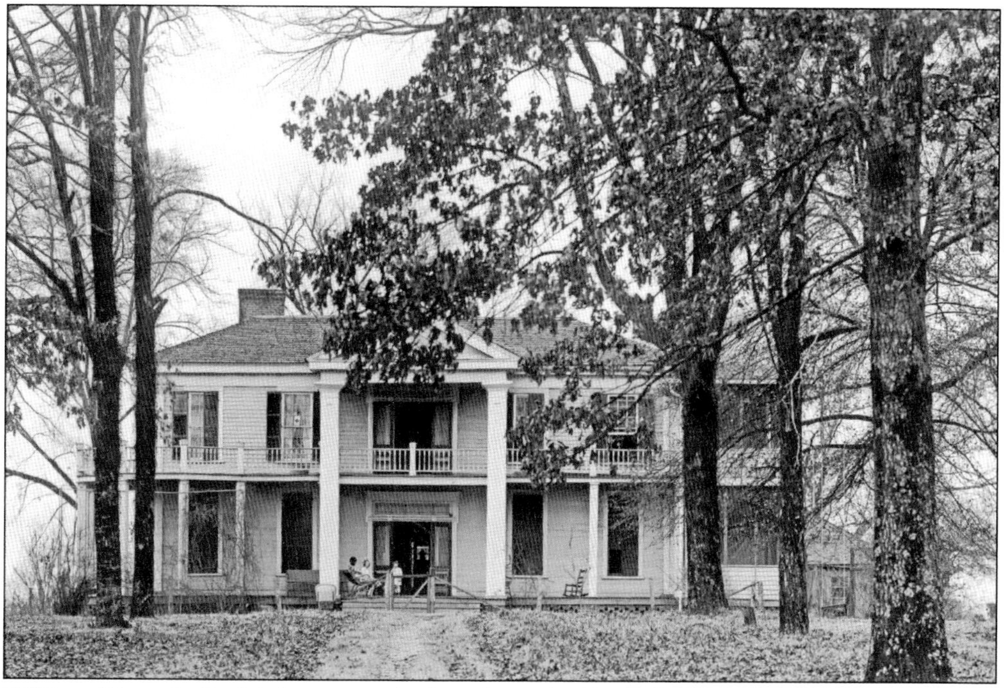

William Wyatt built this house on the lot where the Freewill Baptist Church and the Perry County Water Authority are located. After Wyatt's death, the house became the property of his grandson Houston Lovelace, and most references refer to it as the Houston Lovelace place. It was probably destroyed in the 1920s. (JCA.)

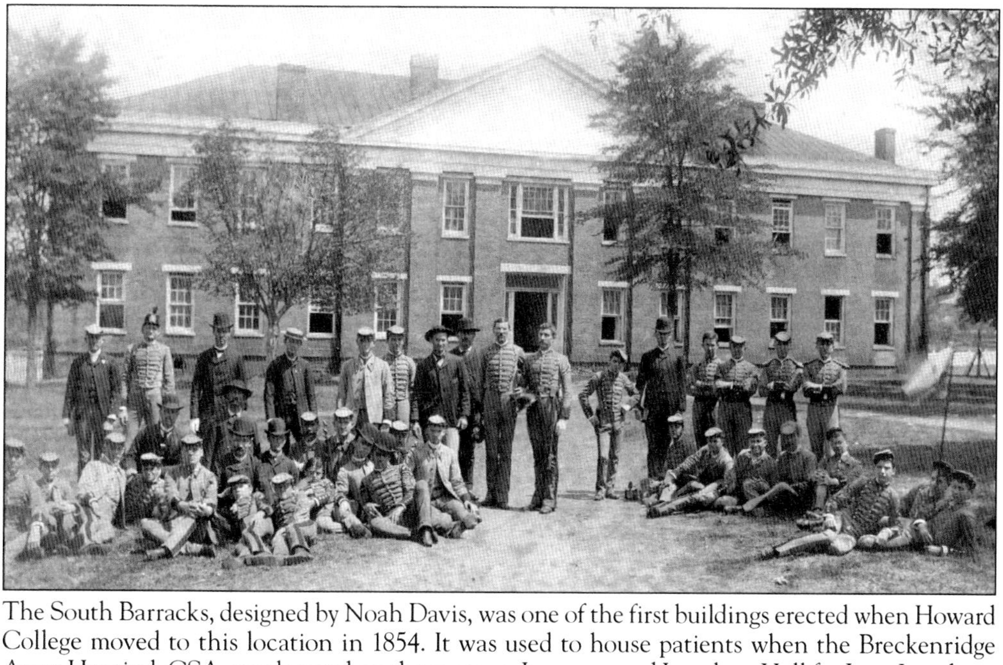

The South Barracks, designed by Noah Davis, was one of the first buildings erected when Howard College moved to this location in 1854. It was used to house patients when the Breckenridge Army Hospital, CSA, was located on the campus. It was named Lovelace Hall for Jesse Lovelace, who was one of the two men credited with saving Howard College from financial ruin in the 1880s. (MMIFA.)

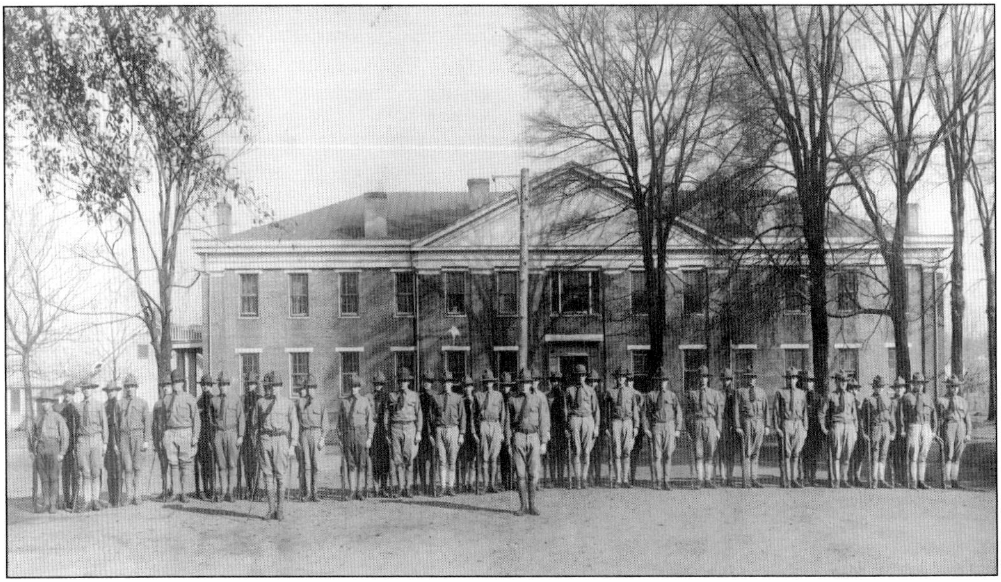

North Barracks was one of the two original buildings erected on the campus of Howard College in 1854. Noah Davis also designed this building. The building became known as Wilkerson Hall for Dr. W. W. Wilkerson, one of the two men who saved Howard College from financial ruin in the 1880s. The photograph shows Company A of the cadet corps in 1918. (MMIFA.)

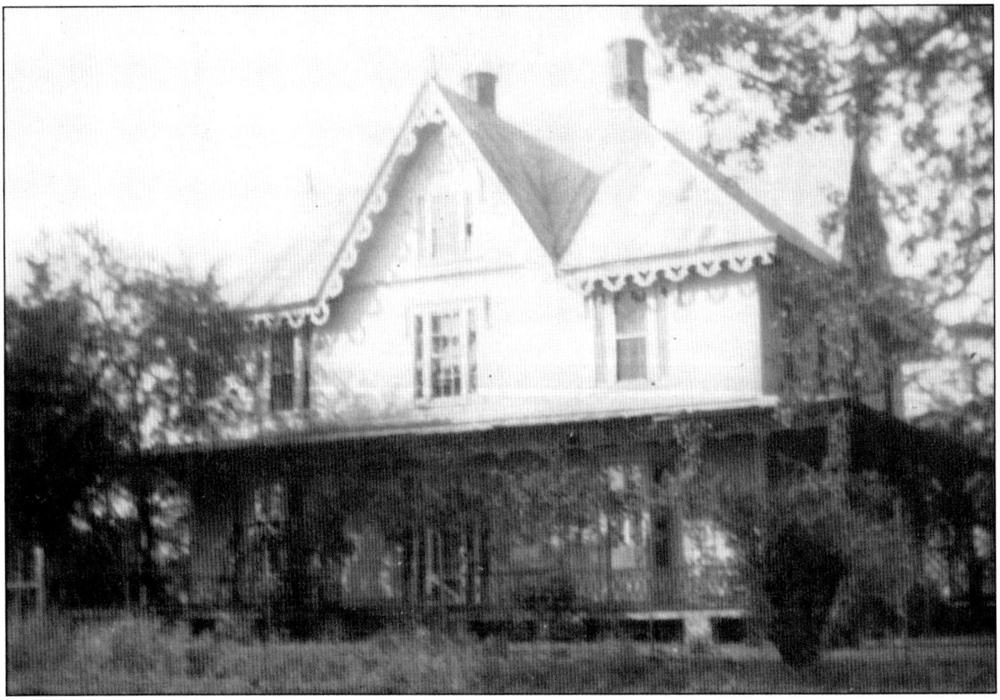

Joseph Selden built Fairhope Plantation, located to the east of Uniontown, in 1854 for his wife, Elizabeth Collier Harrison Minge. Theophilus Gilliam Fowler was the local builder. This Gothic Revival house's porch features elaborate iron grillwork from the Old Peacock Iron Works of Selma. (Courtesy of Wilna W. Kelley.)

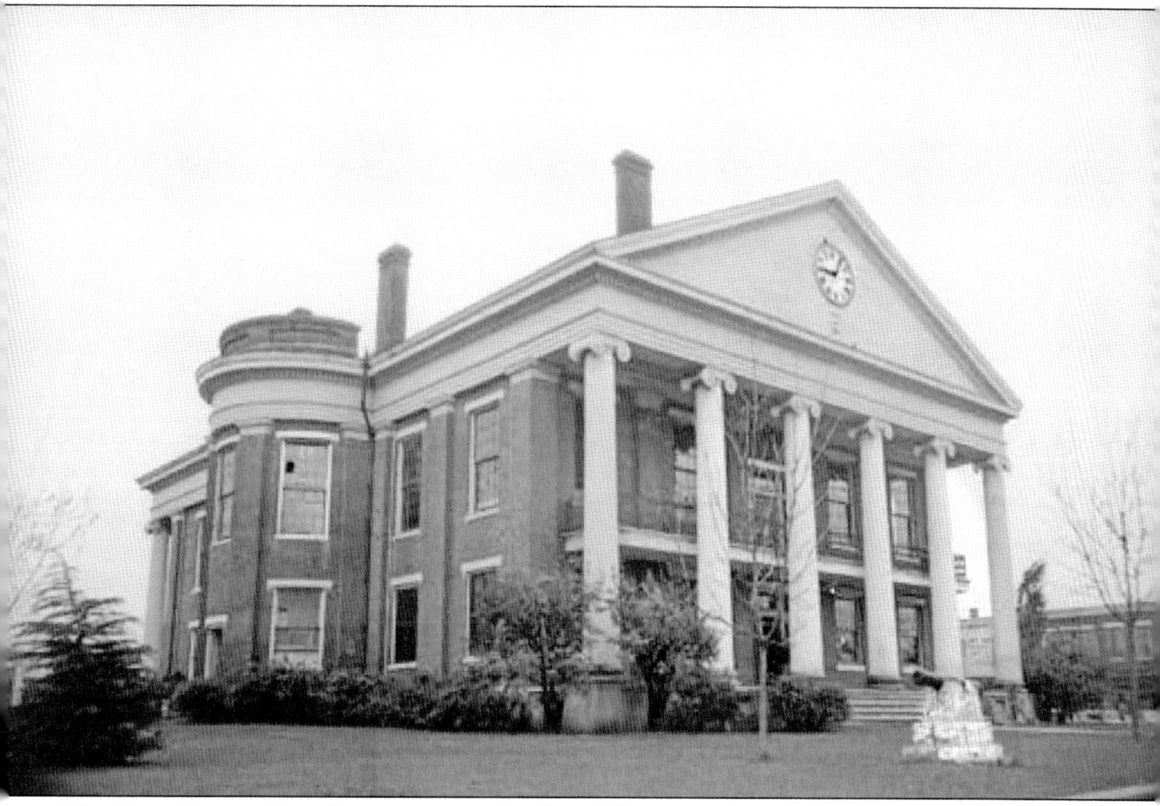

The Perry County Courthouse was completed in 1856. It was the third courthouse erected on the same spot. The first was described as a peculiar looking building with the appearance of a smokehouse with windows and the second as a modest brick building. Benjamin Parsons was the designer, and Larkin Tarrant was the builder. The building exemplifies Greek Revival design. Originally at the center of each side of the building were oval stair towers containing curving staircases with marble steps. The floors of the building were black and white marble from Bibb County, Alabama. The building was renovated in 1954, the oval stair towers were removed, and the marble was replaced with tile. Wings were added on each side for office space, and the marble was sold at auction. The entire building was painted white, since it was impossible to duplicate the color of the original handmade bricks. Records found in the offices date back to the early days of the county. (PCHPS.)

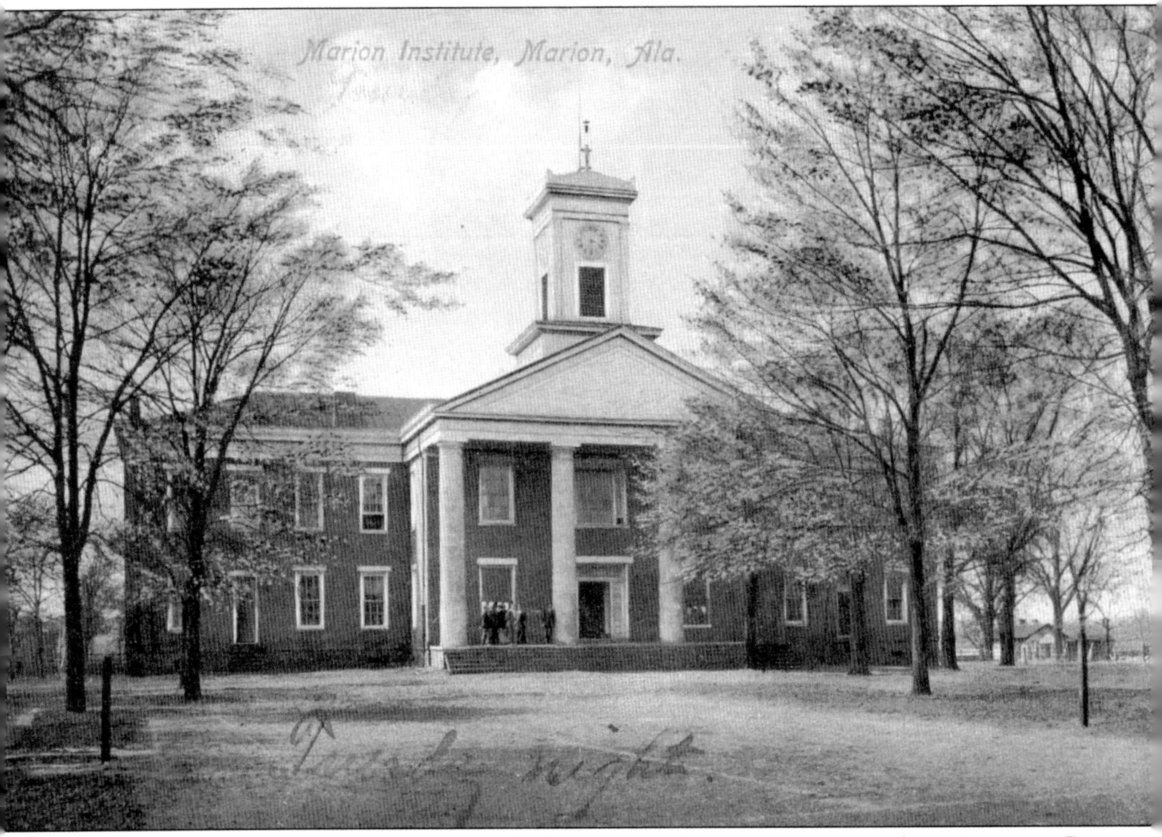

Dr. Noah K. Davis designed the chapel for Howard College, now Marion Military Institute. Dr. Henry Talbird was president of Howard College at the time of the construction. The sun-dried bricks used in its construction were made from clay found on the site. The quality of the brick has made it easy for numerous generations of cadets to carve their names or initials in the bricks on the exterior walls. It was completed in 1857, with Larkin Y. Tarrant as contractor. It is believed to have served as the operating area for the Breckenridge Army Hospital, CSA. It is also thought that it contained some of the offices of the hospital. During the early 1900s, it was known as the Hall of Council and Commons and contained meeting rooms of the literary societies. When he was president of Princeton, Woodrow Wilson visited the campus and spoke to the cadets in this chapel in 1905. Today it serves as the chapel for Marion Military Institute. (MMIFA.)

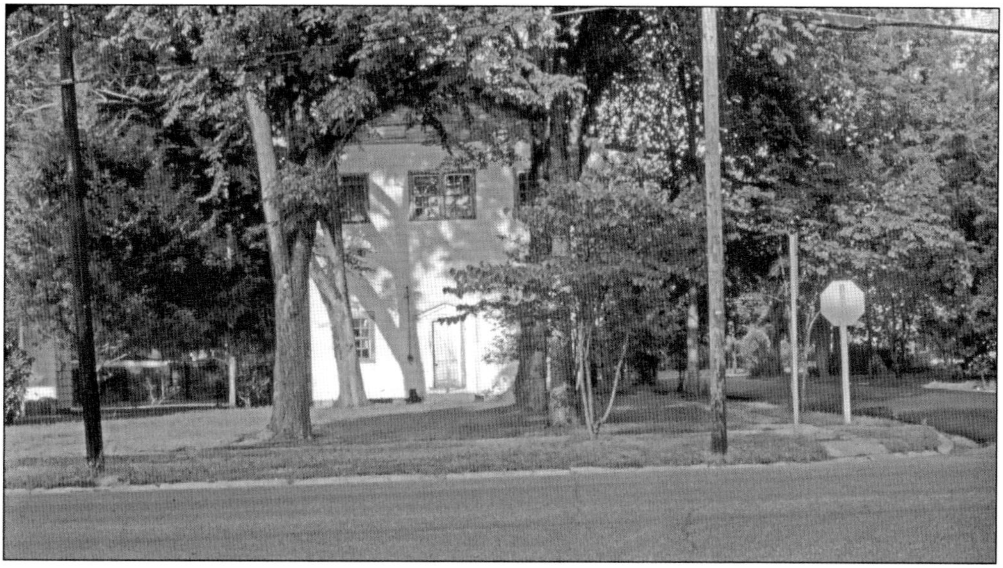

Uniontown Masons bought this lot from the Fitts estate in 1848. The building was erected during the 1850s. Deeds read and others papers indicate joint ownership at times with a boys' academy and with the YMCA. Originally, the stairs to the upper level were open, but they were enclosed after the 1935 Historical American Buildings Survey. In the early 1980s, the building was torn down. (Courtesy of the author.)

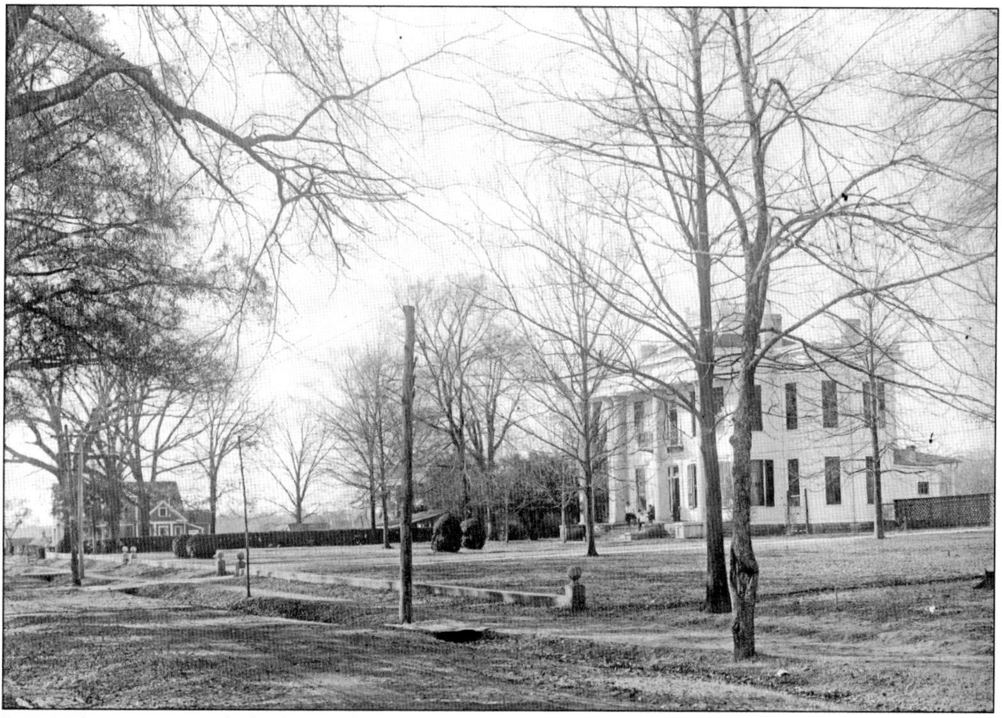

J. T. Whitsett erected the house known as Reverie in 1858 on Lafayette Street in Marion. Of Greek Revival design, this house features a widow's walk with a classical balustrade. The columns across the front are constructed of triangular-shaped handmade bricks covered with stucco. Union officers used it as their headquarters after the War Between the States. (JCA.)

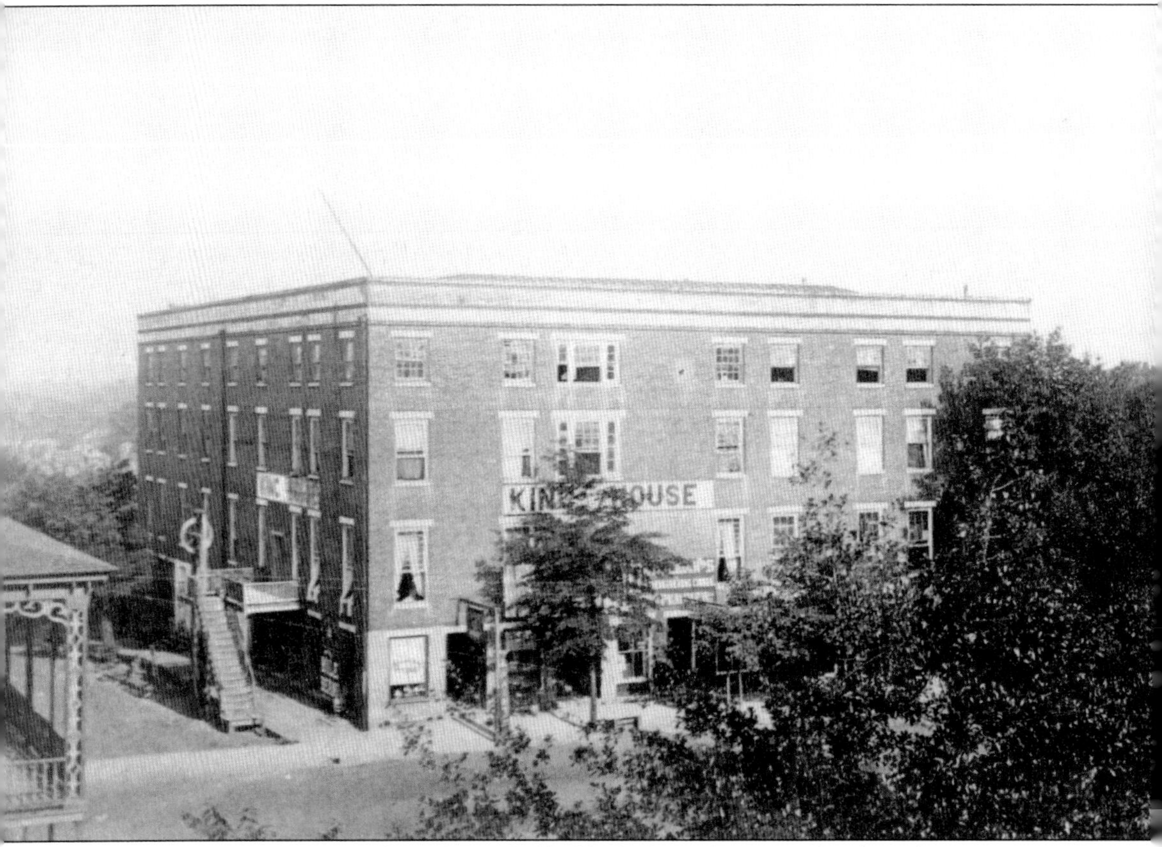

For many years, a hotel took up almost half a block along the west side of Washington Street. It was first known as the King House and then the Bruce House when it was owned and operated by S. C. Bruce. P. McEachin bought and renovated it, advertising it as the Marion Hotel. It has also been known as the King Hotel and the Wheeler House. The original building was four stories. The first floor contained the reception area, the second floor contained the dining hall and a hall used for town meetings, and the third and fourth floors contained rooms for customers. Porches ran across the front of the building, giving customers and townspeople a place to view parades and other activities. Town meetings were held here in the large hall on the second floor. Judson College would move pianos to the hall for concerts by its students. The building burned on February 17, 1921, and was replaced with a two-story building. (PCHPS.)

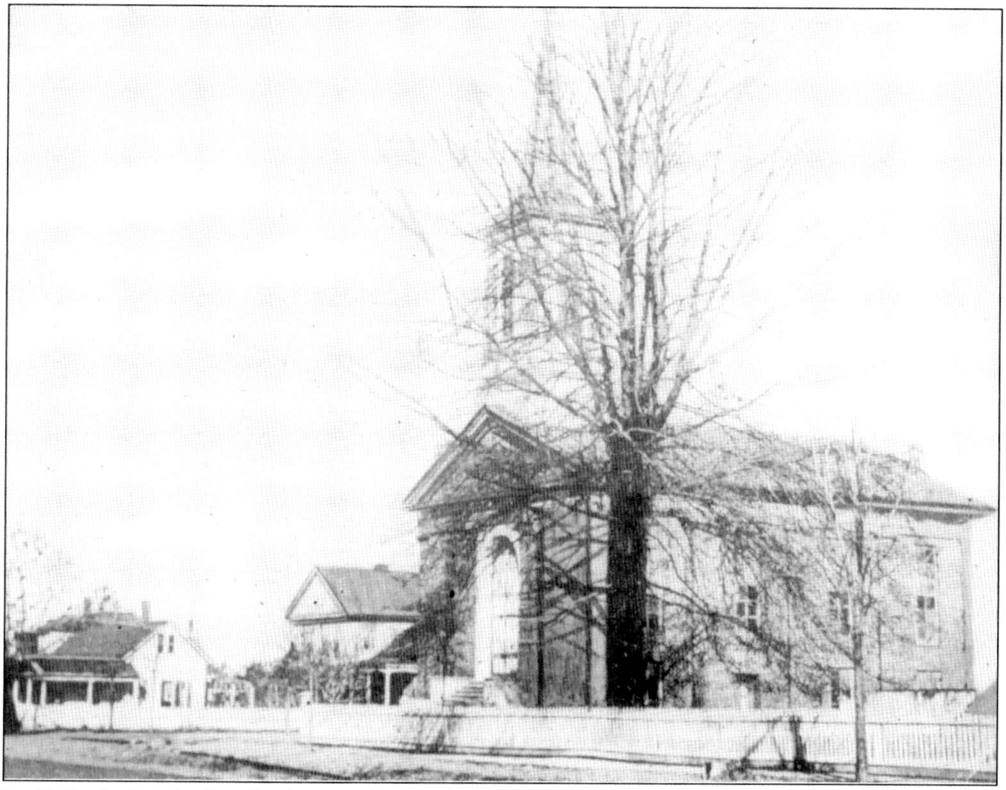

In 1843, the Methodists had a grand ingathering of members in Uniontown. This Greek Revival building was erected in 1858 with the aid of a $500 bequest from Gen. Joseph Boyd Chambers. The contractors were brothers Theophilus Gilliam and John Douglas Fowler. The outside remains much the same as when it was built, except for the stained-glass windows that were added in 1921. (Courtesy of the author.)

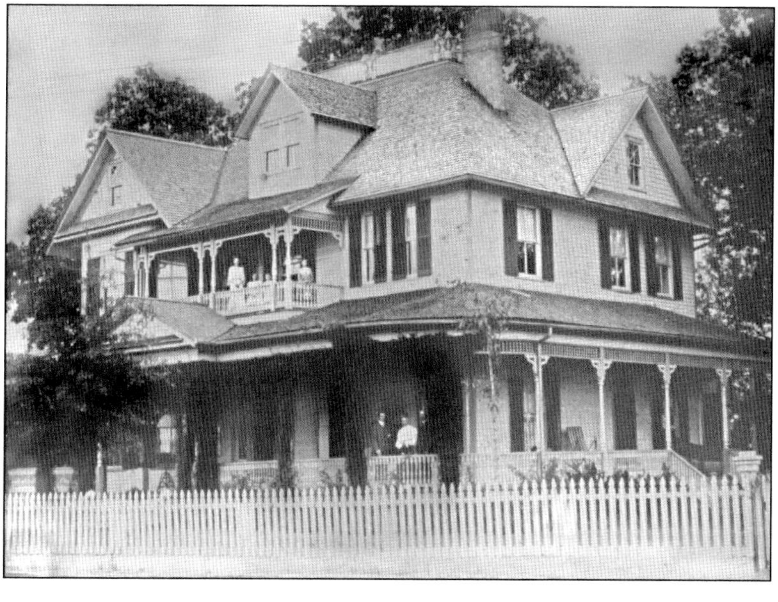

The Henry Pitts family made their home in this large house built by Pitts on North Broadway Street in Uniontown. After some years, the house was sold to the John E. West family. Members of the West family can be seen here on the porches of the house. The house burned prior to 1926. (Courtesy of the author.)

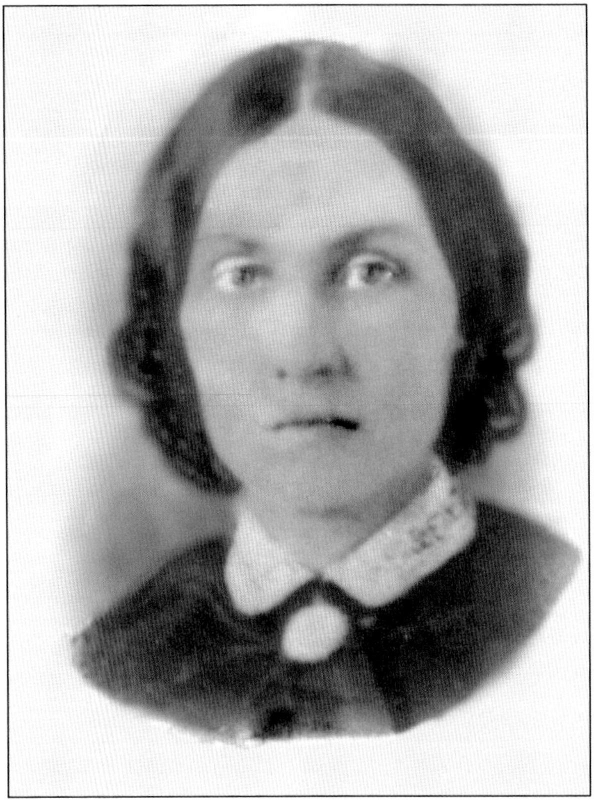

Shown here are Gen. Sam Houston and his wife, Margaret Lea Houston, in the years after they moved to Texas. Margaret's picture was made at the age of 41, while the one of General Houston was taken while he was serving in the U.S. Senate. They made their home in Texas, with very few trips back to her early home in Marion. Margaret spent much of her time alone except for her children, as General Houston was often away for long periods of time on government business. Her mother, Nancy, moved to Texas, along with other members of the Lea family, and spent her last years there. The Houstons made their home in Independence, Texas, and built a home very similar to the Lea house in Marion. (Both, courtesy of Carolyn Sandlin.)

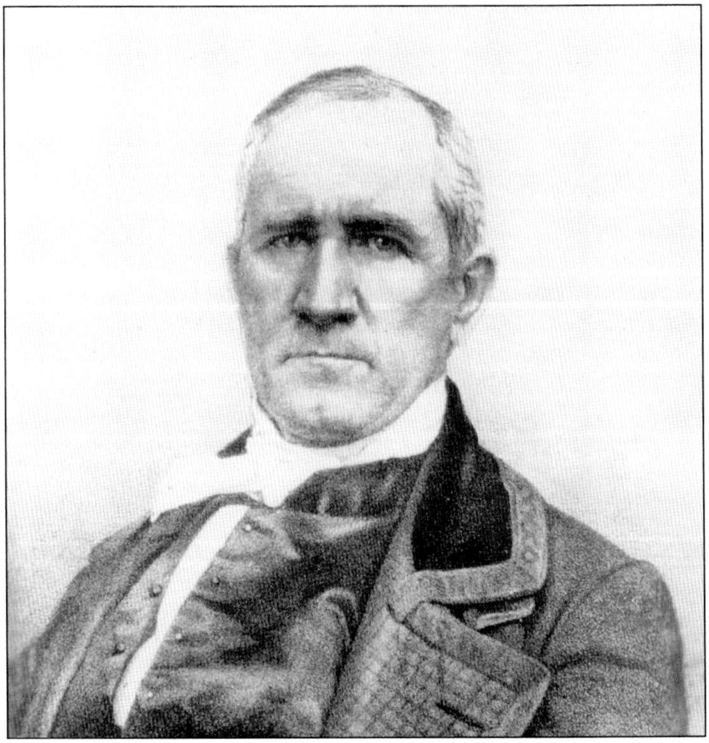

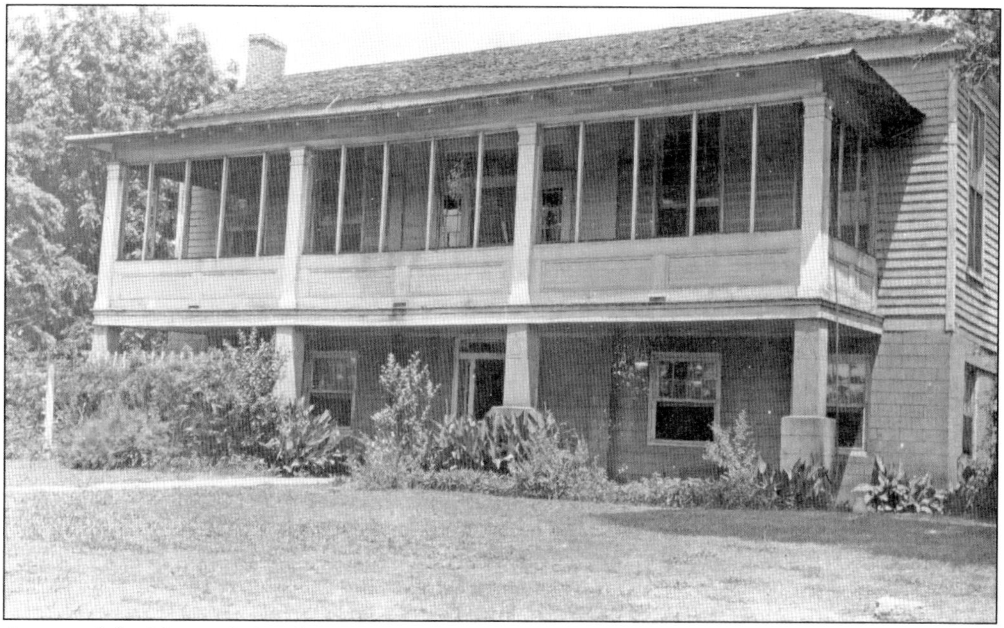

A view of the Henry C. Lea home in Marion as it appeared during the time of the War Between the States shows a change in the front of the house, with a porch running across the second story. During the War Between the States, the house served as a convalescent hospital for Confederate troops. It was known as Soldier's Rest. (Courtesy of Carolyn Sandlin.)

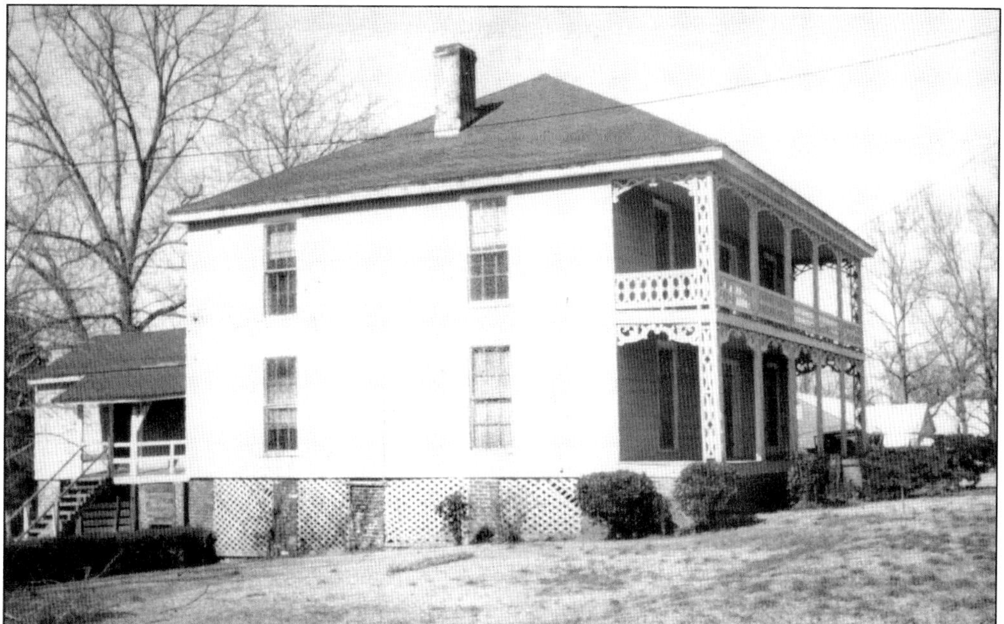

Known as Jubilee, this house sits on the west side of Washington Street in Marion. The house features elaborate saw work, pilasters, banisters, and arches on the front porch. As one can see from the side views, the rear of the house is very high off the ground. (Courtesy of James Barnes.)

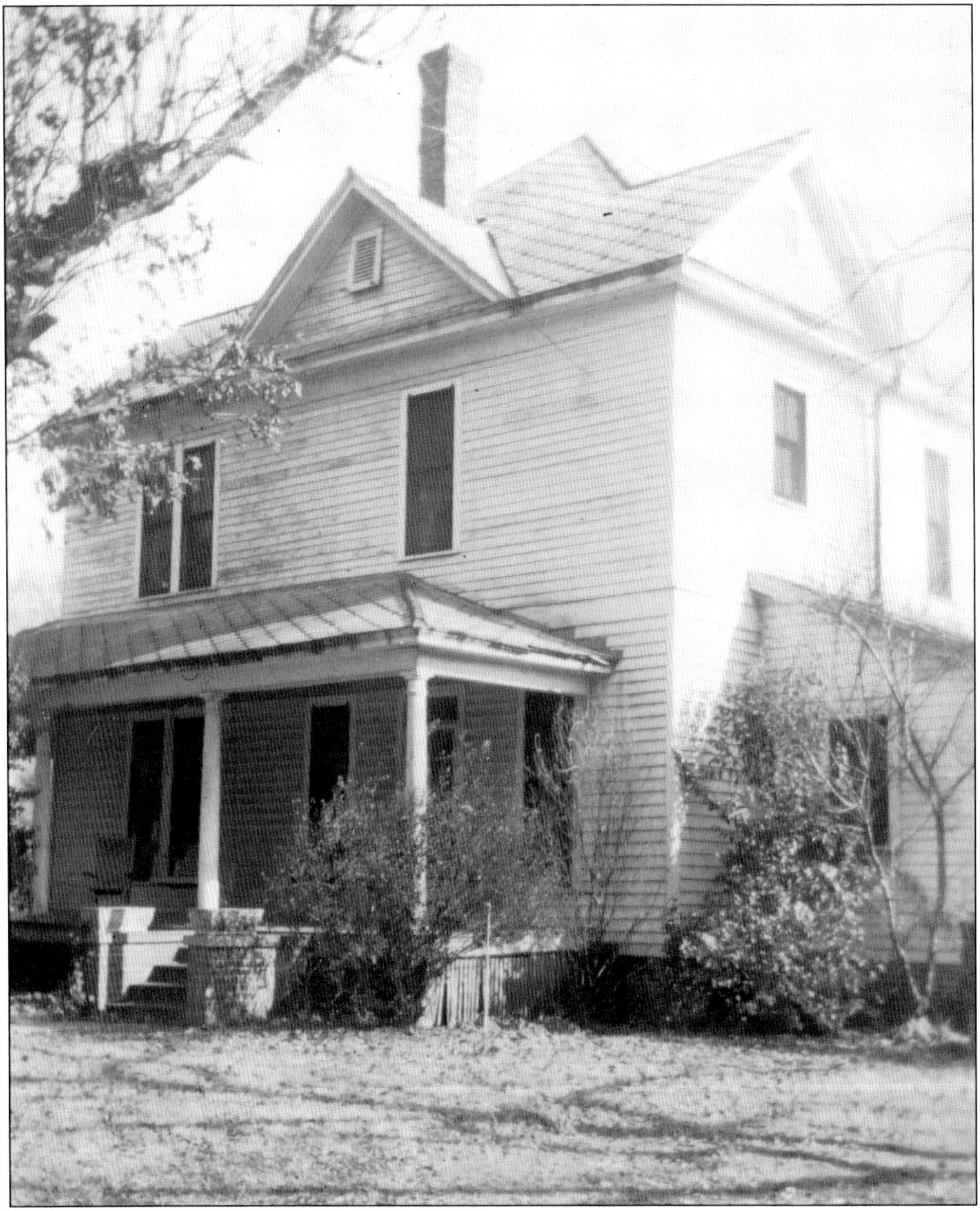

Once located on North Broadway Street in Uniontown, this house was built by a member of the Chambers family. Originally it was a one-story house, the second story being an addition. In later years, it was the home of the Robert Adair and Paul Winn families. The house burned in 1965. (Courtesy of Wilna W. Kelley.)

Three

Two Steps Forward, One Step Backwards

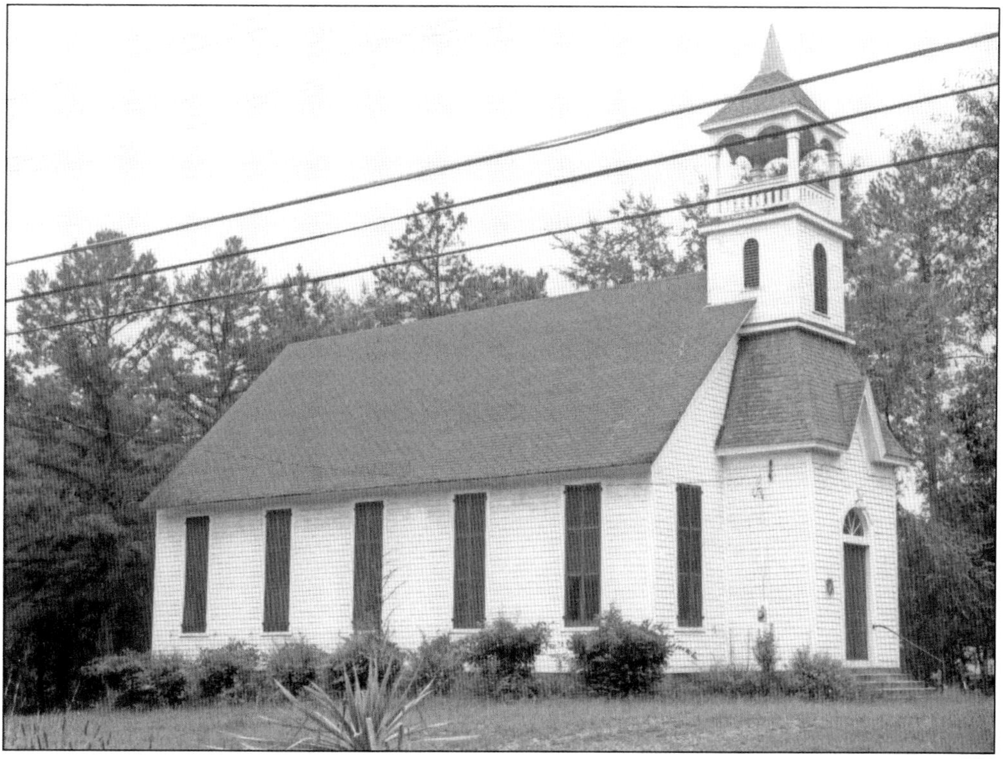

The Congregationalist church was organized in 1869 in Lincoln School by freed slaves and representatives of the American Missionary Association. In 1871, members and friends erected this building. It is the oldest black church in Marion. The architect and contractor was T. C. Stewart. It was here that Andrew Young married Jean Childs. It is still active today. (PCHPS.)

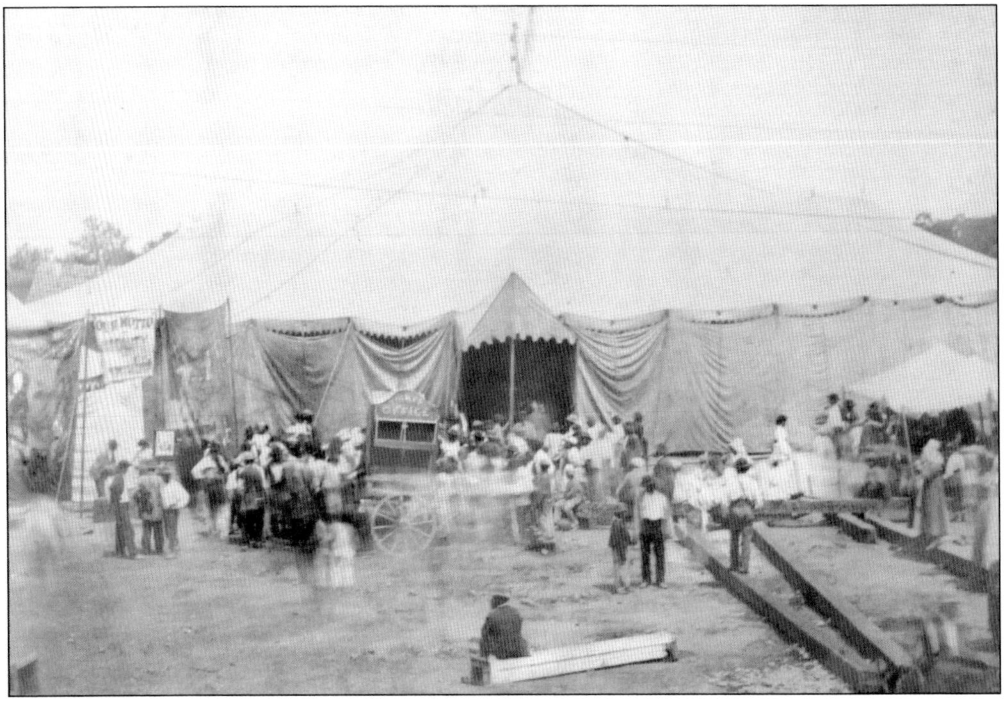

This picture, dated 1874, has a tent of the Queen City Circus in the foreground. Circuses seem to have been a favorite form of entertainment for the citizens of Marion as early as Samuel A. Townes's 1844 *History of Marion, Alabama*, in which he tells of a visit by the circus and the resulting high jinks of some of the town's young men. (SU.)

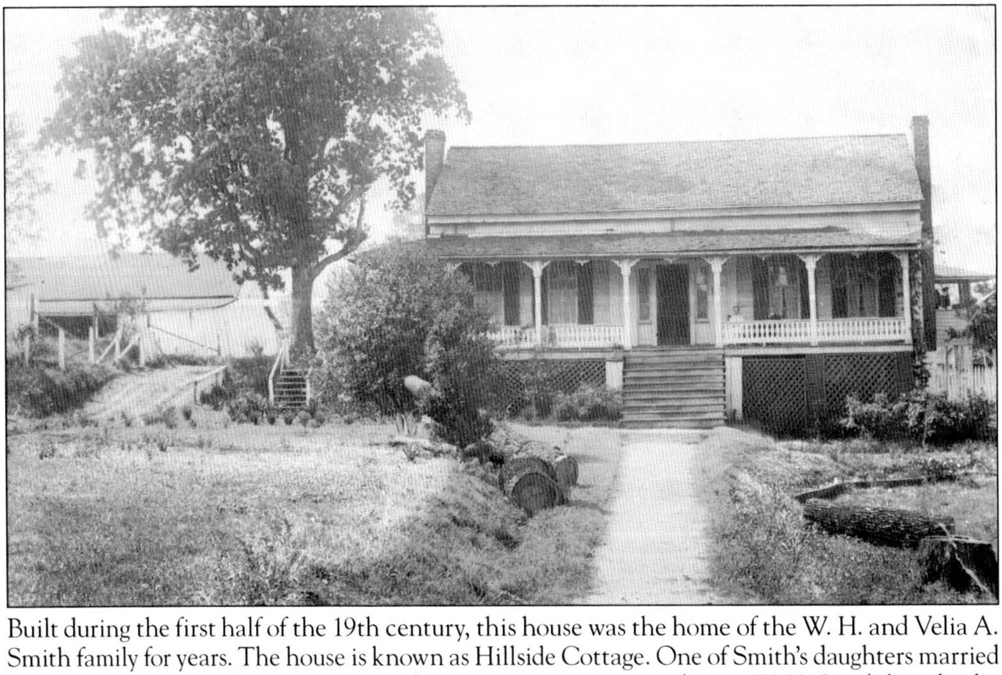

Built during the first half of the 19th century, this house was the home of the W. H. and Velia A. Smith family for years. The house is known as Hillside Cottage. One of Smith's daughters married John C. Mickleboro, who became one of Marion's prominent merchants. W. H. Smith bought the house in 1869, and his heirs sold it to Judson College in January 1930. (PCHPS.)

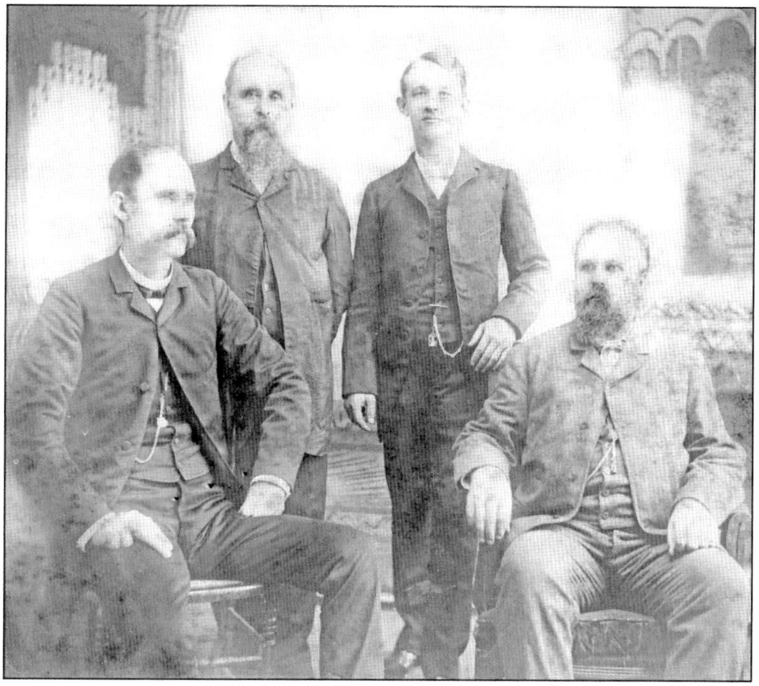

W. H. Smith was a merchant in Marion and then later served as a judge. All four gentlemen seem to be wearing the same pin on their vest, indicating membership in some organization. The room also appears to be a special meeting place. Pictured from left to right are G. R. Johnson, J. M. ?, Ira Davis, and W. H. Smith. (PCHPS.)

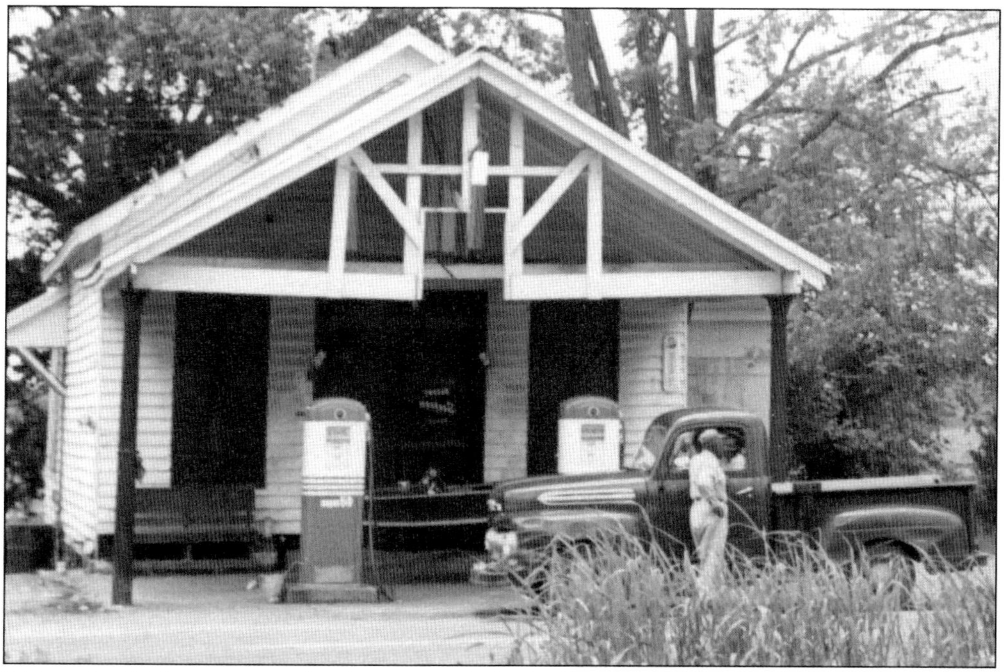

This is the 1875 store located at Holmestead, the William Moore plantation. Inside it appears, today, much like a store that served the people who lived and worked on the plantation. The furnishings are reminiscent of a time gone by. Also on the inside, historic papers, a deed signed by Andrew Jackson, and other items may be viewed. (Courtesy of Charles Holmes.)

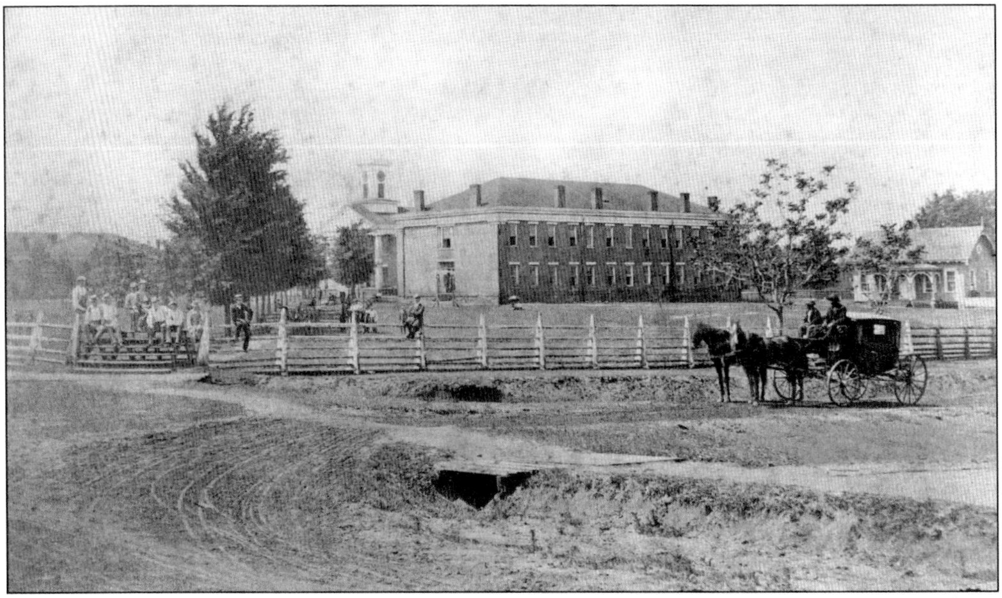

The above scene is from the Howard College campus before it moved to East Lake near Birmingham in 1888. The campus was much smaller at that time than it is today. The campus did not reach Washington Street. Note the enclosed carriage driving by the fence surrounding the campus. That fence had a stile where students gathered to sit and discuss the daily state of affairs. (MMIFA.)

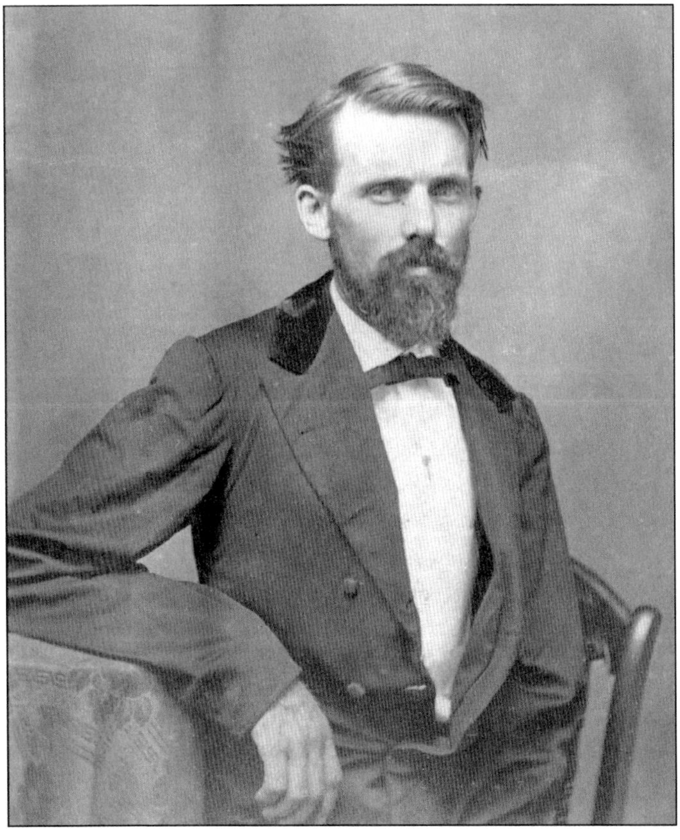

Shown in this photograph dated 1871 is A. L. Oxford. Oxford was a prominent businessman in Marion during the last quarter of the 19th century and the early part of the 20th century. His name is found in many of the land records for the period. (SU.)

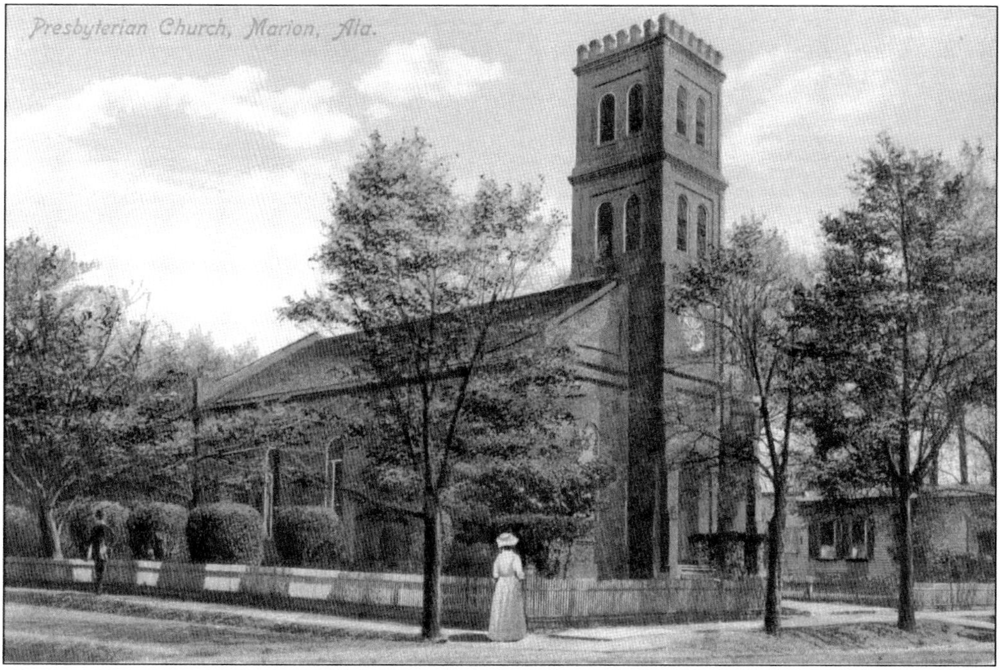

The Presbyterian church in Marion was organized on July 30, 1832. The first pastor was Rev. Robert Nall, a son of Ann Smith, one of Marion's earliest settlers. The building pictured above, of Romanesque architecture, was dedicated on December 30, 1877. A dividing partition remains between the center pews. This is a reminder of the early custom of requiring men and women to sit separately. (JCA.)

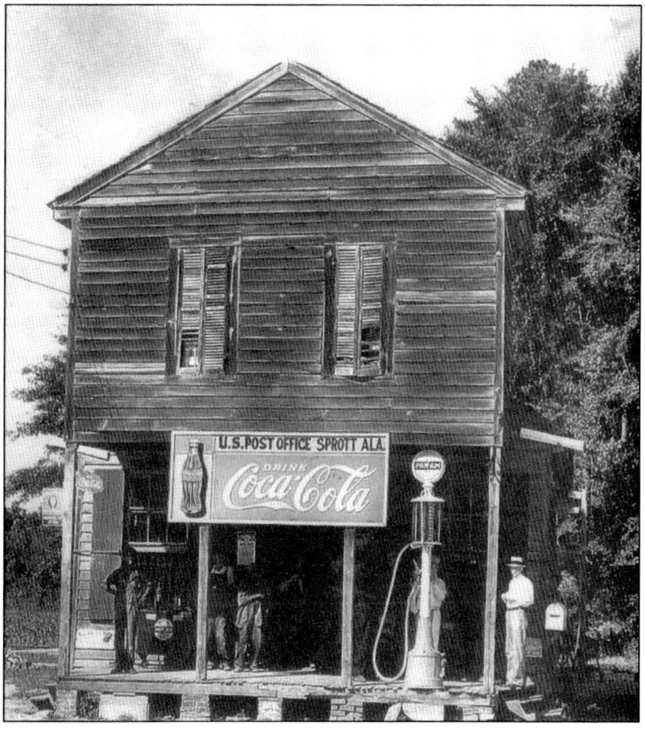

This two-story building was once the post office and general store at Sprott, 7 miles to the east of Marion. It opened in 1881. The post office shared the building with L. B. Sprott General Merchandise and the plantation business office. In 1941, a photograph of the building appeared in *Let Us Now Praise Famous Men* by Walker Evans and James Agee. (PCHPS.)

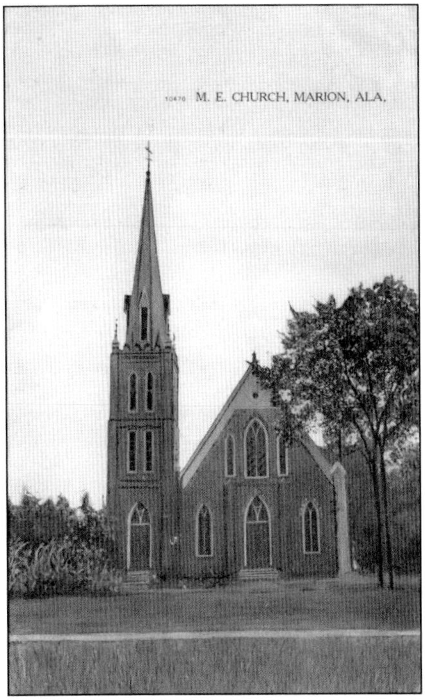

Methodists had been in Marion for many years when they built this High Victorian Gothic-style building in 1882. The polychromatic slate roof remains today, as do most of the medieval-style stained-glass windows. The windows are pointed, as is the steeple. There is a corner tower with a louvered belfry and slender octagonal spire. (Courtesy of Kitty Grey Long.)

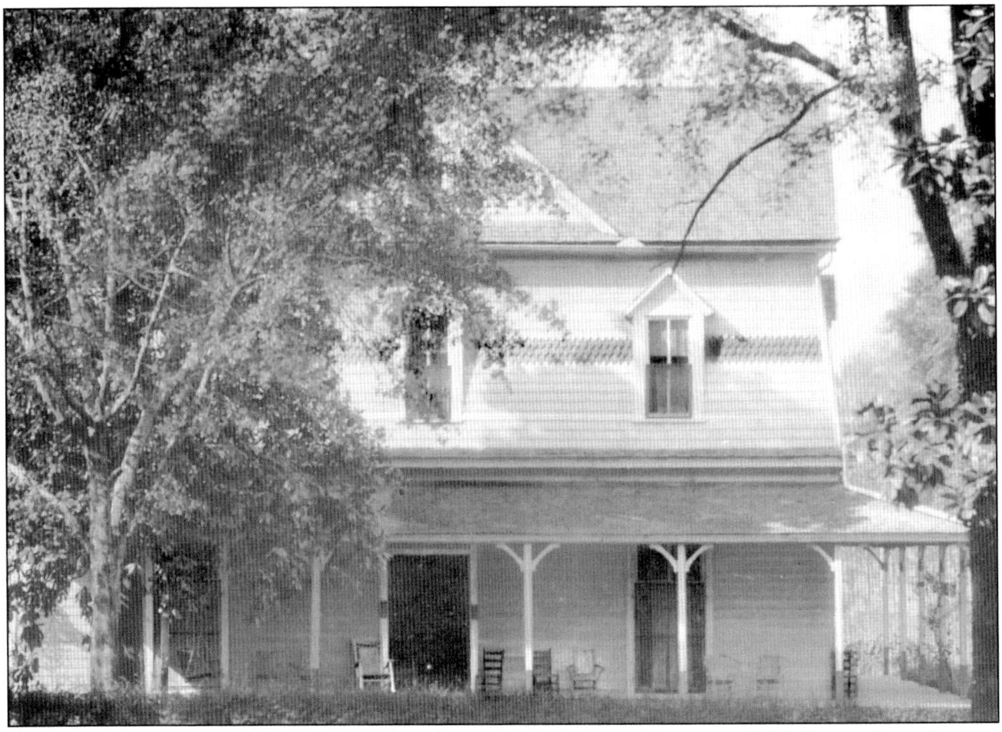

The picture is entitled "Vary Cottage." The cottage sat on a lot across Bibb Street from Jewett, where Bessie Miles Mead Hall is now located. It may have been the house that Dr. Luther Rice Gwaltney bought when he was president of Judson College. Later Amy Vary purchased this property and bequeathed it to her alma mater, Judson College. (PCHPS.)

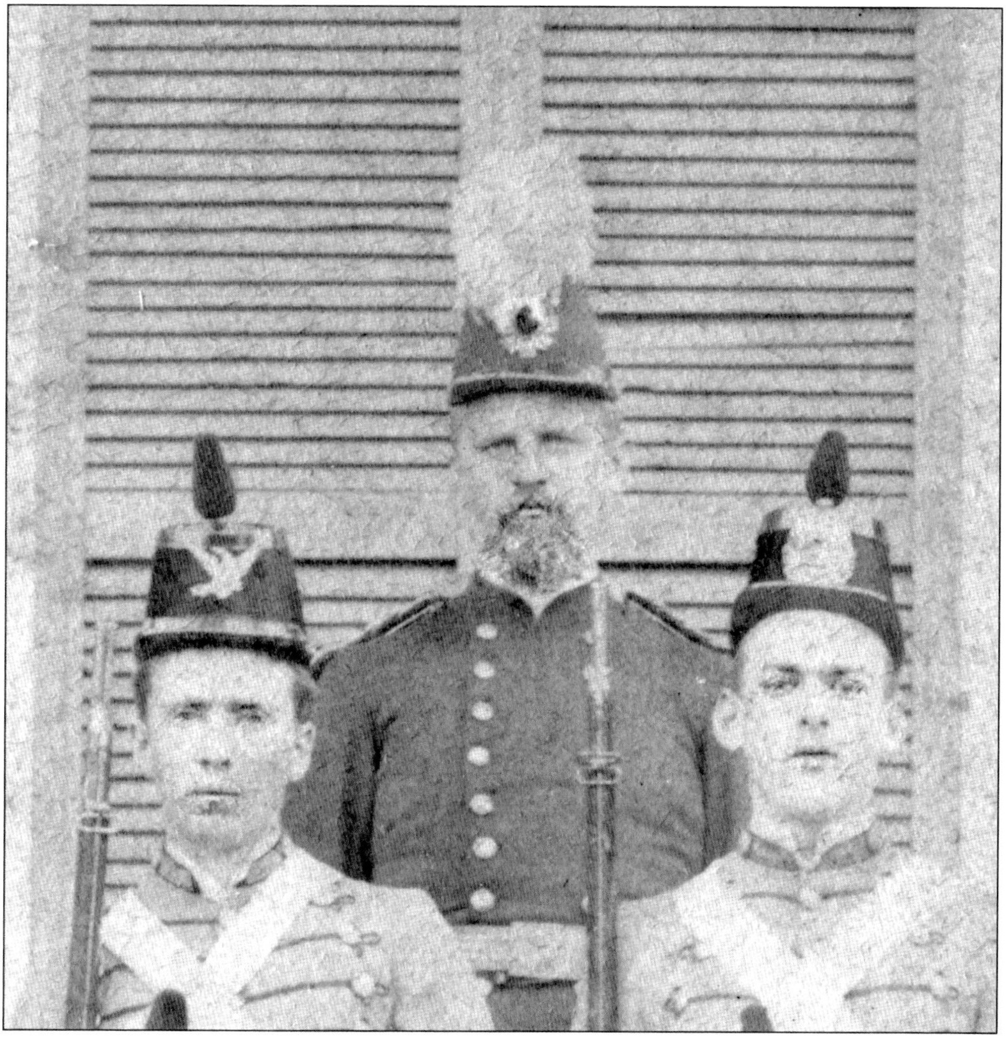

James Thomas Murfee was a graduate of the Virginia Military Institute. He began working at the University of Alabama as a professor and served as the commandant of cadets from 1862 to 1865. Murfee held the rank of colonel of the Alabama troops and was on active duty with the 41st Alabama Regiment during the War Between the States. He was commandant of the cadets when the University of Alabama was attacked by Union troops. He and the cadets retreated to Marion, Alabama. During the years of 1867 to 1869, he was architect and rebuilder of the university. He came to Howard College as president in 1871. He led the school through a difficult period, and when Howard College moved to East Lake, he chose to remain in Marion and establish the Marion Military Institute. While he was president, Woodrow Wilson, then president of Princeton, came to Marion Military Institute to speak to the cadets. Murfee retired in 1906. He has been inducted into the Alabama Men's Hall of Fame. (MMIFA.)

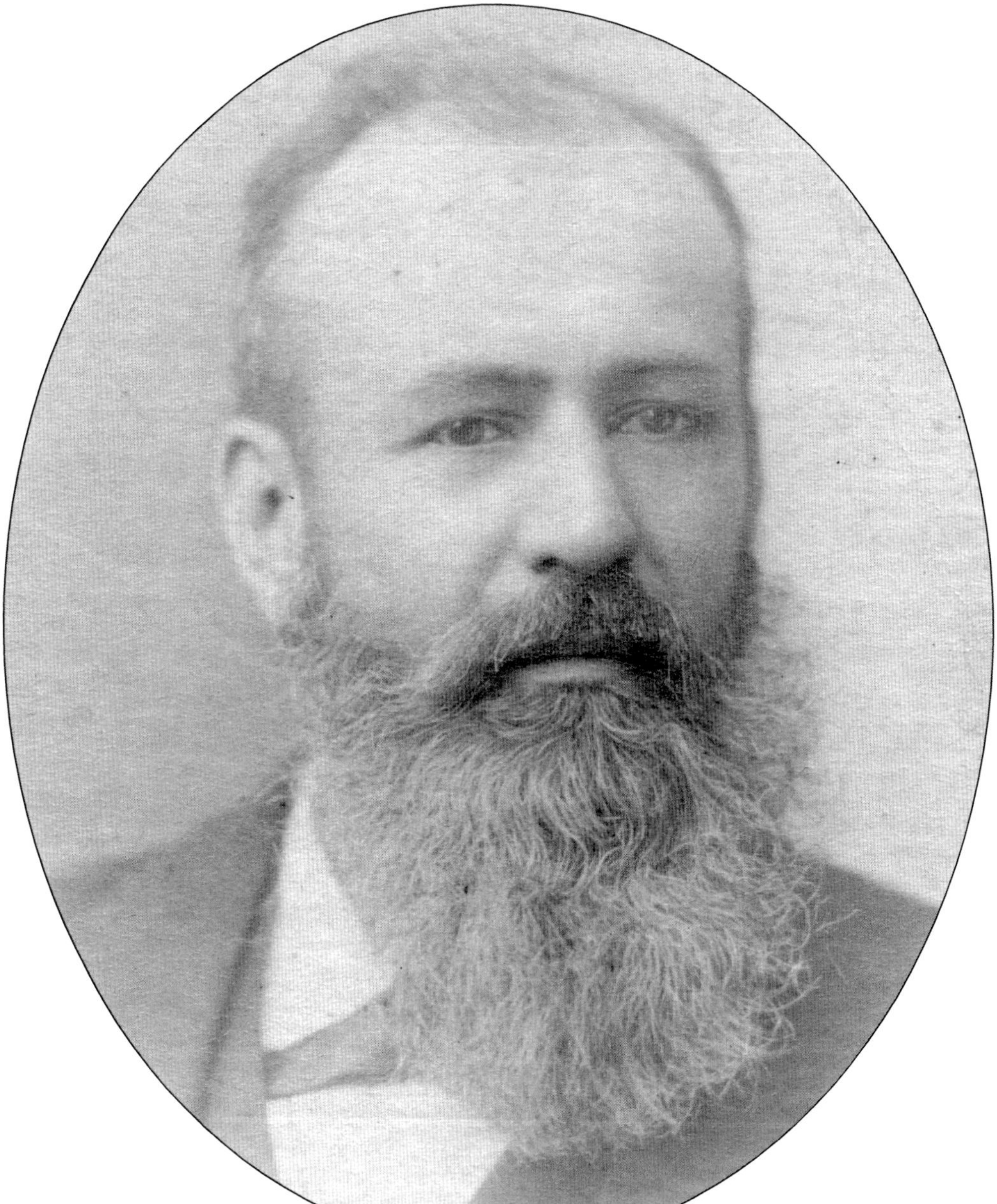

W. W. Wilkerson attended the University of Alabama and received his medical degree from the Jefferson Medical College of Philadelphia, Pennsylvania, in 1855. He served as an assistant surgeon during the War Between the States. When he returned home, he became very prominent in the civic and religious affairs of the town. An active Baptist, he, along with others, brought the *Alabama Baptist* back to Marion. For several years, he was on the board of trustees of both Howard College and Judson College. He, along with Jesse B. Lovelace, saved Howard College from financial ruin during the 1880s. The North Barracks on the Marion Military Institute Campus is named for him. He was invaluable in establishing Marion Military Institute in the buildings vacated by Howard College. At the time of his death, he was chairman of the board of trustees at Judson College. (JCA.)

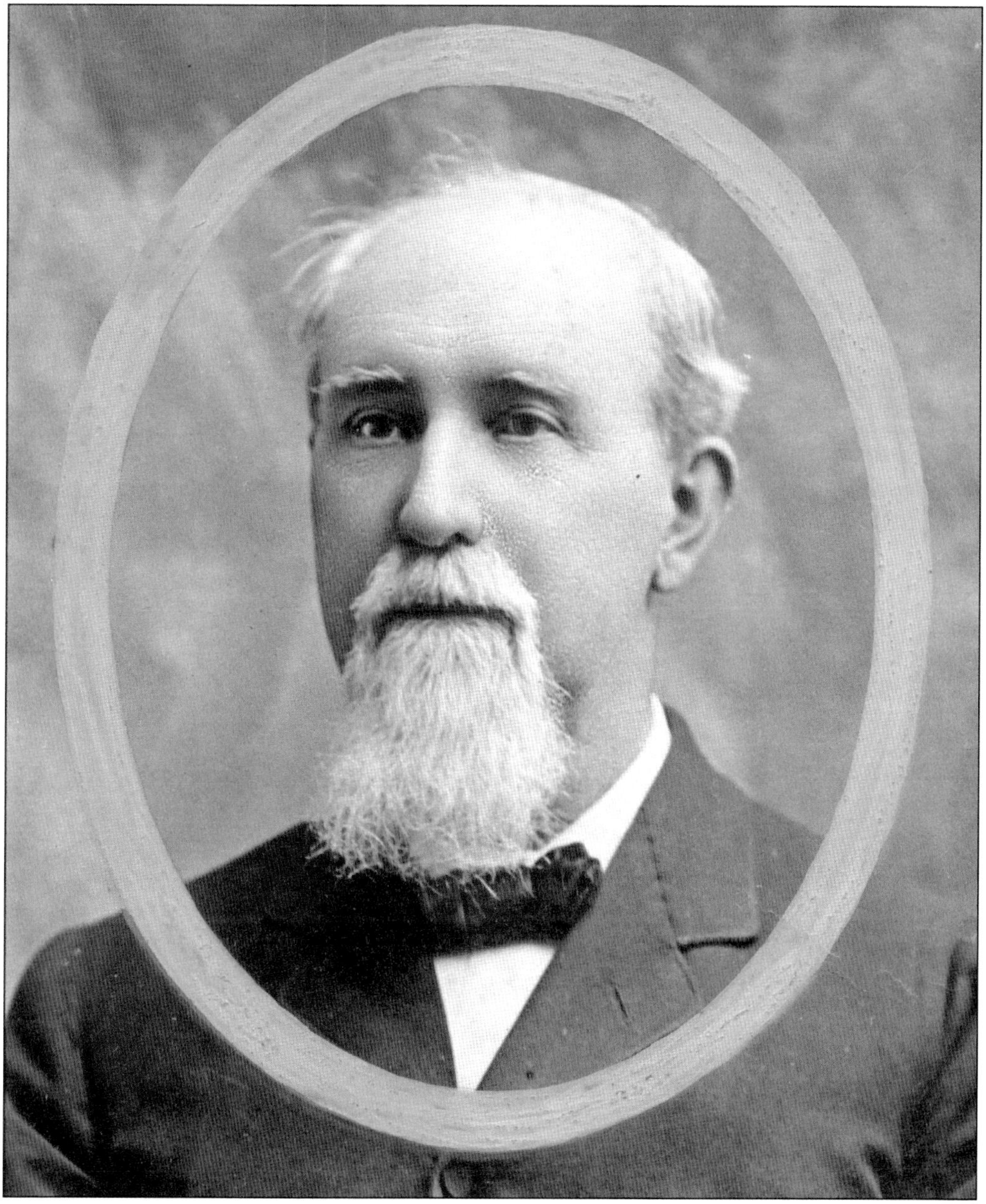

Jesse B. Lovelace was active in the operation of Judson College and Howard College for many years. His first wife, Mary Wyatt, was the daughter of William Wyatt, one of the early presidents of the board of trustees of Judson College. She also served as the first president of the Alumnae Association. Lovelace and Wilkerson partnered in many activities involving Howard College and Judson College, as well as in other facets of Baptist life in Marion. Together with Rev. Edwin T. Winkler and W. W. Wilkerson, he supported the *Alabama Baptist* newspaper until they gave it to the Alabama Baptist Convention. He, along with Wilkerson, saved Howard College from financial ruin in the 1880s. After Wilkerson's death, Lovelace became president of Judson College's board of trustees. There is a window near the pulpit in the Siloam Baptist Church inscribed, "In Memory of Jesse B. Lovelace and Mary P. Lovelace." It was a gift by their children to the church. A fire in the educational building destroyed the window, but it was replaced with insurance money. (JCA.)

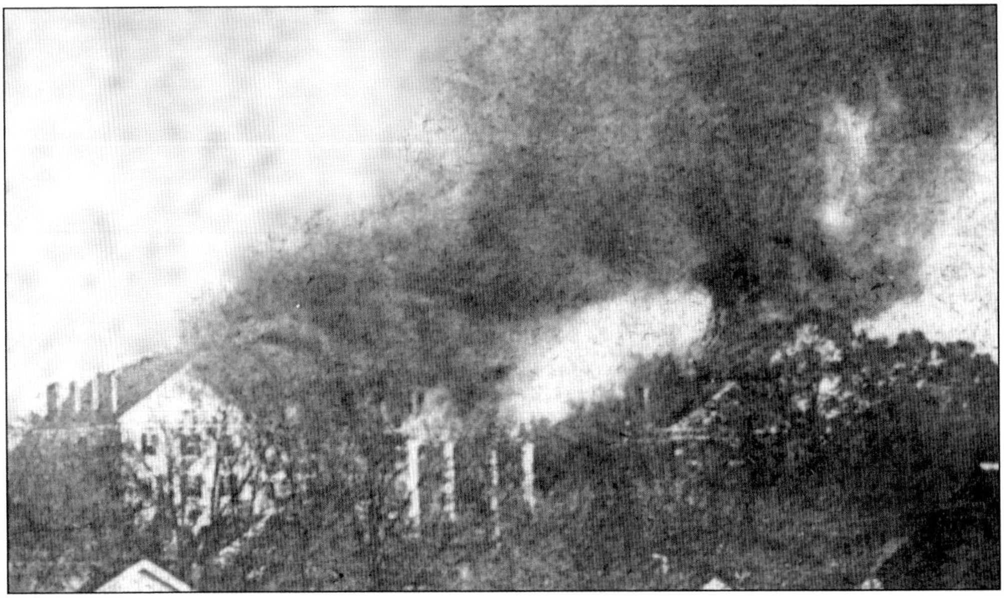

On November 24, 1888, tragedy struck Judson when a slow-burning chimney fire burst into flames. Evidently one of the chimneys caught fire, causing sparks and pieces of soot to drift and fall on the shingle roof. From the center portion, the fire quickly spread to both wings, and the entire building was destroyed within four hours. In just a few days, plans were underway for rebuilding Judson. (JCA.)

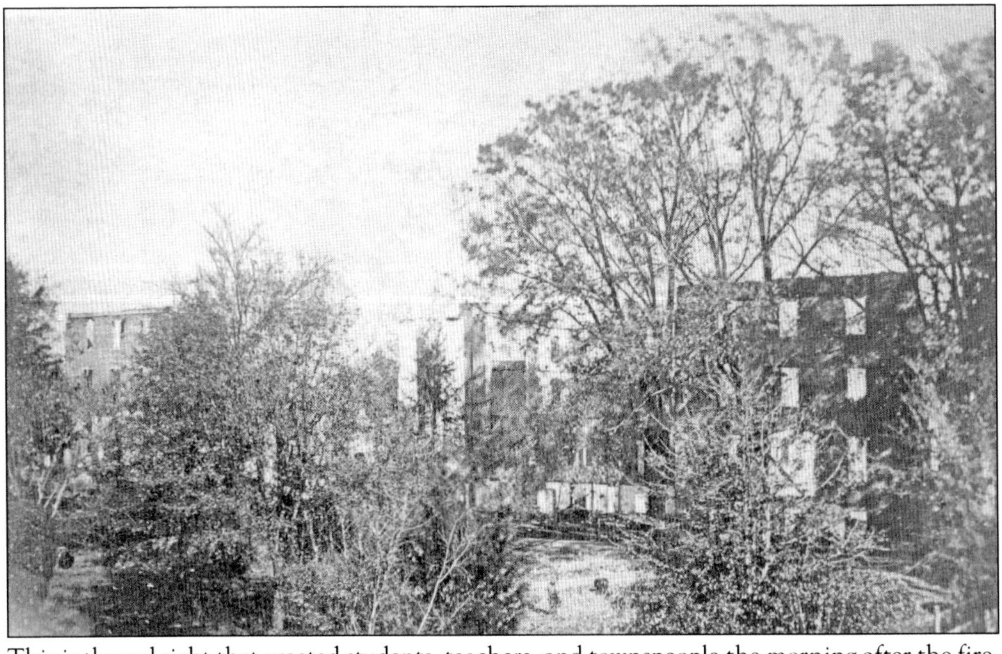

This is the sad sight that greeted students, teachers, and townspeople the morning after the fire. The ruins were enough to inspire all of these groups, along with the alumnae and trustees, to band together to rebuild "the Judson," as it was called, and that planning began immediately. (JCA.)

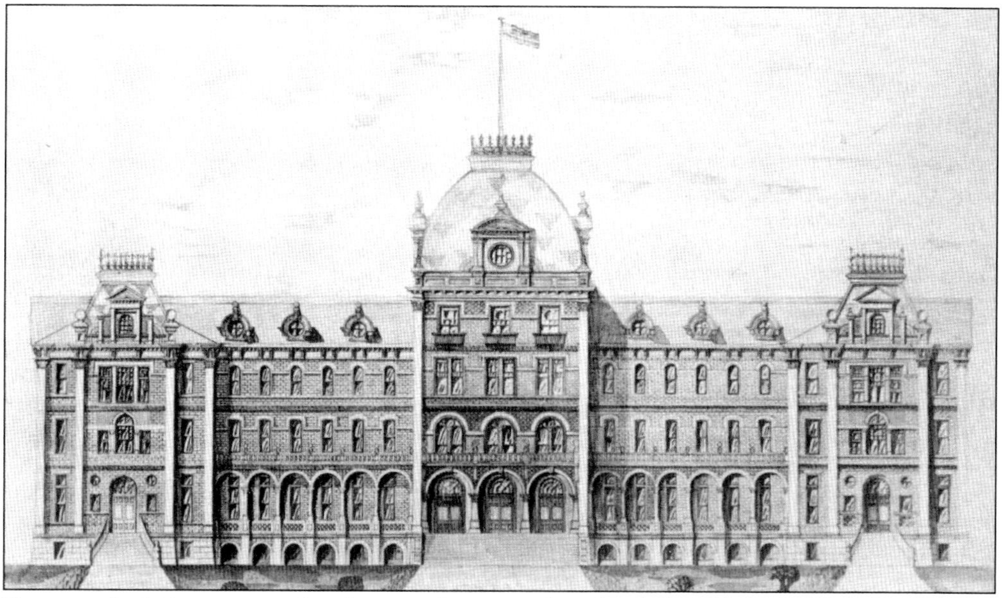

Plans to rebuild began immediately: an architect was hired and plans drawn. This is the proposed building. The actual building was not quite the same as seen here, but this was very similar to the new building that greeted students less than a year after the fire. (JCA.)

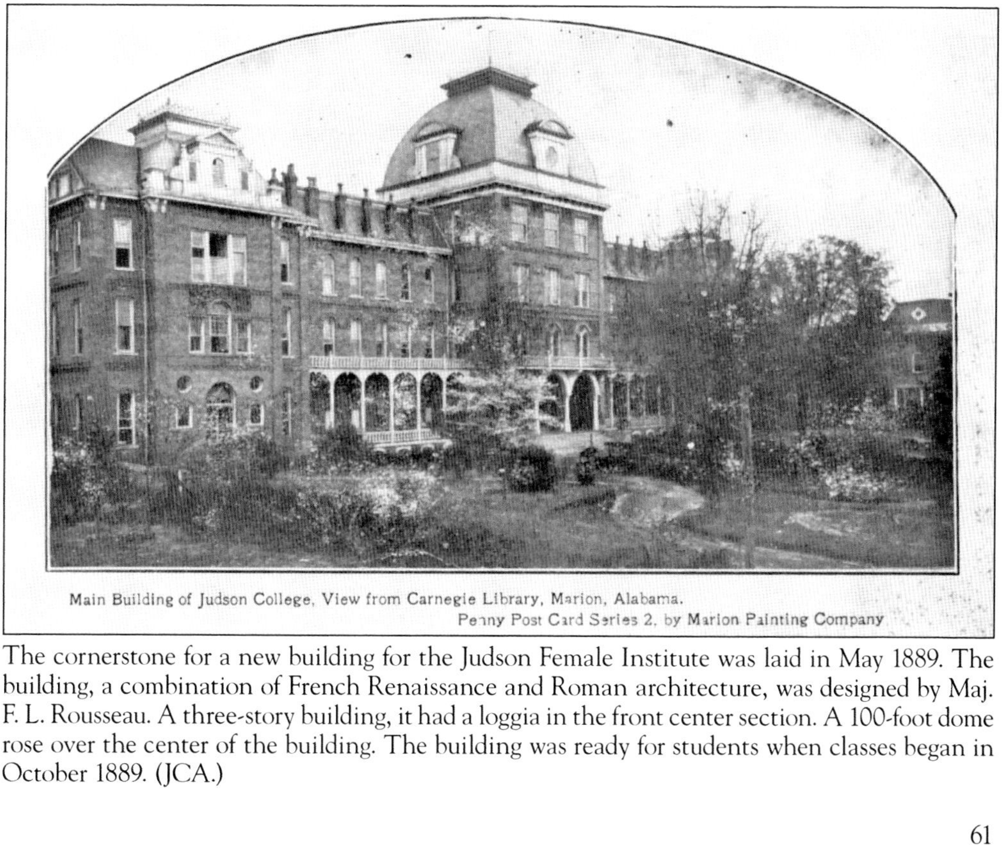

The cornerstone for a new building for the Judson Female Institute was laid in May 1889. The building, a combination of French Renaissance and Roman architecture, was designed by Maj. F. L. Rousseau. A three-story building, it had a loggia in the front center section. A 100-foot dome rose over the center of the building. The building was ready for students when classes began in October 1889. (JCA.)

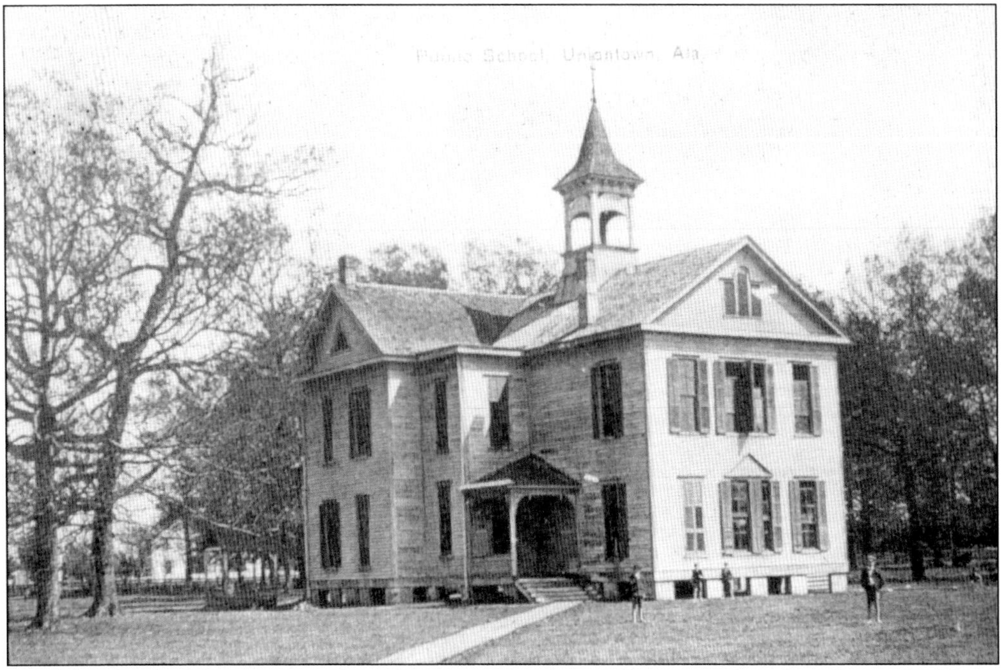

Land for this building was purchased in 1888. Students affectionately referred it as St. Elmo. Probably the use of the name St. Elmo can be attributed to the influence of Augusta Evans Wilson, the writer. She had two sisters who lived in Uniontown, Carrie Jones and Sarah Bush. (Courtesy of the author.)

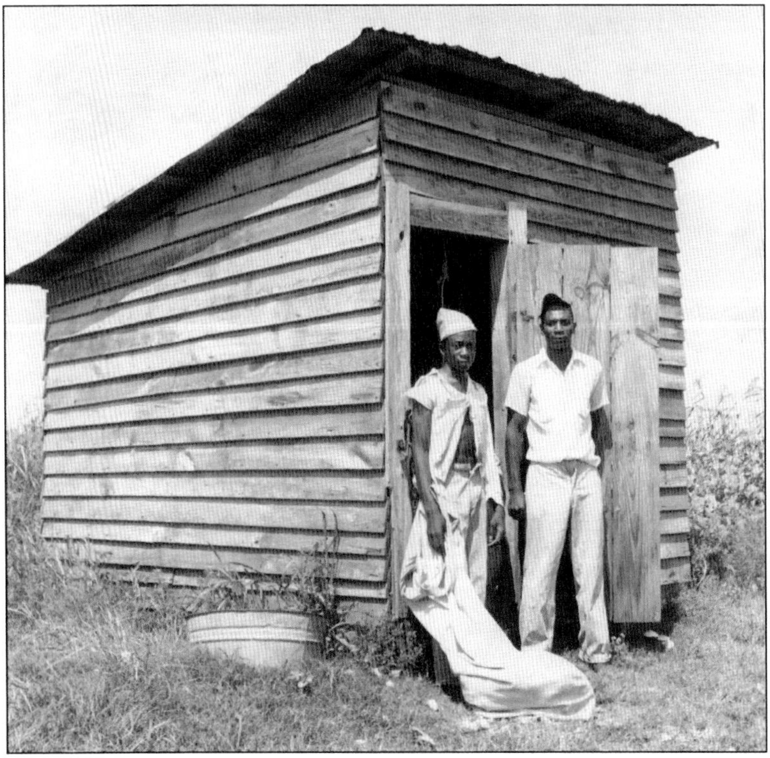

This small building on the Moore plantation is a temporary cotton storage building. It served as a place to store filled and partially filled cotton sacks. These sacks held between 70 to 90 pounds each. The filled sacks were loaded onto wagons and taken to the gin. (Courtesy of Charles Holmes.)

Again on the Moore plantation, one sees a picture of the scaffold for a cotton scale. Each farm had its own scales so that it could determine when it had enough cotton picked to make a bale. The pickers were also paid by the amount they picked, so the ability to weigh the bags daily was a necessity. (Courtesy of Charles Holmes.)

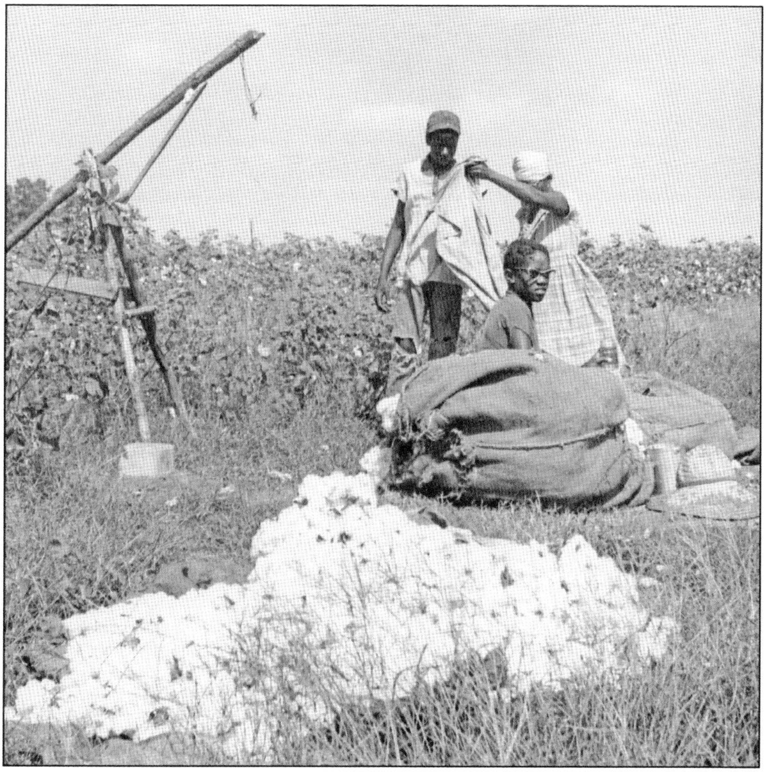

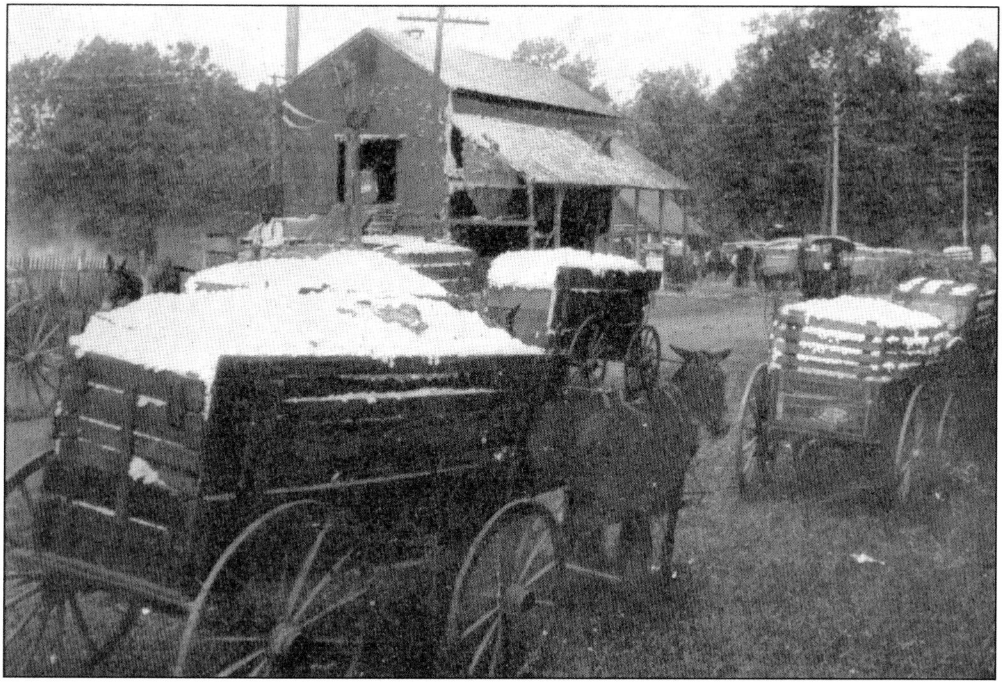

Pictured above are lines of wagons filled with cotton and awaiting their time at the gin. This time of waiting gave the drivers, be they farm owners or hired hands, a chance to visit and catch up on the news of the day. These visits were often the highlight of the day for the drivers. (PCHPS.)

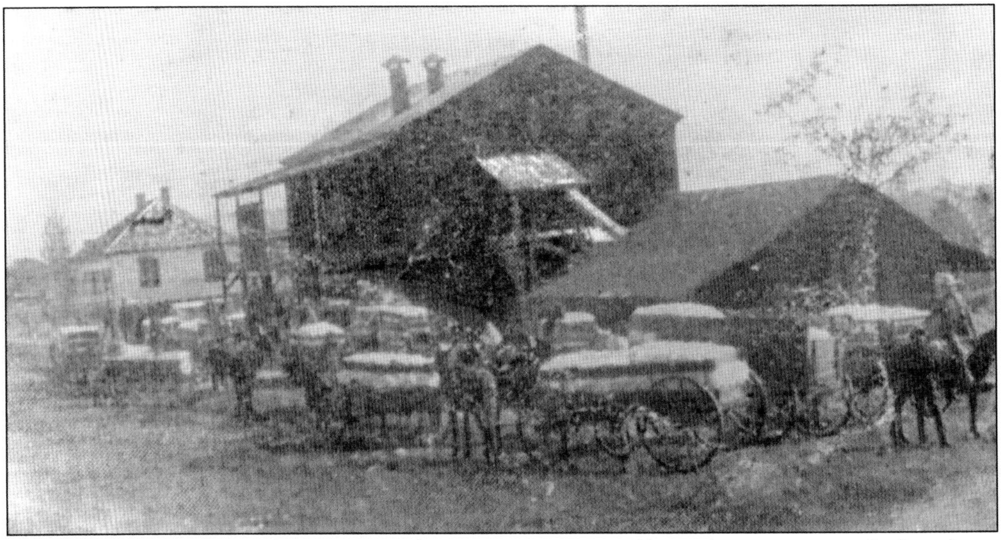

The Millie Davis gin on Fikes Ferry Road in Marion is pictured here. Again one sees the long lines of wagons waiting their turn. Gins were located in Marion and Uniontown as well as in the smaller communities throughout the county. The gin was located near the railroad station. (PCHPS.)

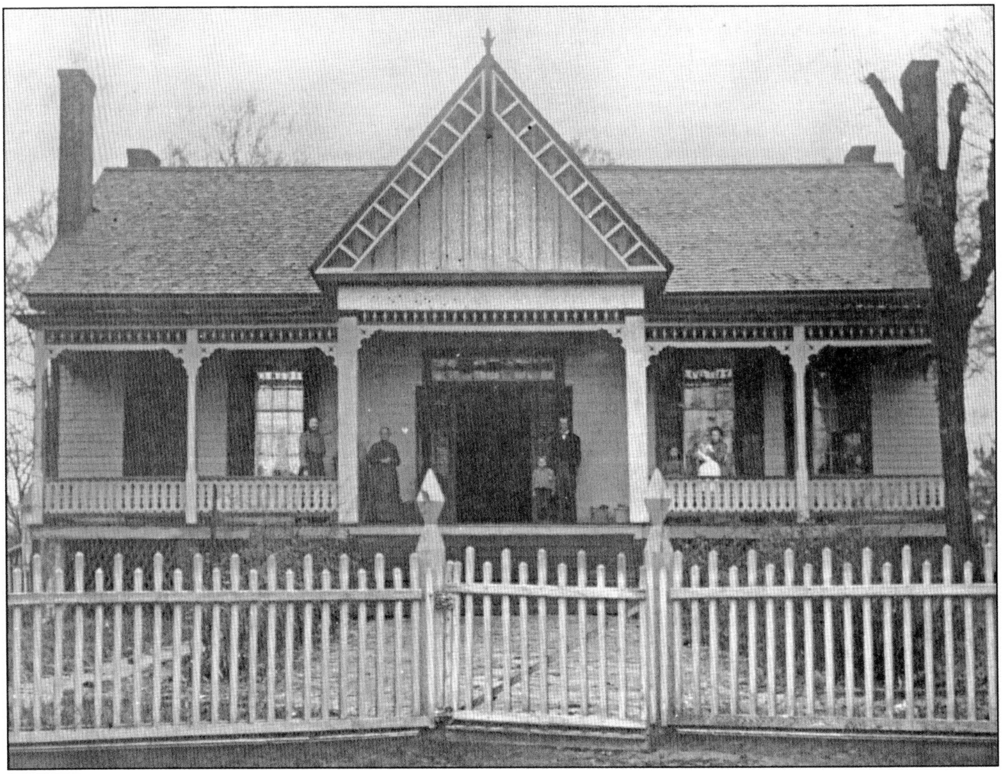

Located on Dekalb Street in Marion, this was the home of Cecil Mickleboro and his family. His father, John C. Mickleboro, lived next door, and Cecil obtained the land on which to build the house from him. Cecil worked with his father in the J. C. Mickleboro Jewelry and Gift Store for many years. The house was built about 1922 in the Craftsman style of architecture. (PCHPS.)

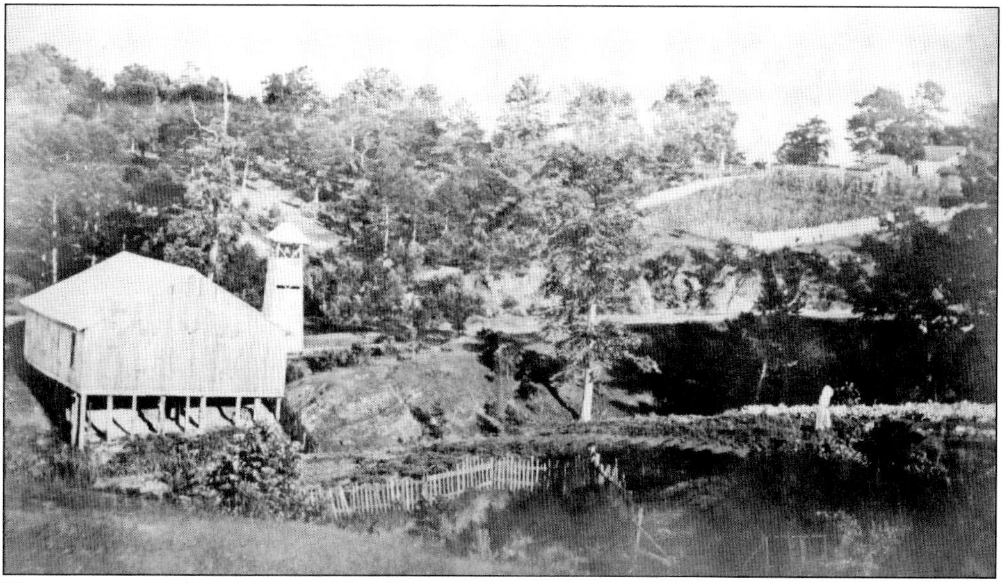

This picture was found in an 1872 collection. It was identified as a black church in Marion. The church appears to be in the country, and what is seen is probably the rear of the building. There seems to be a bell tower beside it. The church was probably to the north or east of town since the terrain is hilly. (SU.)

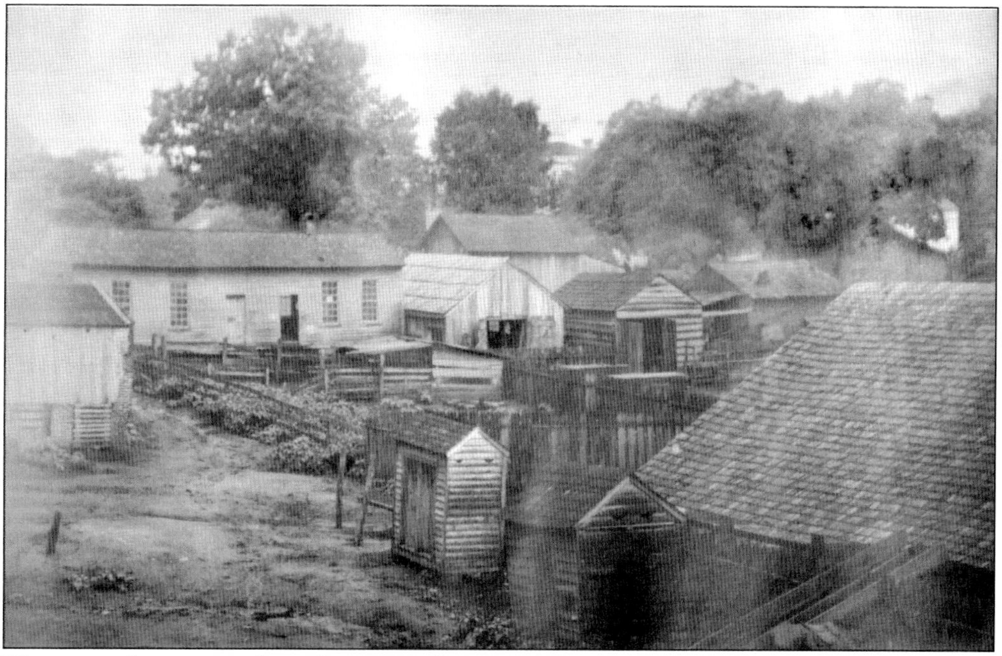

This is another picture from the 1872 collection of photographs. It is believed to be a group of buildings in a backyard or adjoining backyards in Marion. At this time, almost all homes had several buildings, including a stable for their horses, a barn for their cow, a pen for their hogs, a coop for their chickens, an outhouse, and others. (SU.)

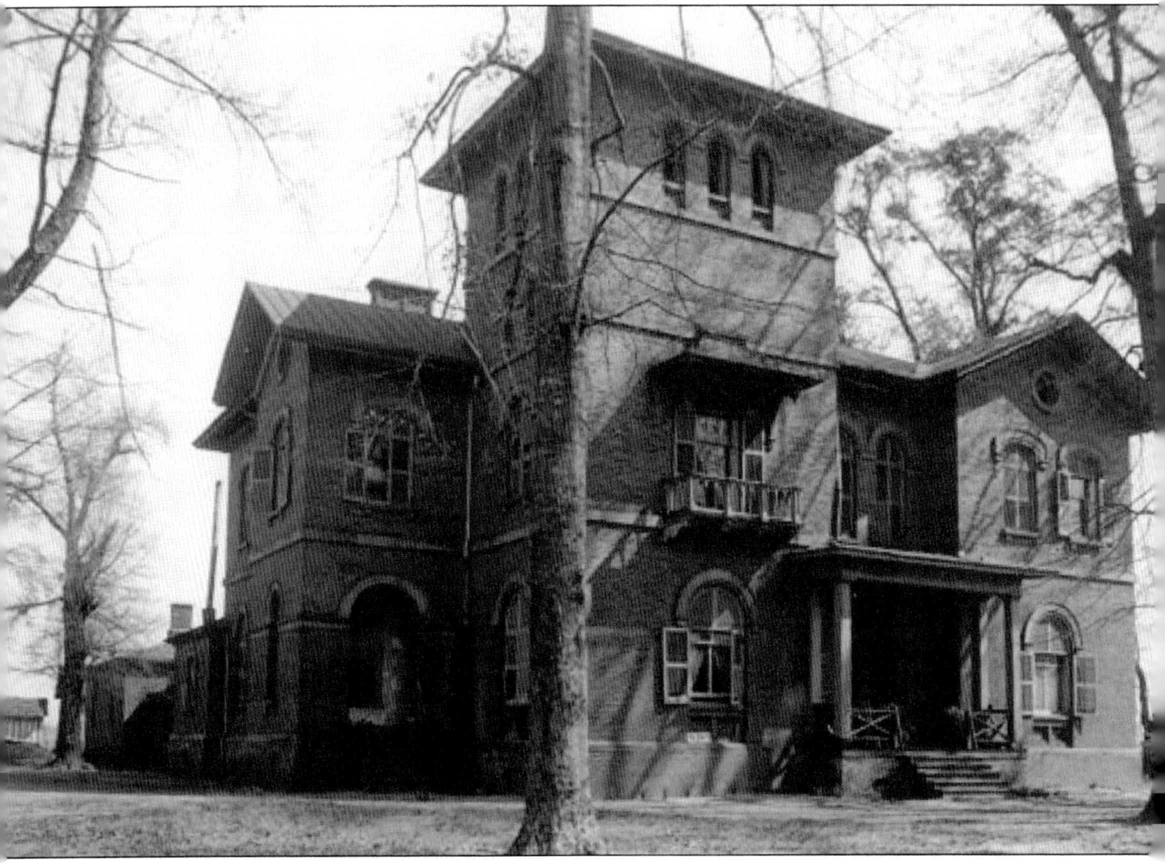

This is Carlisle, or Kenworthy, Hall during the 1870s. At that time, the Carlisle owner lived in Selma and only came to Marion in the summer. A daughter supposedly jumped from the tower when she thought the message she received meant that her fiancé had been killed in battle during the War Between the States. Her story appears in Kathryn Tucker Windham's *Thirteen Alabama Ghosts and Jeffrey*. (SU.)

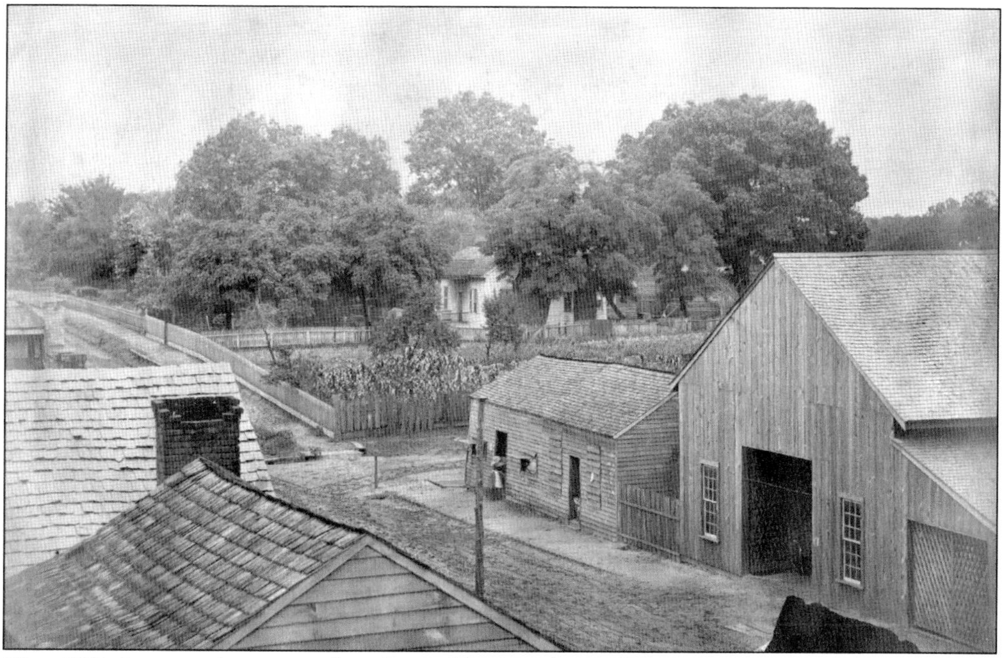

This 1872 photograph seems to be of a road leading from a business section of Marion to homes in the distance. On the right is what appears to be a livery stable and smaller buildings. One seems to be a house with someone standing in the doorway. Next to it on the right is a cornfield. Notice the picket fence that runs for quite some distance. (SU.)

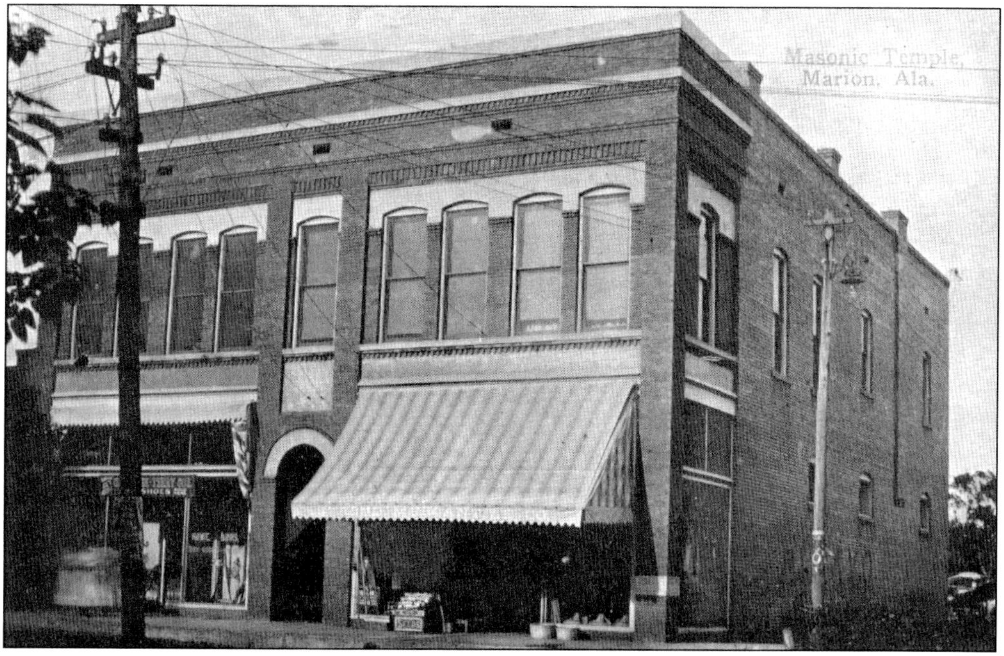

The buildings in this Marion scene are on the northeast corner of Washington and Lafayette Streets. The corner building has been covered with a metal facing and is not recognizable as being the one in the photograph. The other building is the print shop. Although altered, the doorway that led up to the Masonic temple is still visible. (PCHPS.)

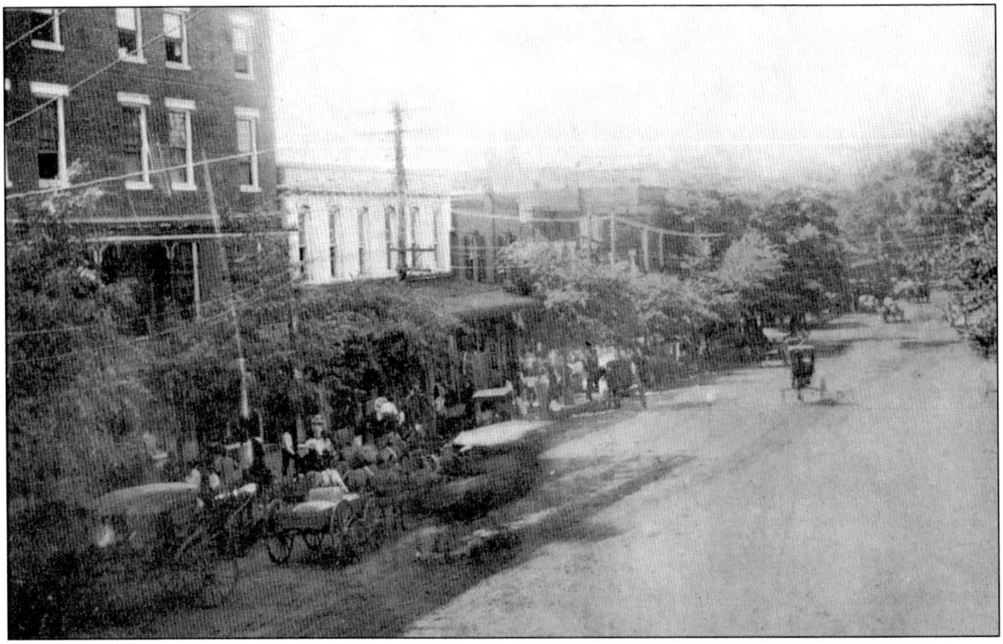

This is a scene of Washington Street in Marion looking north. On the west side of the street is the old four-story King Hotel. Trees hide the front of the buildings farther up the street, making identification of the buildings impossible. Across the street to the east is the Courthouse Square. (PCHPS.)

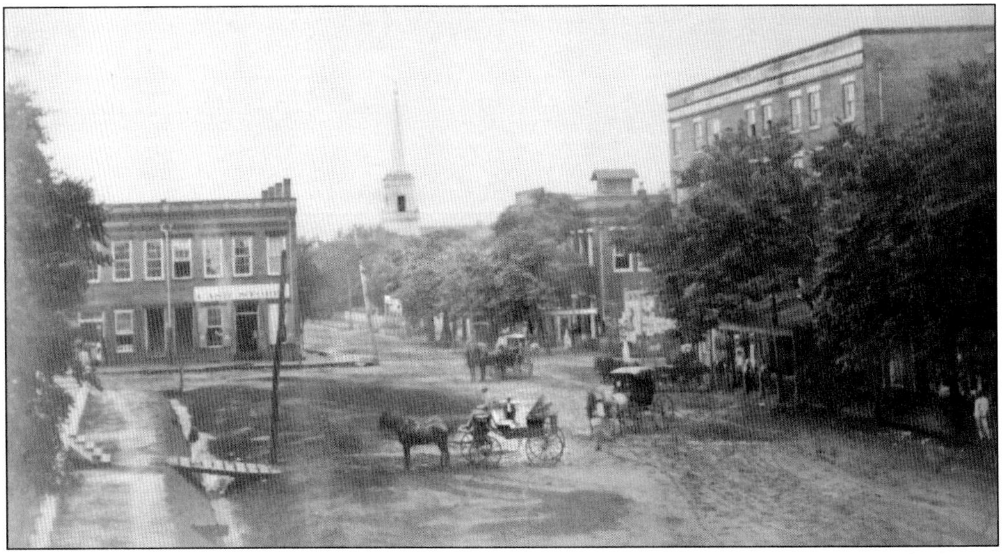

Looking south on Washington Street, the four-story King Hotel is on the right and what is now Nathan Harris and Son just past it. At one point, an elevated walkway connected the two buildings on the second floor. Straight ahead is what was the People's Bank, but at the time of the picture, the sign says "Cash Store." (SU.)

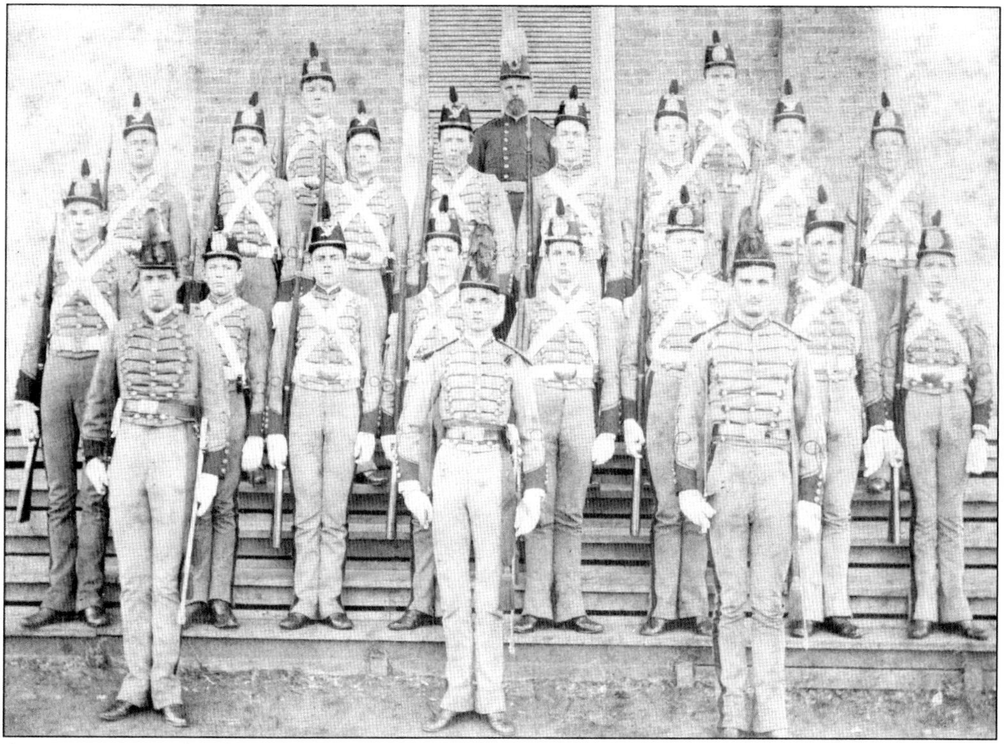

An 1880 group of cadets from Howard College stands on the steps of the chapel. To the rear of the group is a gentleman believed to be James Thomas Murfee, president. The uniforms with the hats and cockades are very fancy for a boys' school in west Alabama. (MMIFA.)

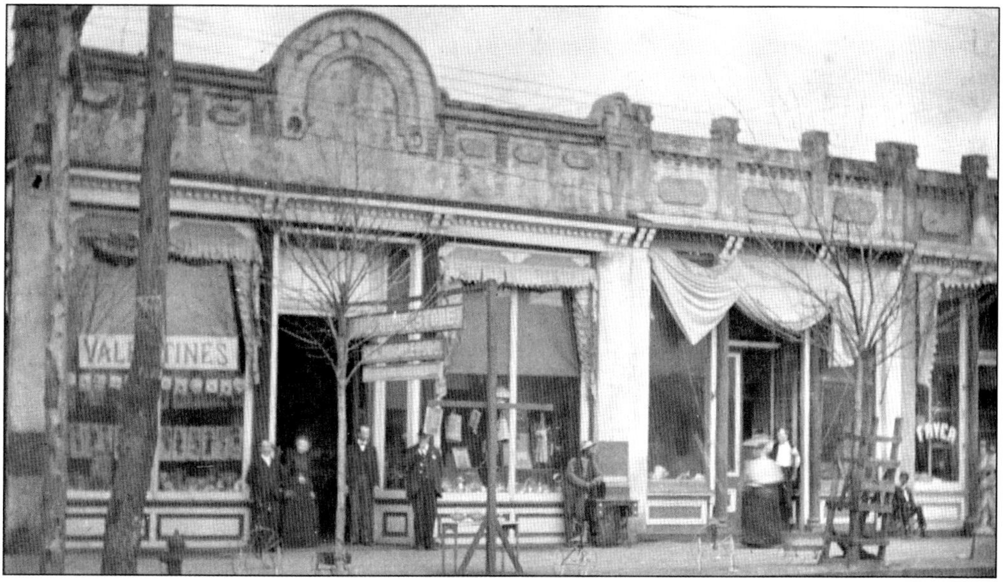

The building on the corner is the original J. C. Mickleboro Jewelry store in Marion. J. C. Mickleboro became very noted for his line of jewelry and other items normally found in this type of store. Many postcards of this time are marked J. C. Mickleboro. It is on the northwest corner of Washington and Lafayette Streets. (PCHPS.)

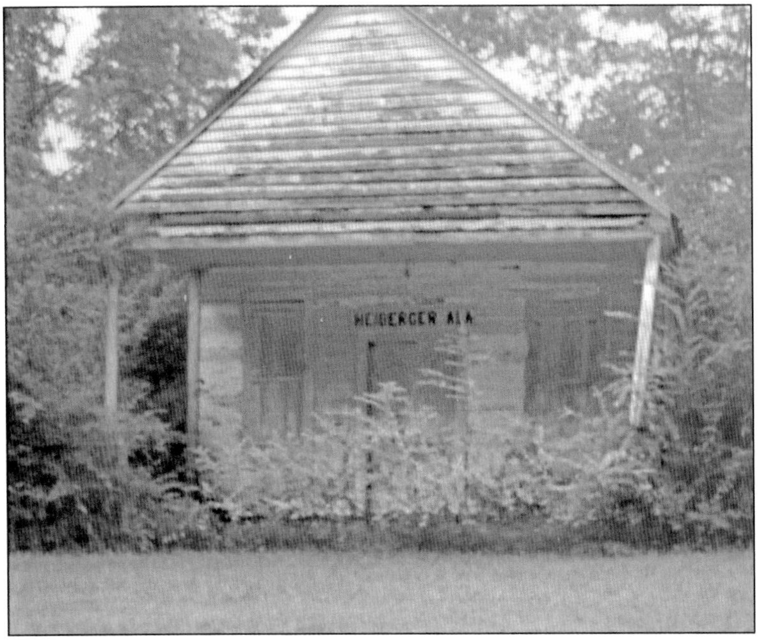

Heiberger started out as Wilmore, but since an Alabama community already used the name, the postmaster submitted the name Heiberger. He was of German descent, and his family had lived in Heidelburg, Germany. This is the post office as it appeared for quite a number of years. In 2006–2007, a member of the Moore family had it restored. (PCHPS.)

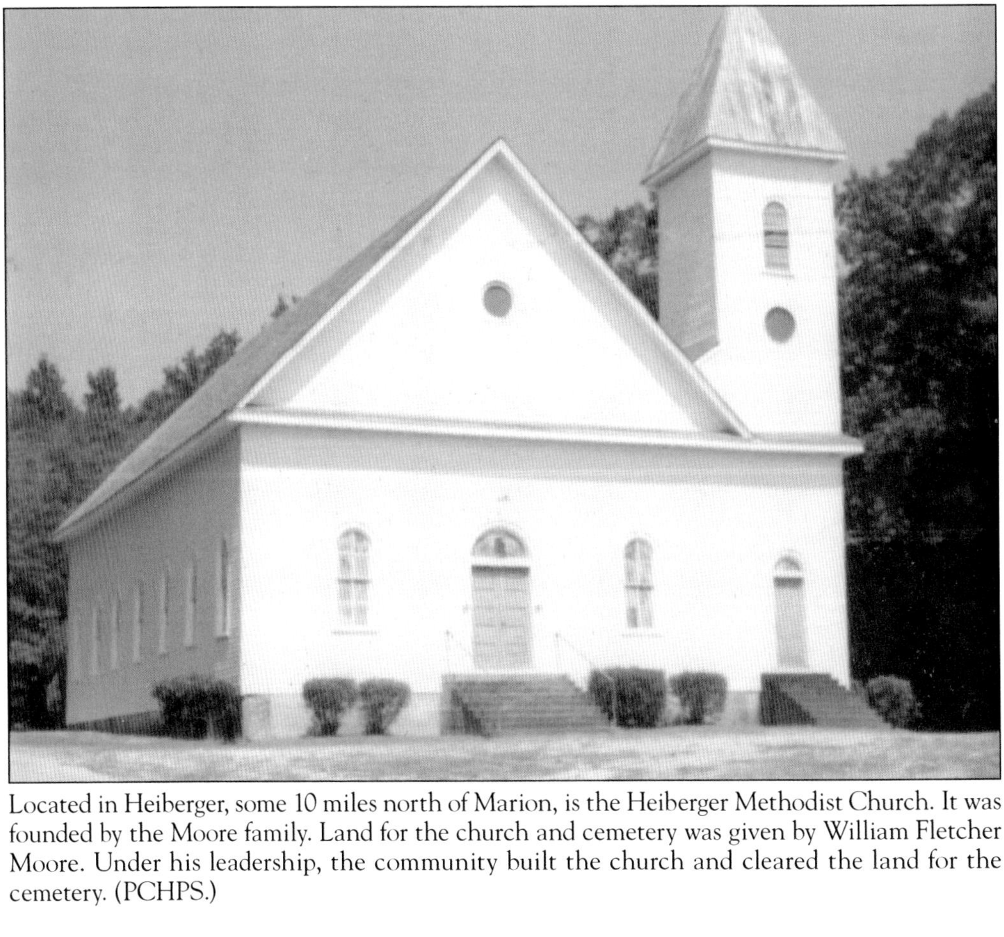

Located in Heiberger, some 10 miles north of Marion, is the Heiberger Methodist Church. It was founded by the Moore family. Land for the church and cemetery was given by William Fletcher Moore. Under his leadership, the community built the church and cleared the land for the cemetery. (PCHPS.)

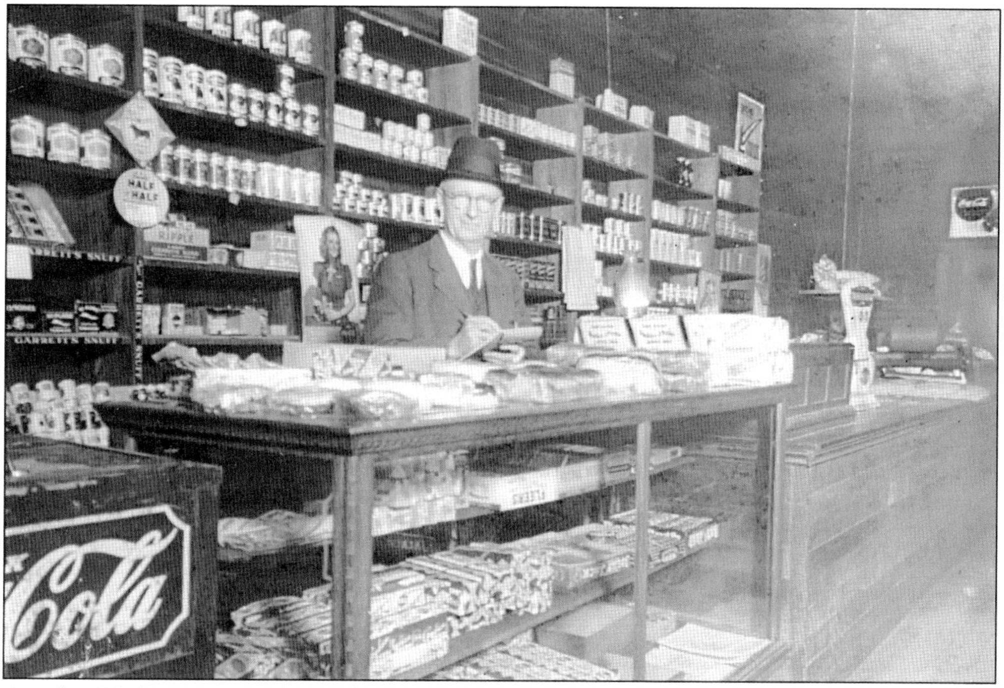

Another Heiberger scene shows the inside of an old country store once located there. Nothing is known about the owner or operator. As with most small communities today, the businesses once located in them are no more. The advent of the automobile and the large supermarkets have made small country stores a thing of the past. The people have remained, but the businesses have moved away. (PCHPS.)

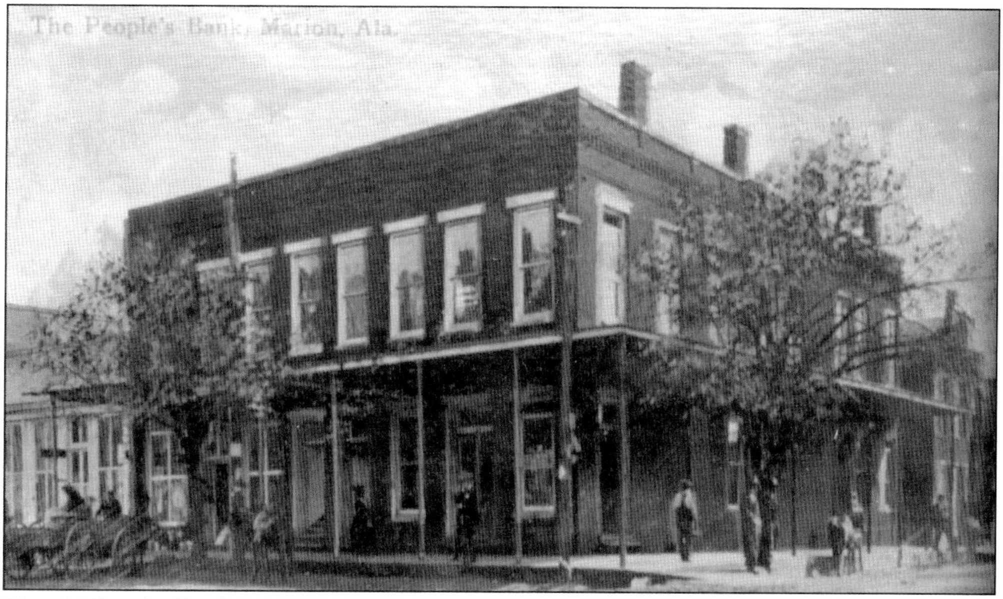

The old Peoples Bank in Marion is shown in the above picture. The building is located on the southeast corner of Washington and Jefferson Streets. The bank operated for many years but closed its doors during the Depression. The building to the right is believed to be the oldest commercial building in downtown Marion. (Courtesy of Charles Holmes.)

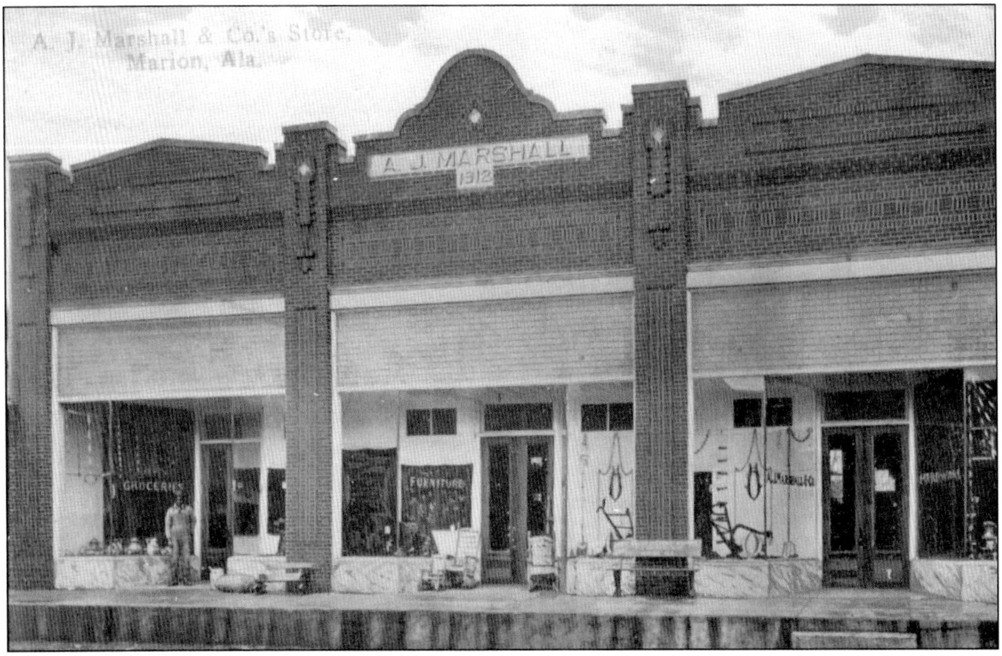

These stores are on the east side of Washington Street, north of the courthouse square. As one can see from the photograph, the middle one is identified as belonging to A. J. Marshall. For many years, the one to the right was occupied by Mickleboro Jewelry. (Courtesy of John Allen Clark.)

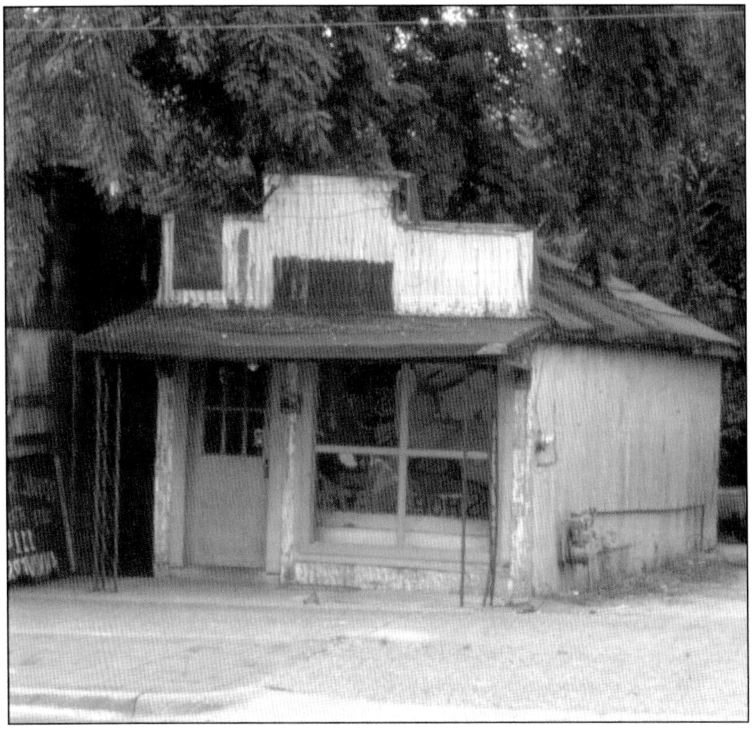

The Royal Shoe Shop was located in Uniontown on U.S. Highway 80. Before it went out of business in the last quarter of the 20th century, it was the oldest continuously operating business in Perry County at the time. Laura Royal, being the last family member, was actively involved in the business. (Courtesy of the author.)

The Episcopalians were organized in Marion in 1838 as St. Michael's Parish. The first rector was Rev. Andrew Matthews. In 1883, it became St. Wilfrid's. The building, which had served the congregation since 1849, was destroyed by fire in 1896. Rebuilt, the new building shown here and the rectory were destroyed by fire in 1907. (PCHPS.)

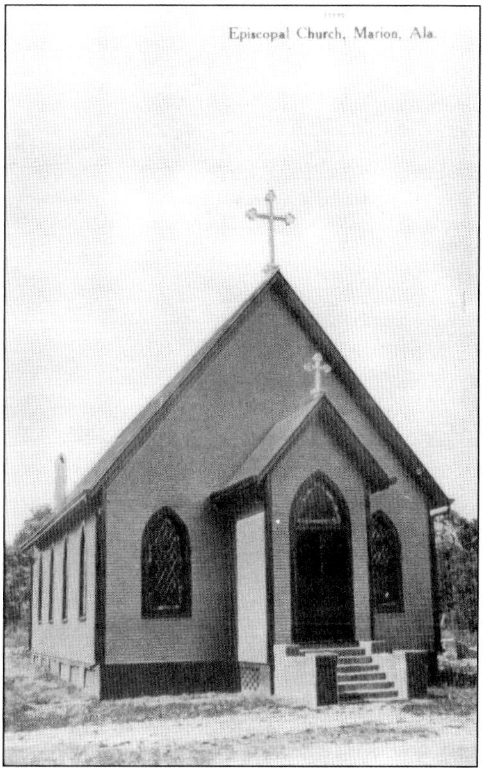

Episcopalians organized Union Parish in 1844 in Uniontown. The first members were four women. Rev. E. C. Murdaugh came as rector in 1845. In November 1864, the Uniontown church was consecrated as the Church of the Holy Cross. A new building, erected in 1900, is thought to be the best example of the English Arts and Crafts style in Alabama. (Courtesy of Emma Glass Beasley.)

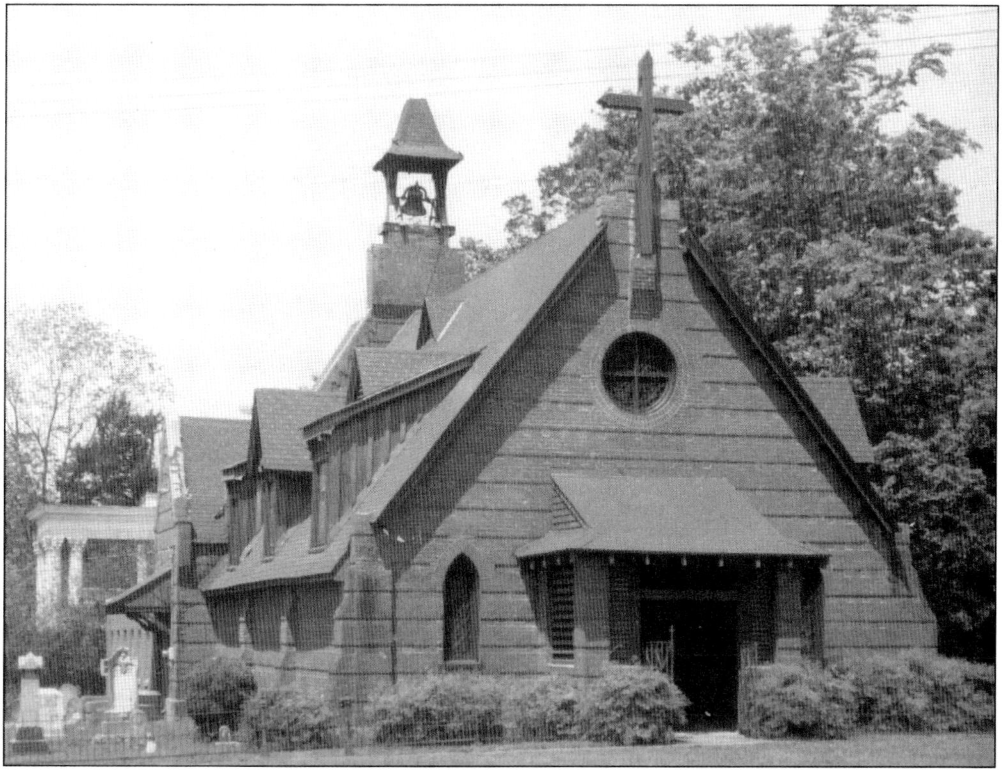

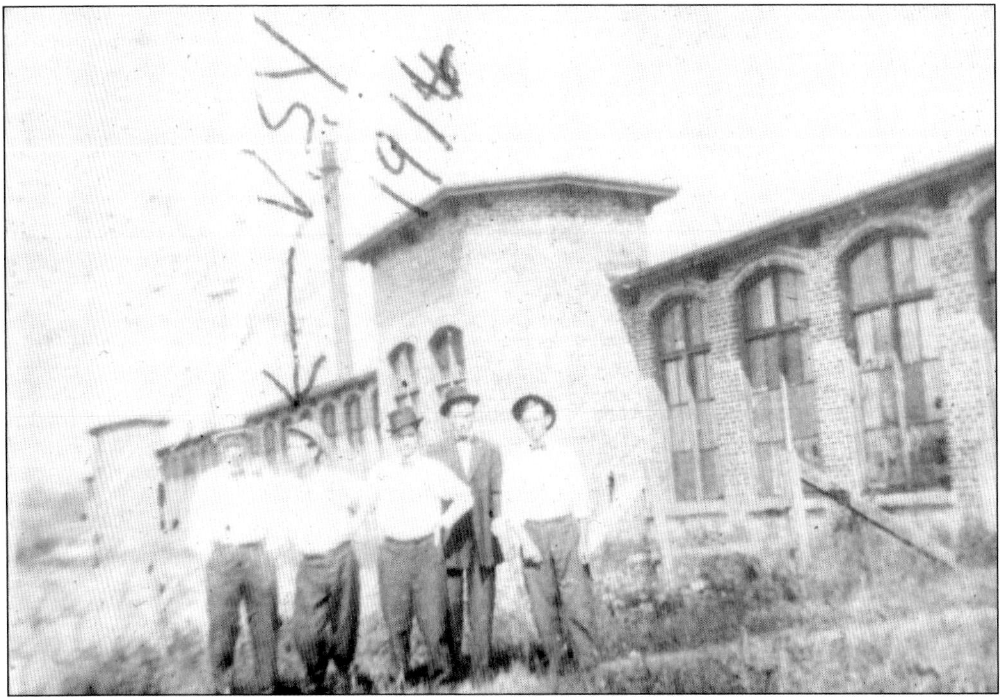

A group of Uniontown businessmen established a cotton mill in 1899. Ella White Cotton Mill was incorporated on November 10, 1899. It was named for the wife of one of the owners, J. H. White. The cotton mill operated in Uniontown until 1954. This picture has a 1914 date, and the gentleman to whom the arrow is pointing is V. S. Yelverton. (Courtesy of the author.)

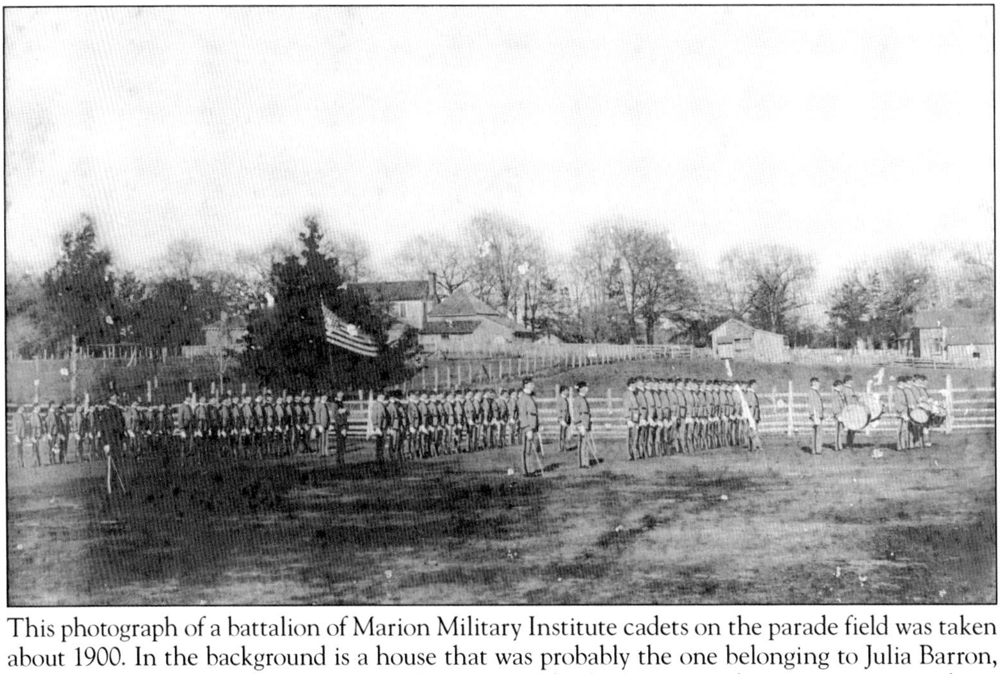

This photograph of a battalion of Marion Military Institute cadets on the parade field was taken about 1900. In the background is a house that was probably the one belonging to Julia Barron, which was located in the general area. If it is, it was the first two-story house in Marion and was built about 1828. (MMIFA.)

Four

Grow, Grow, Grow, Grow

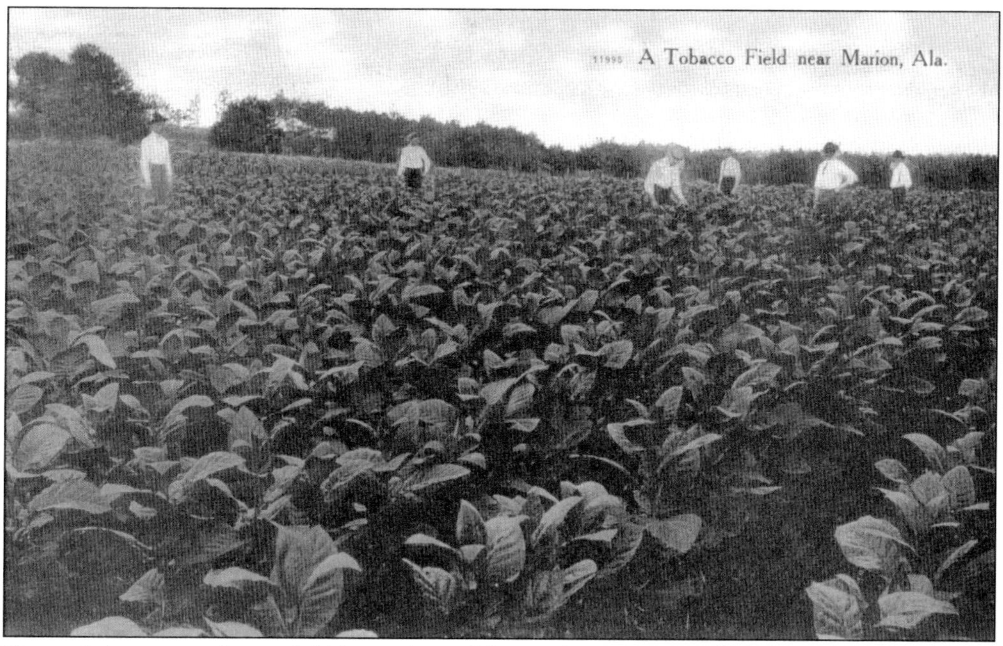

Pictured above is a tobacco field located near Marion. It is not generally known that tobacco was grown in the area, however, it seemed noteworthy enough for someone to take a picture and have postcards made with the scene on it. At about the same time tobacco was being grown in Perry County, soy beans also were being planted. (Courtesy of Kitty Grey Long.)

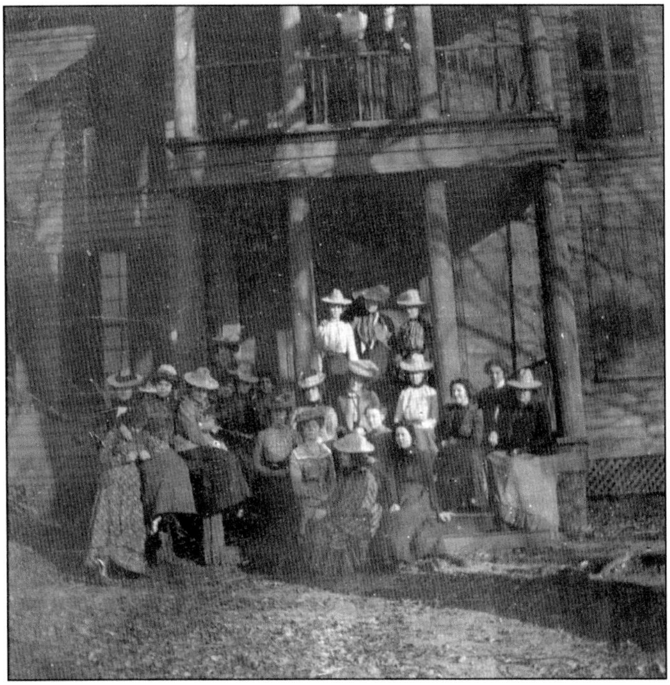

This photograph, taken in 1902, depicts students in front of what was once the home of Milo P. Jewett and his family. They purchased this house in 1844 from Mary Griffin. It was located a block south of the present campus. The Jewetts sold the house to Edward A. Blount in 1855. It was destroyed by fire some time after this photograph was taken. (JCA.)

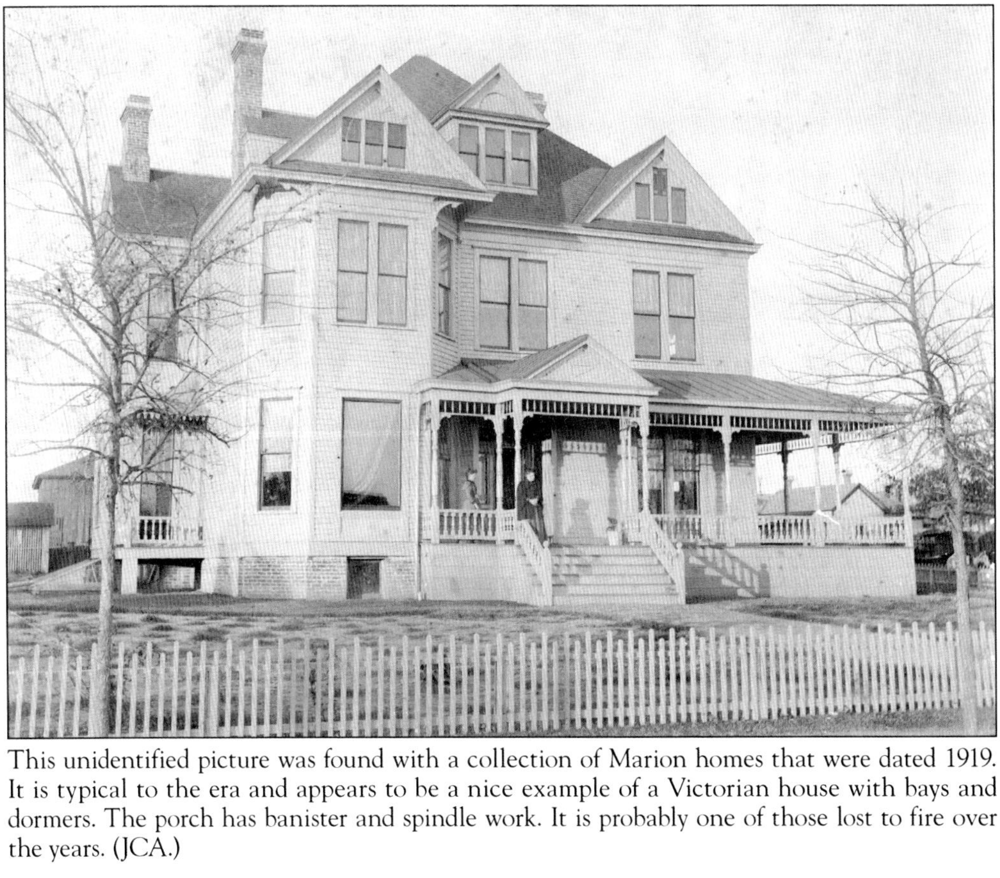

This unidentified picture was found with a collection of Marion homes that were dated 1919. It is typical to the era and appears to be a nice example of a Victorian house with bays and dormers. The porch has banister and spindle work. It is probably one of those lost to fire over the years. (JCA.)

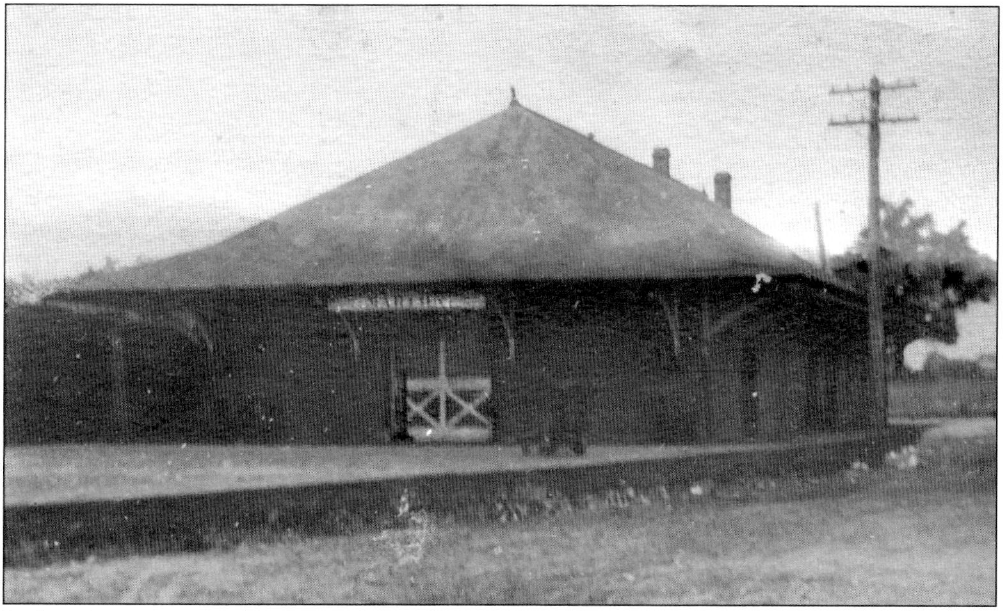

Railroads were a part of Marion scenery from at least 1854 (maybe earlier) until the early 1990s. The Marion Alabama River Transportation Company purchased land in this area in 1854. This building, erected about 1908, replaced one that had burned. For many years, college students came through this building on their way to and from local colleges. (Courtesy of Judy B. Martin.)

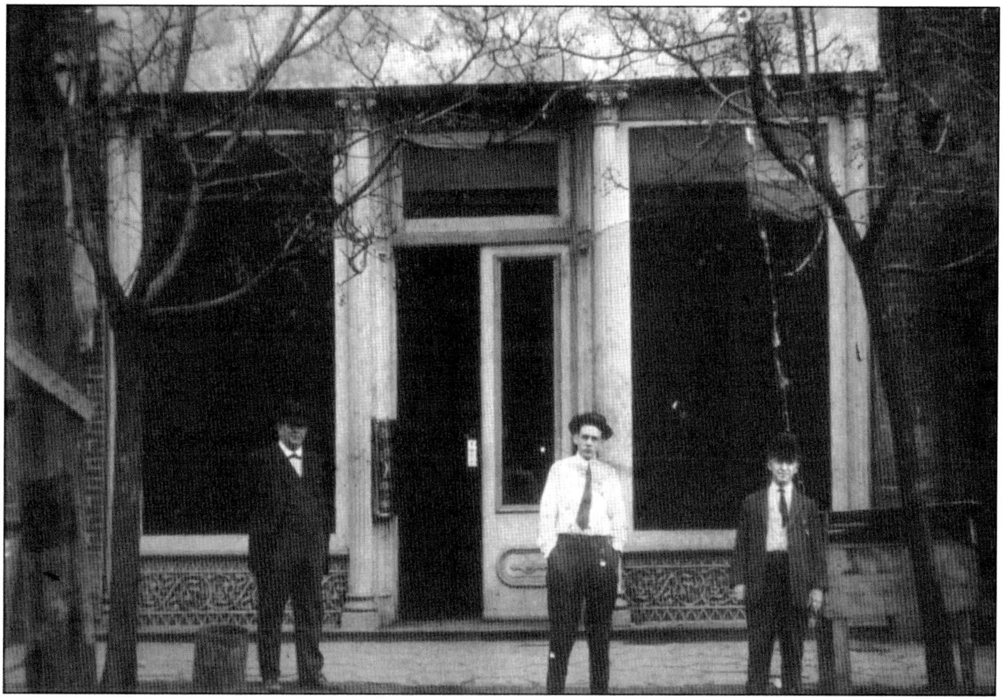

The Ernst Brothers Bank was located in this building on the west side of Water Street in Uniontown. It later was home to the Planters and Merchants Bank until 1926. Today a brick facade covers the original front of the building. J. Hardie Bradford, a former president of the bank, is in the middle of the above photograph. (Courtesy of the author.)

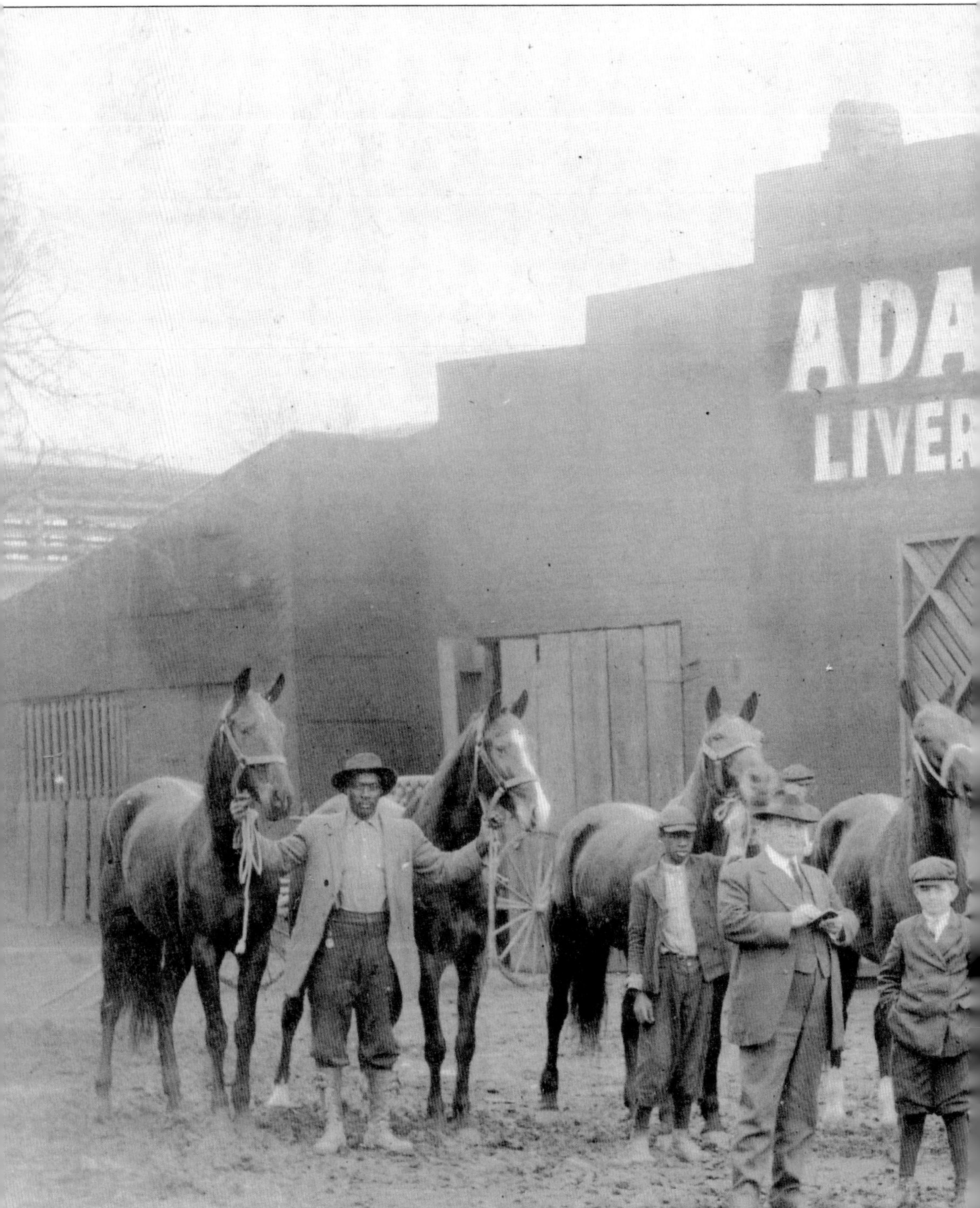

The Adair Brothers Livery, Feed, and Sale Stable in Uniontown was as necessary during the 19th and early 20th centuries as the service station is today. In fact, there is a service station located in the same spot where the Adair livery stable was located. Robert Adair, the owner, is the only

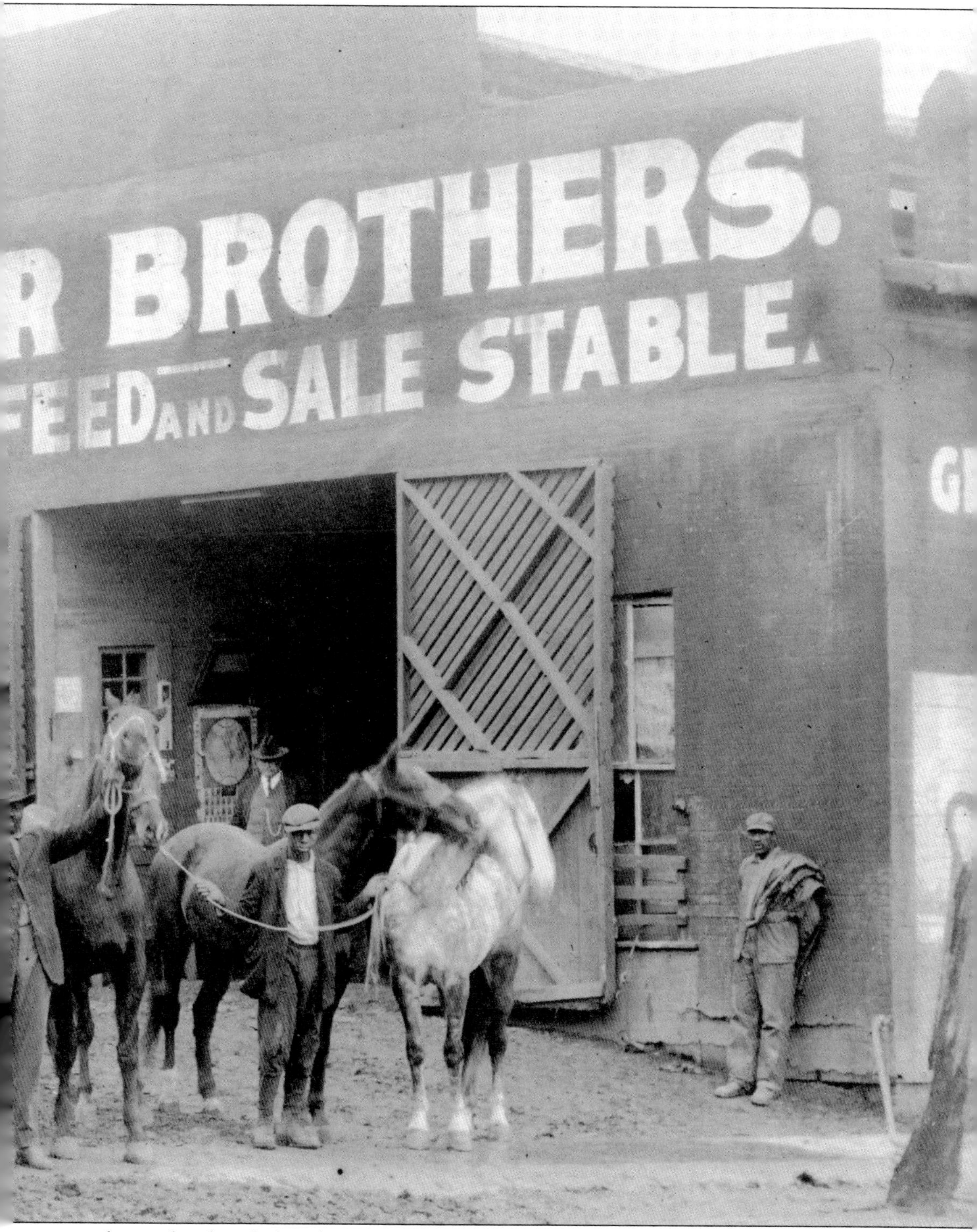

one who can be identified in the picture. He is standing in front of the others with a young boy, believed to be his oldest son, who later ran the business. It is possible that this picture was to be used as advertisement for the sale of the owner's livestock. (Courtesy of Wilna W. Kelley.)

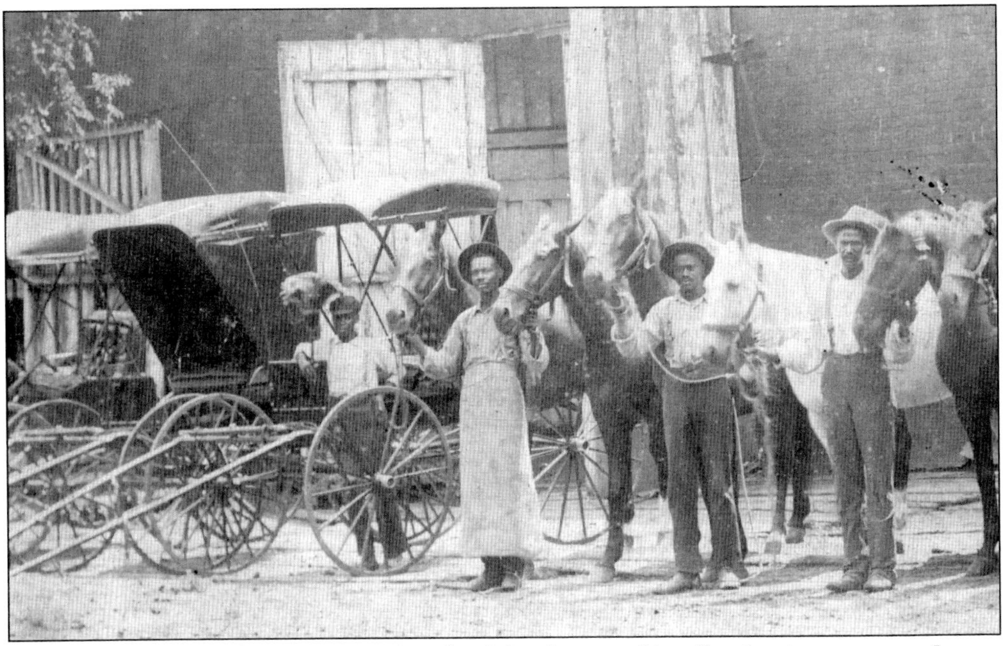

These two pictures indicate services that the Adair livery stable offered to its customers. In one are buggies, and in the other are carriages. The owner had matched pairs of horses on hand. On Sunday, the young men of the town would rent buggies with a matched pair to take their lady friends for a ride. Today, if one needs a ride, one might call a taxi cab. Before automobiles, carriages were often the taxi cab of the day. Carriages would meet the train to carry incoming passengers to their destination and take passengers to catch their outgoing train. (Both, courtesy of Wilna W. Kelley.)

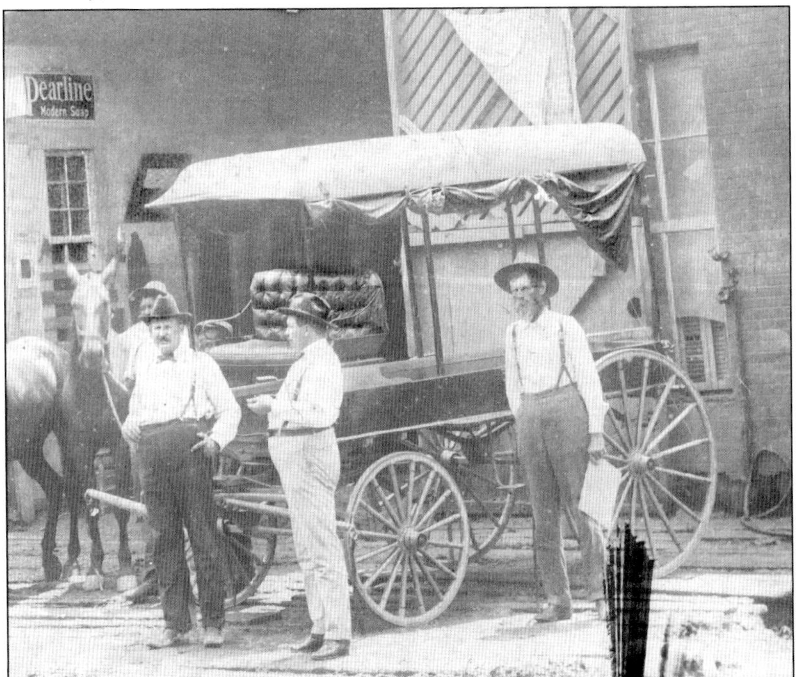

Out for a buggy ride are the Adair children of Uniontown. Seated in the front are Robert and Wilna, and in the rear are, from left to right, Evelyn, Marian, and Kathleen. Their father operated the Adair livery stable. The house is unidentified. (Courtesy of Wilna W. Kelley.)

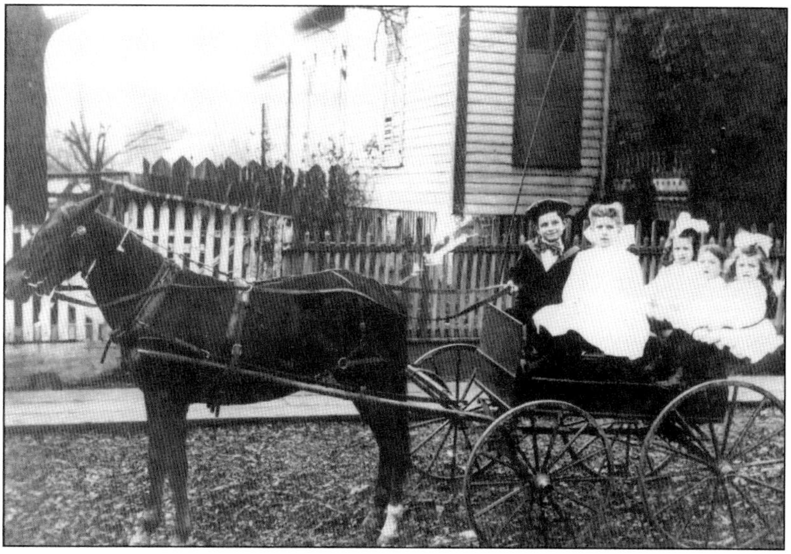

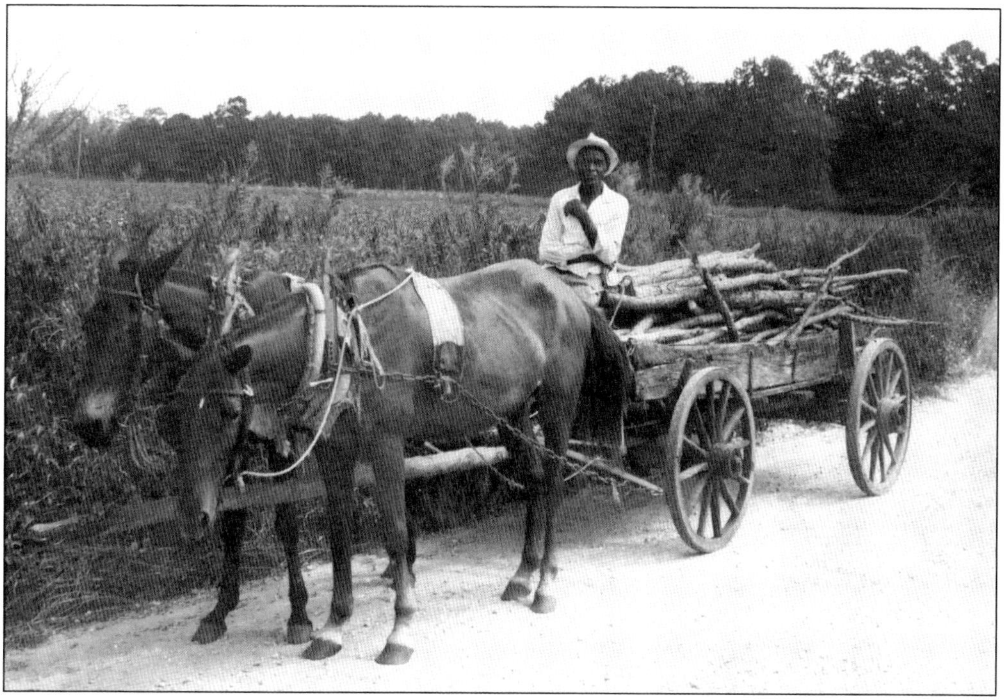

Just as a livery stable was a necessity during this time, heating was done mostly by wood and, later, coal-burning fireplaces and stoves. Above is a picture of a wagon loaded with wood on the William Moore plantation. The driver had probably been to the nearest woods to cut and load the wagon and was planning to store it in a wood shed. (Courtesy of Charles Holmes.)

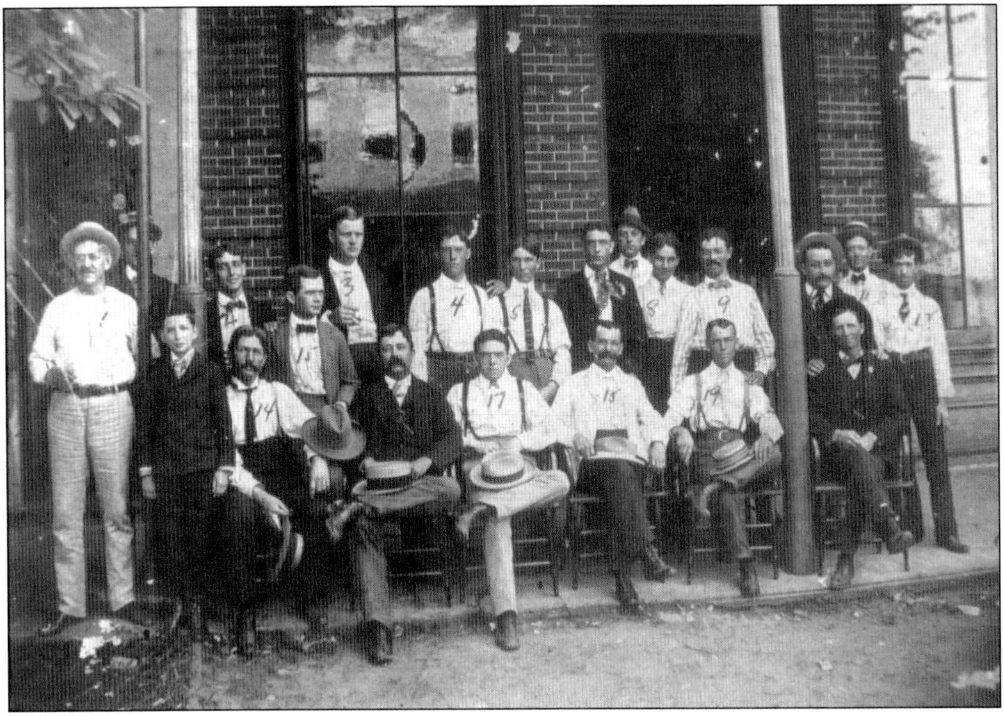

White Mercantile Company, located on the northeast corner of Water and Front Streets in Uniontown, sold a variety of items, including coffins. In fact, the complete title was "J. H. White and Co., Wholesale and Retail Dealers in Staples and Fancy Dry Goods, Clothing, Hats, Boots, Shoes, Notions, Groceries, Provision, Furniture, Etc." (Courtesy of the author.)

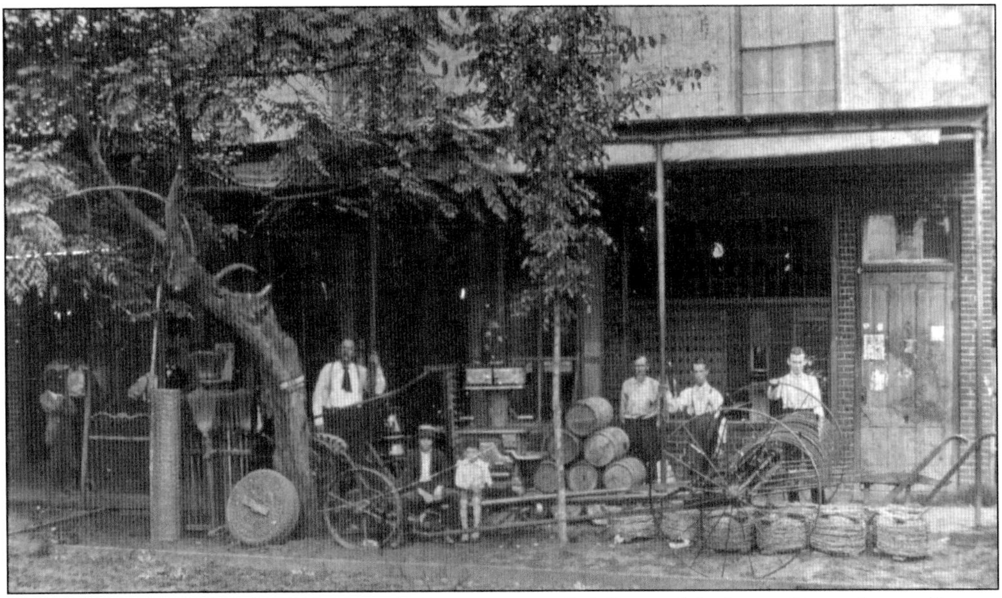

On the same block as White Mercantile Company was J. J. Brown Hardware. James Joyner Brown began this business in 1880. Notice the farm equipment sitting in front of the building. Brown also employed a tinsmith who made gutters, buckets, and other such items. An array of available merchandise is seen across the front of the store. (Courtesy of the author.)

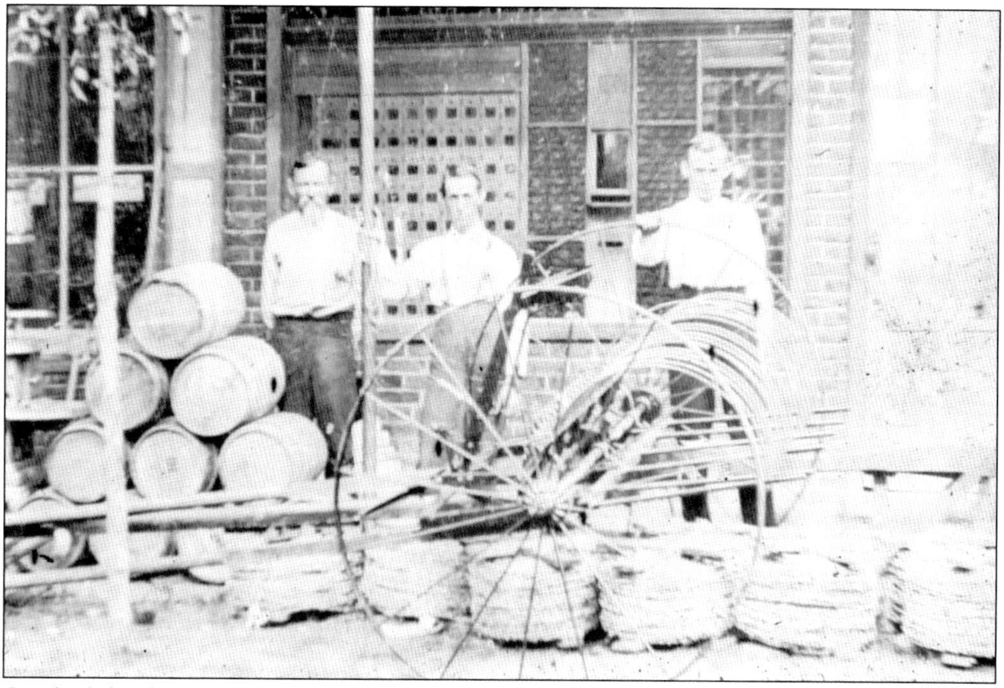

On the left side of the J. J. Brown Hardware building were the post office boxes for the citizens of the town. These boxes opened to the street side; thus, citizens could have access to their mail at all times. Brown served as postmaster during one of President Cleveland's terms. (Courtesy of the author.)

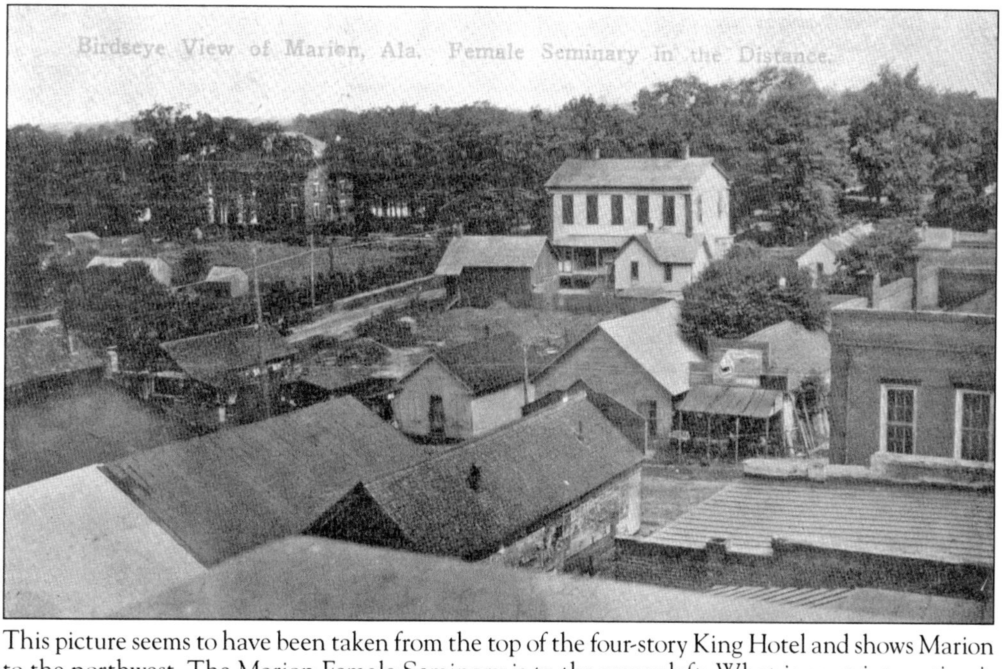

This picture seems to have been taken from the top of the four-story King Hotel and shows Marion to the northwest. The Marion Female Seminary is to the upper left. What is most interesting is the building toward the middle of the picture. It seems to be a large white house but resembles what could have at one time been a church. (Courtesy of Kitty Grey Long.)

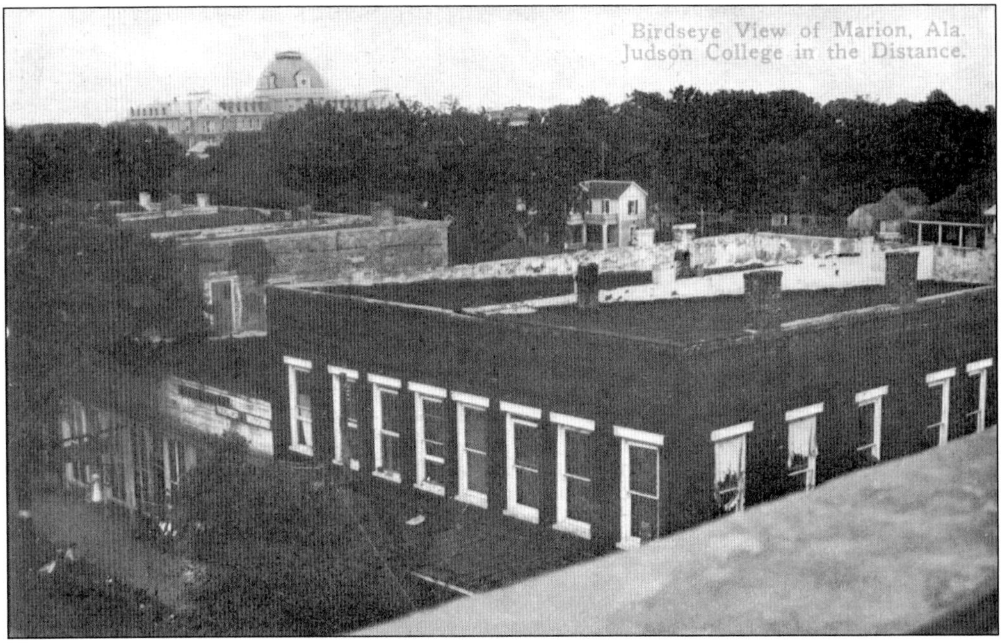

This scene also seems to have been taken from the top of the four-story King Hotel and shows a scene to the southeast. Obvious is the dome of the Judson on the Judson College campus. If a close examination is made of the white house in the middle of the scene, a Greek Revival front is visible. (Courtesy of Kitty Grey Long.)

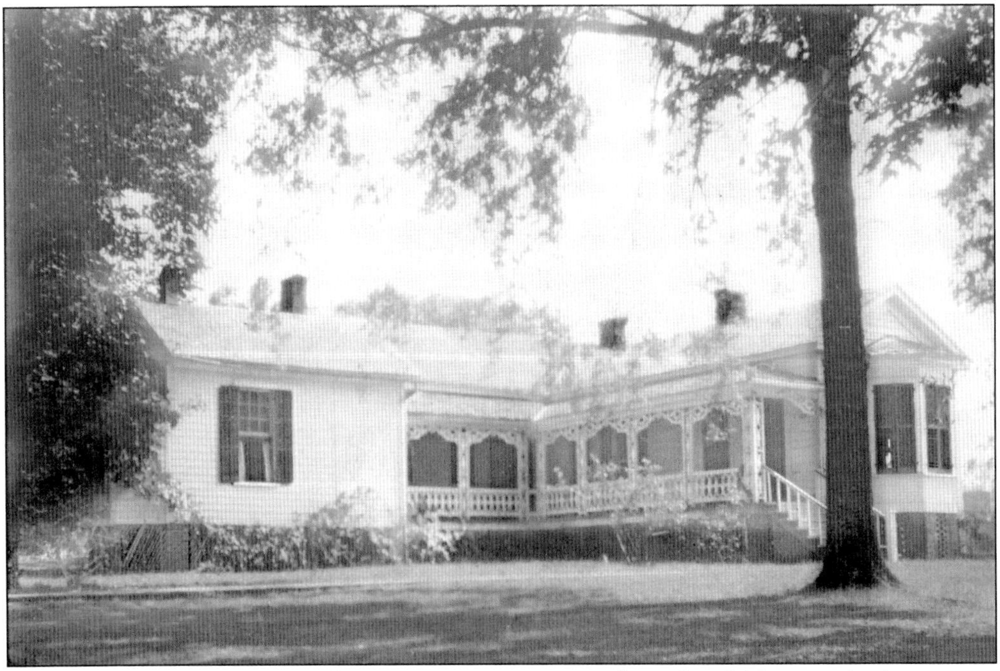

The house, known as the McAllister Cottage, once sat to the right of Alumnae Auditorium on the Judson College campus. It was the home of Dr. W. T. McAllister, a Marion physician. Later it served as a home for Judson presidents until a president's home was built. It may be the house that was moved a block to allow for new construction on campus. (JCA.)

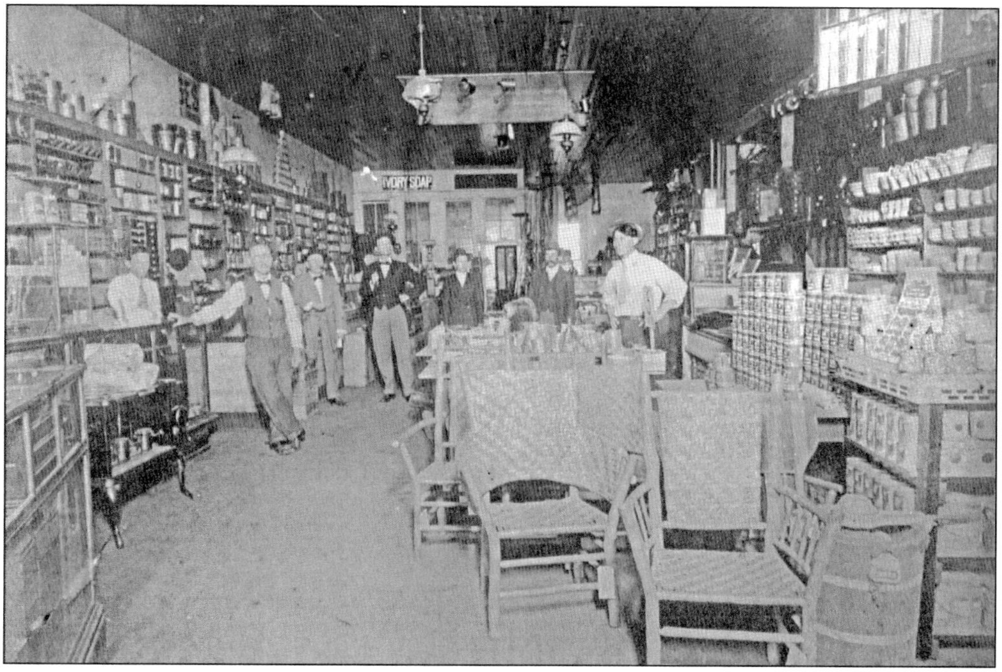

These are scenes from an old-fashioned general store in Marion, probably about the turn of the century. There is no identification of the clerks, but due to the number, it seems to have been a fairly large operation. Notice the produce in baskets along the left side of the picture below. The glass-front display cases are not the type seen in use today. The tall shelves would indicate that this was not a self-serve store. A rolling ladder is probably out of sight. Another item of interest was the chairs to the right of the picture above. This is not something found in a grocery store today. (Both, SU.)

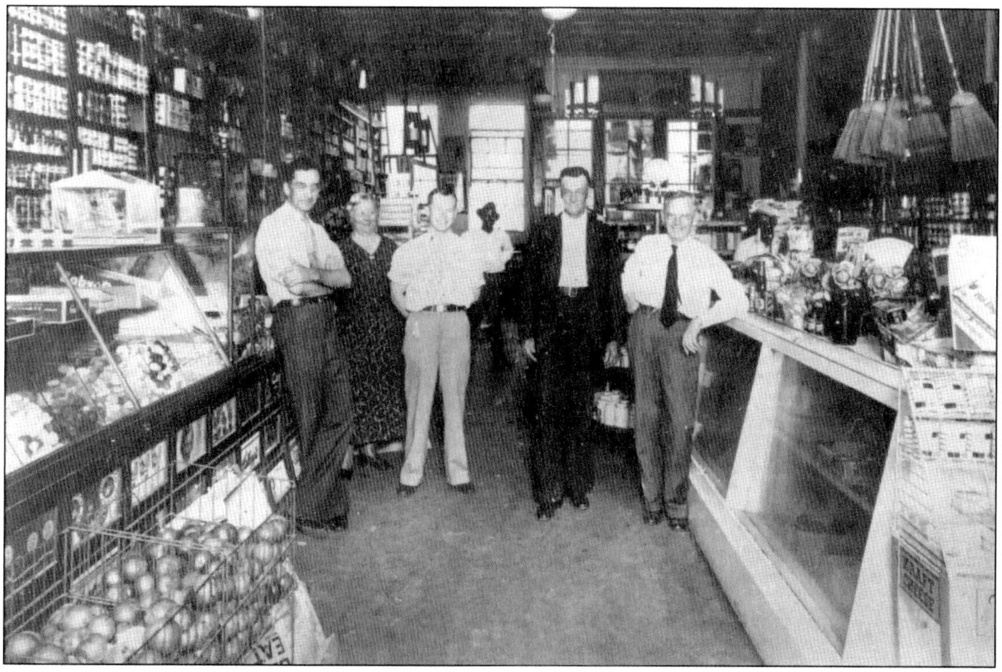

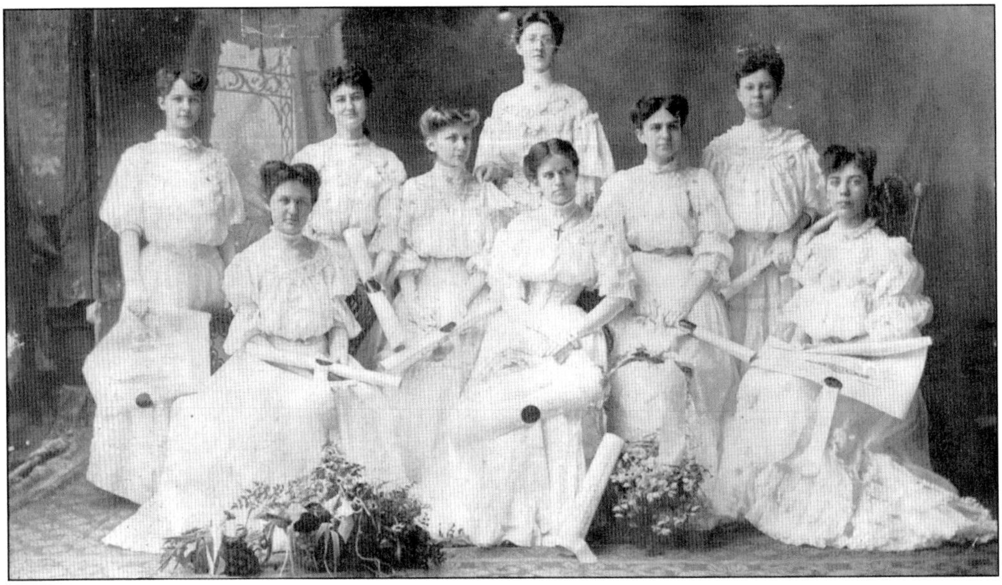

A picture of the 1905 graduating class of the Marion Female Institute shows a group of young ladies dressed very elegantly in all white dresses. They are holding their diplomas, some rolled up and others unfurled. They were very much larger than those awarded today. Each year thereafter, the class grew smaller, until the school closed in 1915. (PCHPS.)

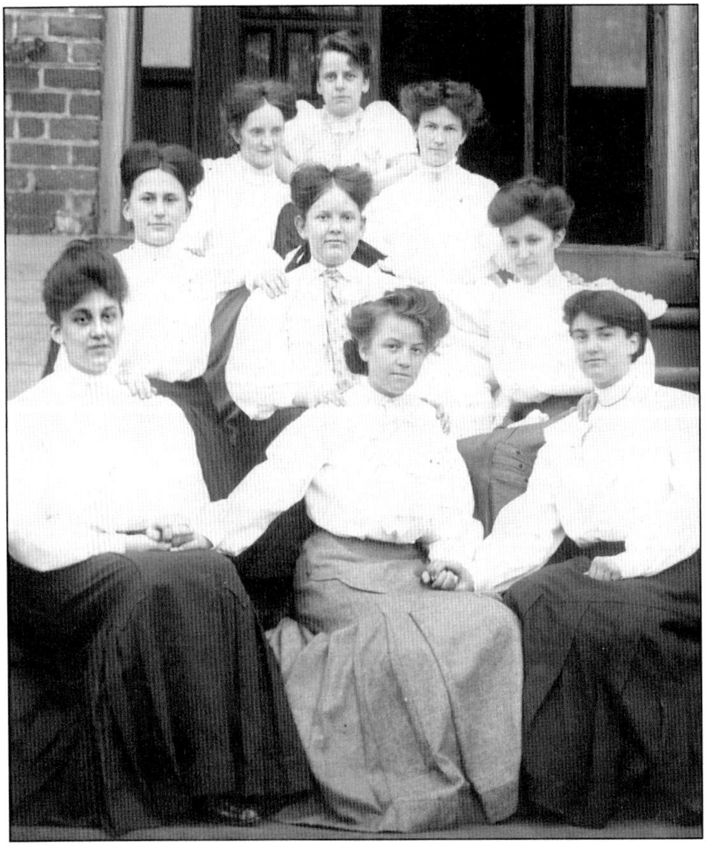

Throughout the *Conversationalist*, Judson College's yearbook of the early 1900s, many pictures of clubs have appeared. Most have names, and their purpose for being is evident by their names. The 1906 yearbook labeled this group the Tee Low Club. Pictured from left to right are (first row) Mary Moseley, Nell Ellis, and Gene Burks; (second row) Annelu Burns, Murelle Mason, and Bessie Massey; (third row) Ida Holly, Mae Auxford, and Mary Lou Dean. (JCA.)

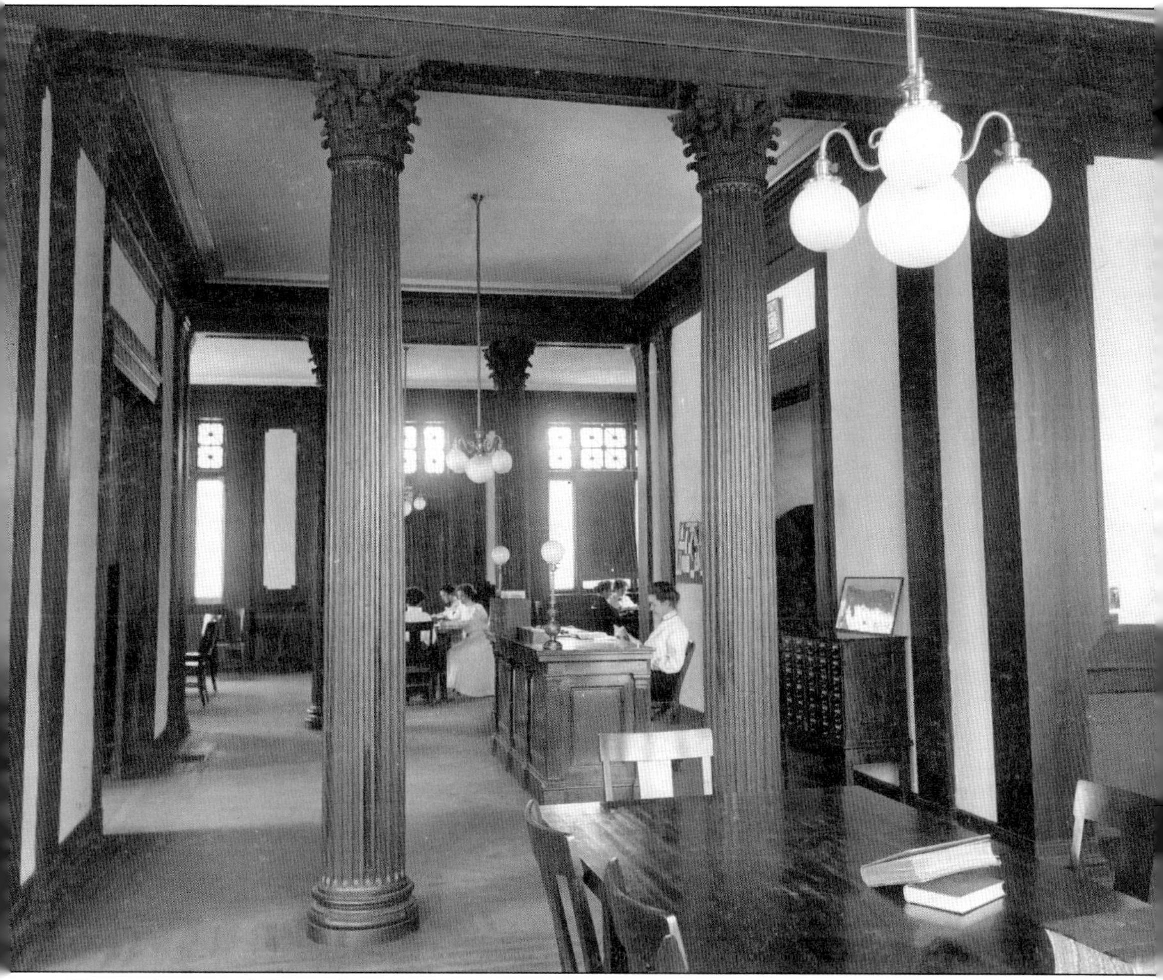

The early part of the 20th century was a period of expansion for Judson College: enrollment increased, land was bought, and buildings were erected. With a gift that Dr. Robert Patrick had solicited from the Carnegie Foundation, the Carnegie Library was built on the Judson College campus in 1908. It is known today as A. Howard Bean Hall and is home to the Alabama Women's Hall of Fame. This is an inside view from the right side of the building. The desk, which sits in the center as one enters the building, is the same one that was placed there in 1908. Above it in a transom was a piece of white milk glass that said "Silence." It is no longer there. After reading *They Called Me Kay*, a book about a former student and librarian, the answer to what happened to the sign was solved. It seems that students and others did not like it, so they took it down and put it in the trash. (JCA.)

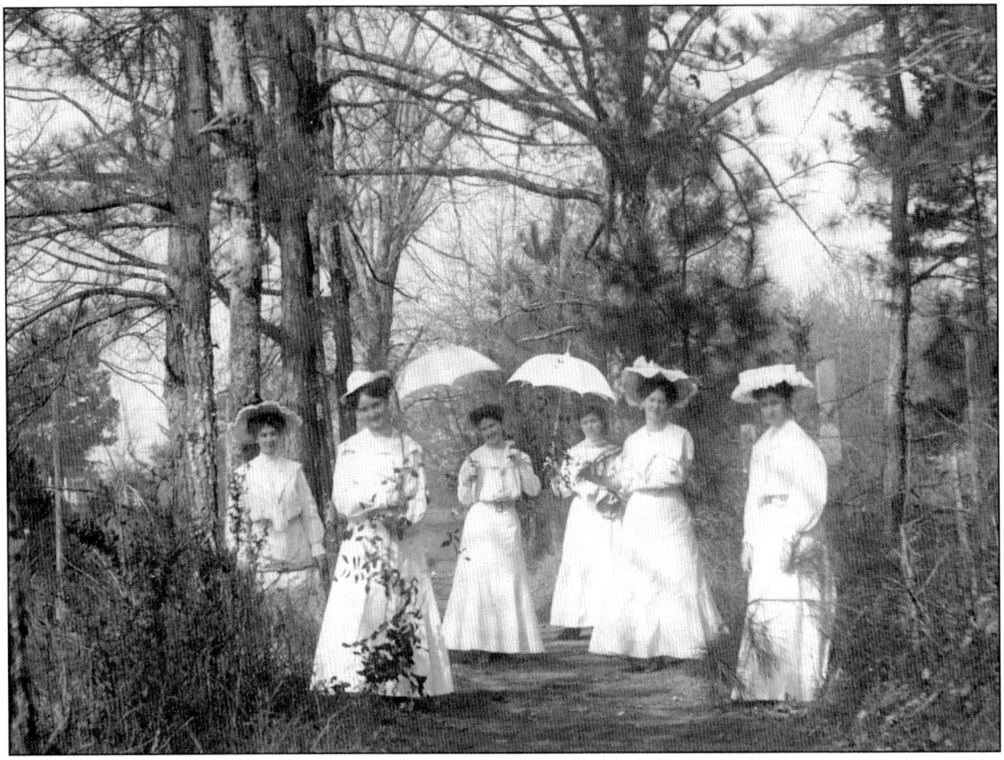

Shown are a group of Judson students out for a stroll. The picture in the *Conversationalist*, the college yearbook, is entitled "The Strollers." Often pictures show students out walking in the country surrounding the school. In all of the pictures, the young ladies are always dressed as if they were going visiting. Likely one of the group is a chaperone, since rules stated that they must be accompanied by a chaperone when off campus. (JCA.)

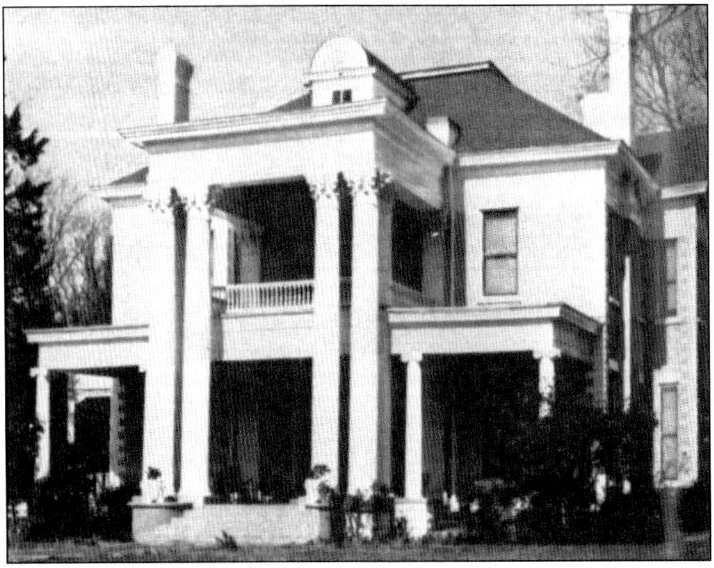

Dr. Solon Lycurgus Coleman bought this property in 1906 and erected this neoclassical house. The house is especially adapted to entertaining on a large scale. Corinthian columns are used on the porches. The house is known as Co-Nita Manor for the wife of a former owner. (Courtesy of Linda and Roy Calhoun.)

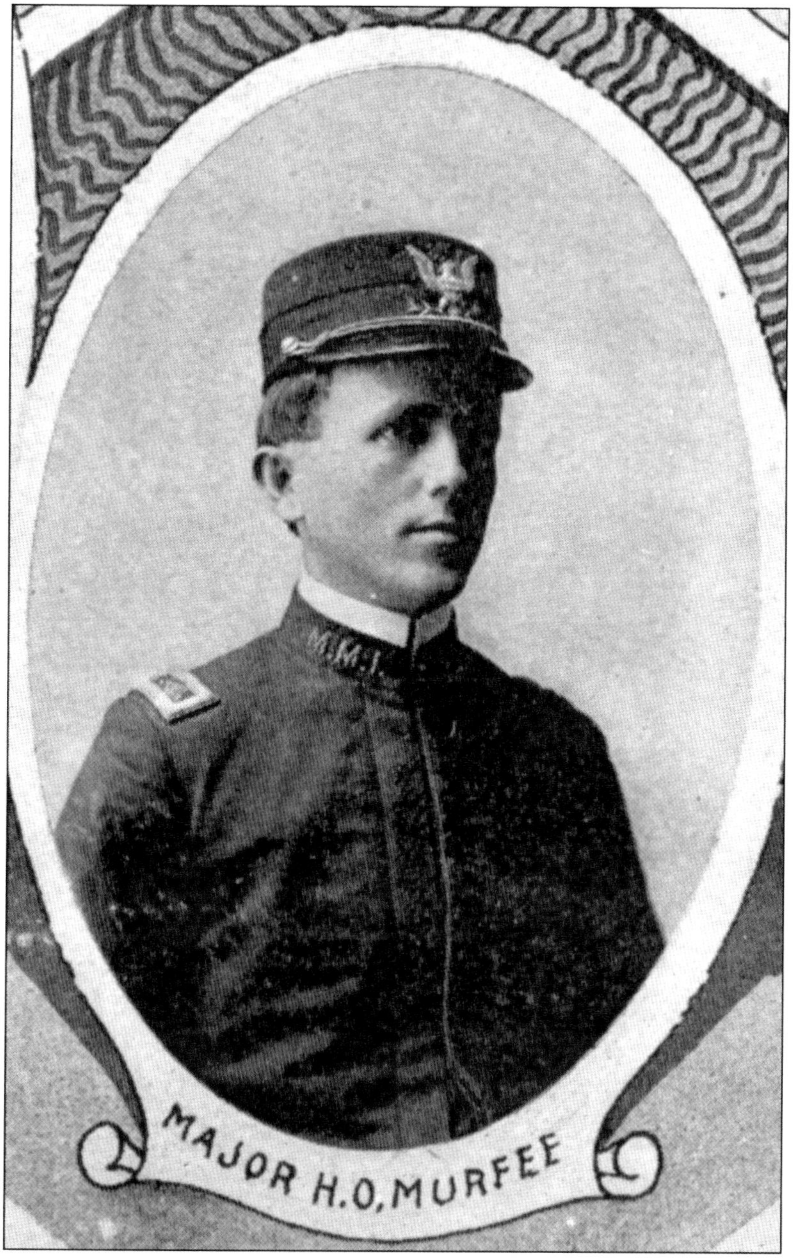

Hopson Owen Murfee, the son of James T. Murfee, was educated at Marion Military Institute, the University of Virginia, and the University of Alabama. While at the University of Virginia, he served as president of the Young Men's Christian Association and the Tennis Association. Murfee was also involved with the tennis championship games while there. Before returning to teach at Marion Military Institute in 1900, he taught at the University of Virginia and the University of Chicago. In 1906, he succeeded his father as president of Marion Military Institute. Pres. Theodore Roosevelt appointed him to the Board of Visitors of the U.S. Naval Academy in 1906. He, along with his brother Walter Lee, was foremost in leading Marion Military Institute to establishing a national reputation. Together they also were able to draw students from all the states and territories, as well as from foreign countries. (MMIFA.)

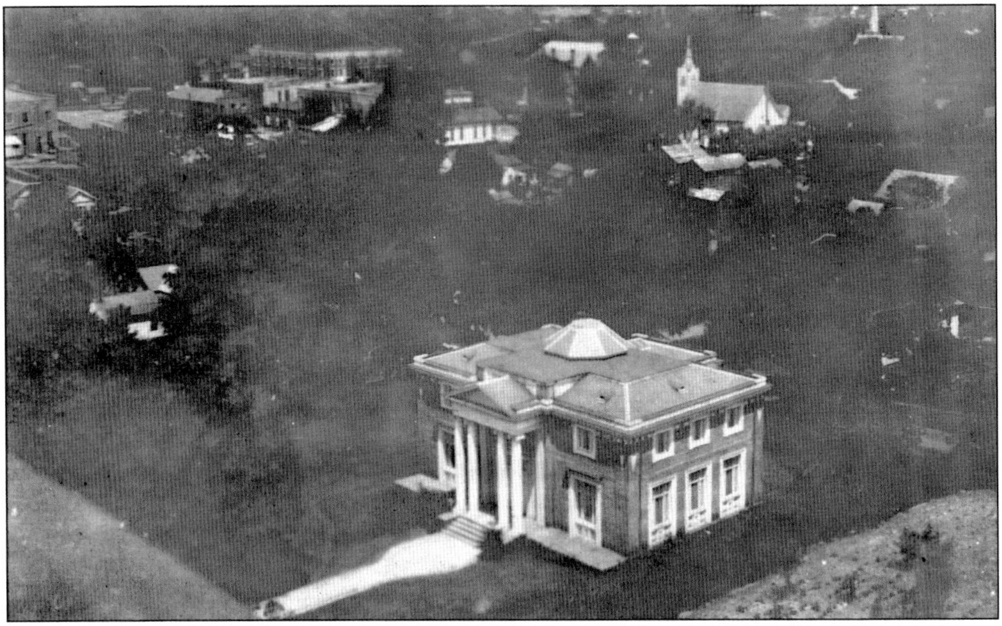

This picture was made some time after 1908. It was probably taken from the Sky Parlor atop Jewett Hall. The Carnegie Library (now A. Howard Bean Hall) was erected in 1908. As one can see, it has a sky dome. Also, it looks northwest toward downtown Marion. (JCA.)

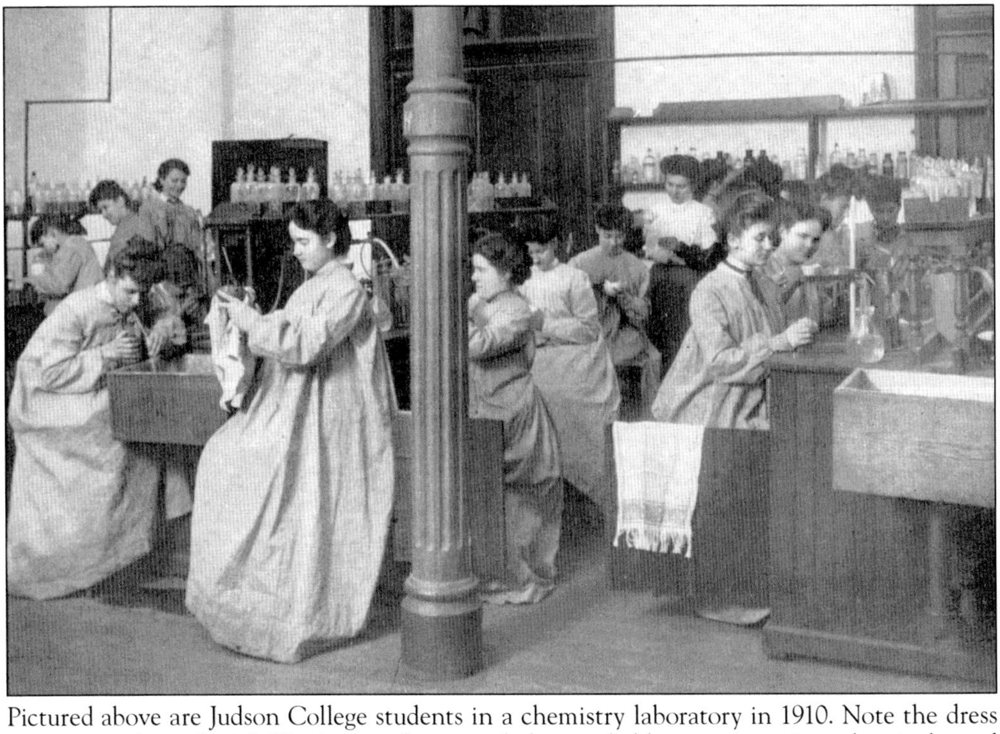

Pictured above are Judson College students in a chemistry laboratory in 1910. Note the dress covers worn by each girl. The jars on the open shelves probably contain various chemicals used in their laboratory work. Even at this early date, it is interesting to note the provisions made for the study of science by women. (JCA.)

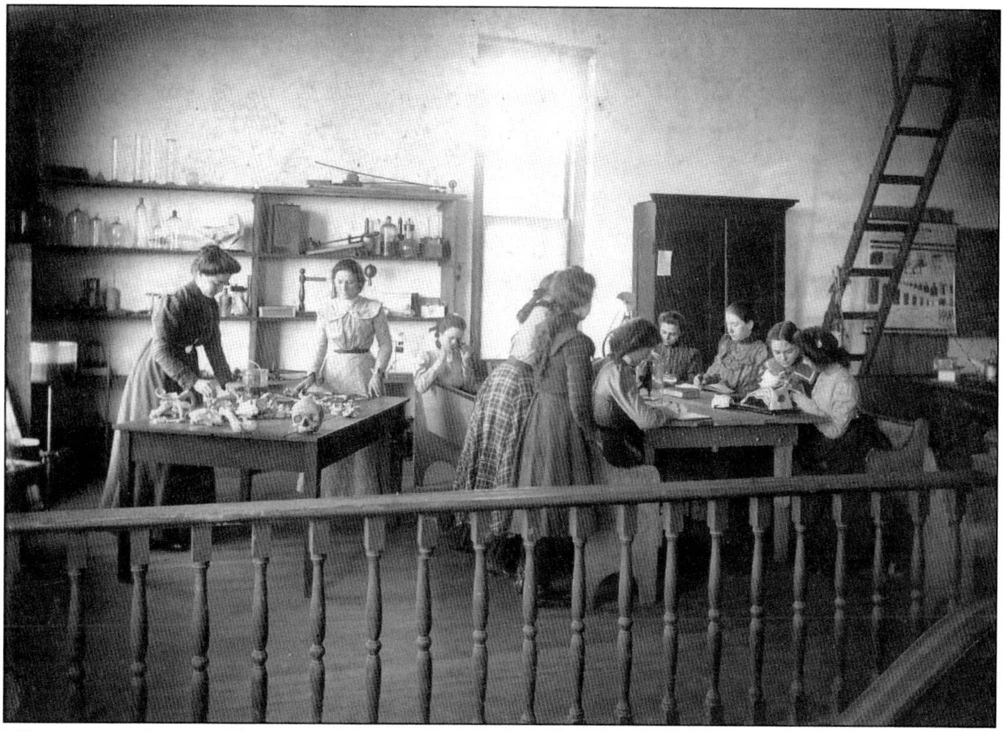

This picture shows students in what is probably a biology laboratory in 1910. Notice the bones on the table to the left. Were they working on putting a skeleton together, or were they identifying bones? No covering dresses were needed for this laboratory. The architecture indicates that both of these laboratories were located in the Judson. (JCA.)

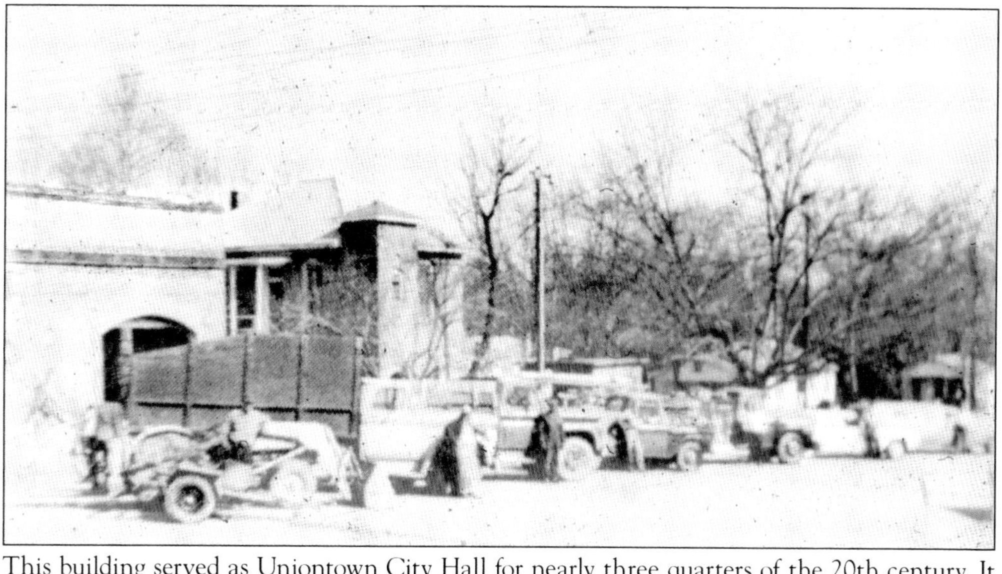

This building served as Uniontown City Hall for nearly three quarters of the 20th century. It was torn down and a new city hall was built in the same area. The first floor of the old building was the volunteer fire department and held the fire truck and firefighting equipment. The second floor, which was reached only by outside steps, contained all the city offices. (Courtesy of the author.)

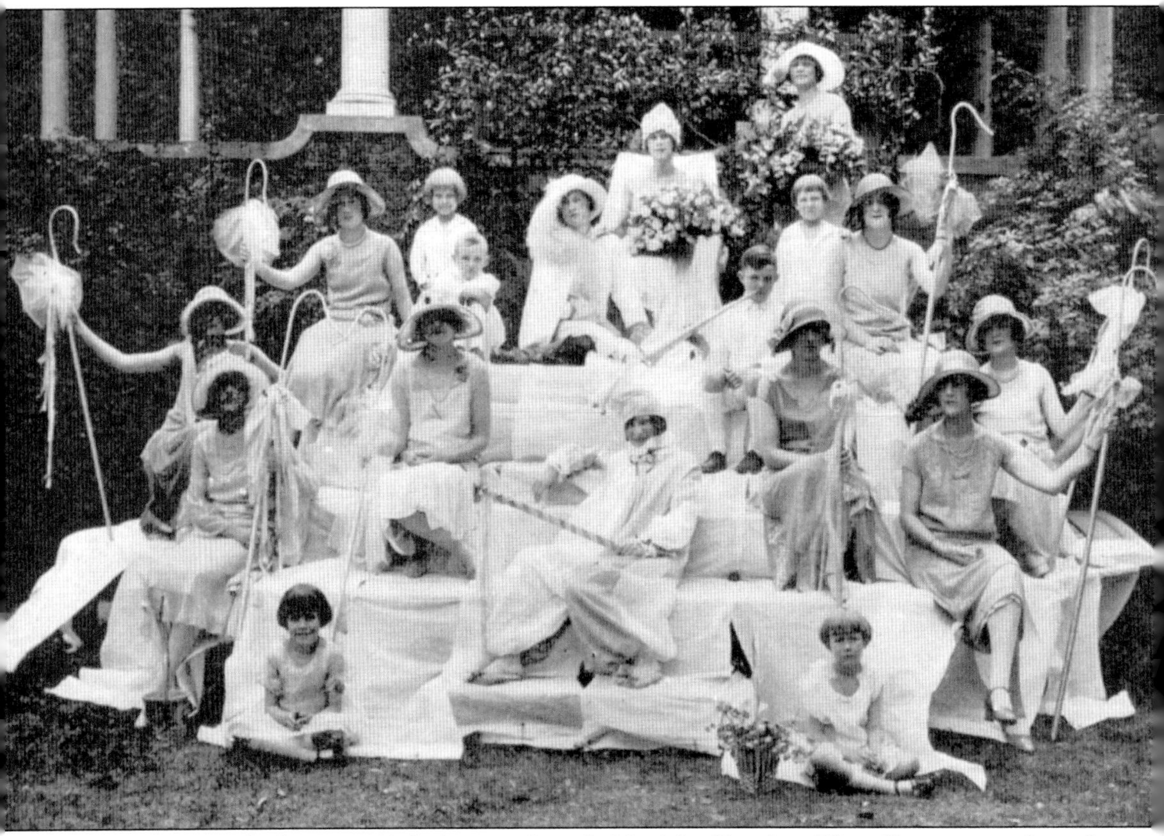

History records that in 1893, Judson students held a May Day fete. The affair was simple and decorous. On that day in 1893 "one of the girls was crowned queen after which we took our tea by a little table out on the lawn just at sunset and had a little programme in the parlor." As the years progressed, the programs became very elaborate with a theme for the day, and the appropriate costumes, scenery, and other trappings were used. This began a tradition at Judson College that continues to this day. In this picture, the girl is referred to as Queen O'May and Court. Today the event is called J Day, which is the school's homecoming, and a J Day Queen and her court are presented to the alumnae in an afternoon ceremony. The festivities have returned to the simple form of their beginnings. (JCA.)

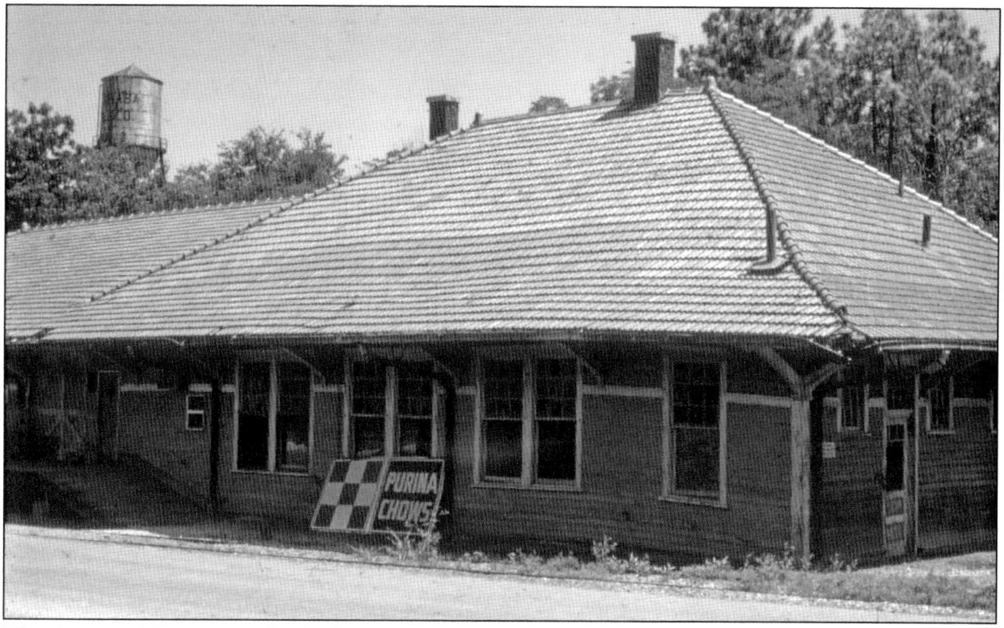

The depot in Uniontown, built about 1913, was similar to many found over the state. The Alabama and Mississippi Rivers Railroad came through Uniontown before the War Between the States. It served as the Southern Railroad station until it was no longer profitable to maintain a station in Uniontown. It was torn down during the early 1980s. (Courtesy of the author.)

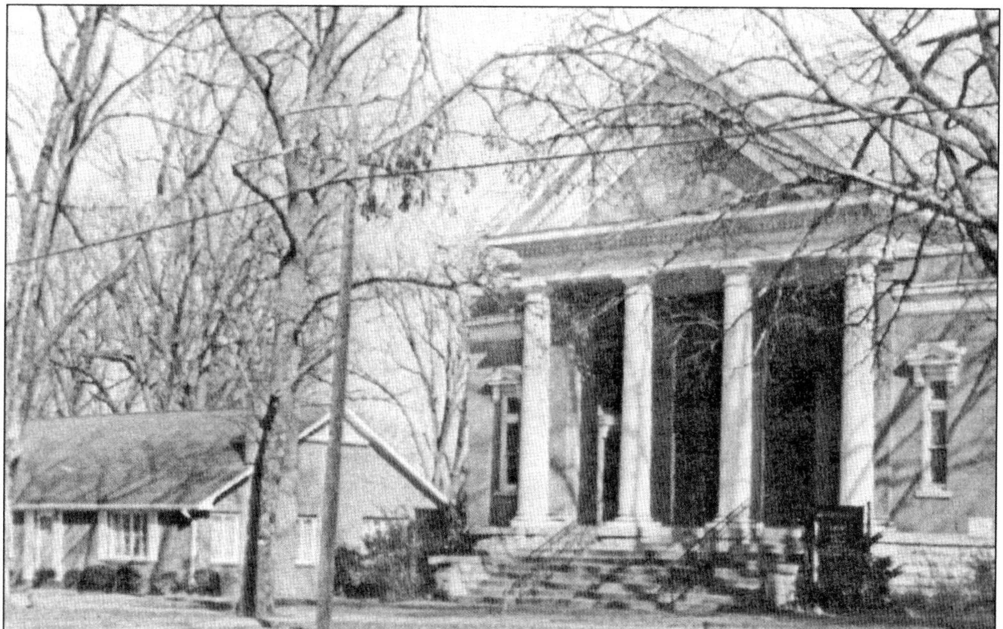

Several Presbyterian congregations in the vicinity joined together in 1853 to form the First Presbyterian Church in Uniontown. This building, neoclassical in style, is located on Water Street. It was ready for services in 1914. One of the features of the 1854 building, a memorial window, was installed in the center of the north wall of the new sanctuary. (Courtesy of Linda and Roy Calhoun.)

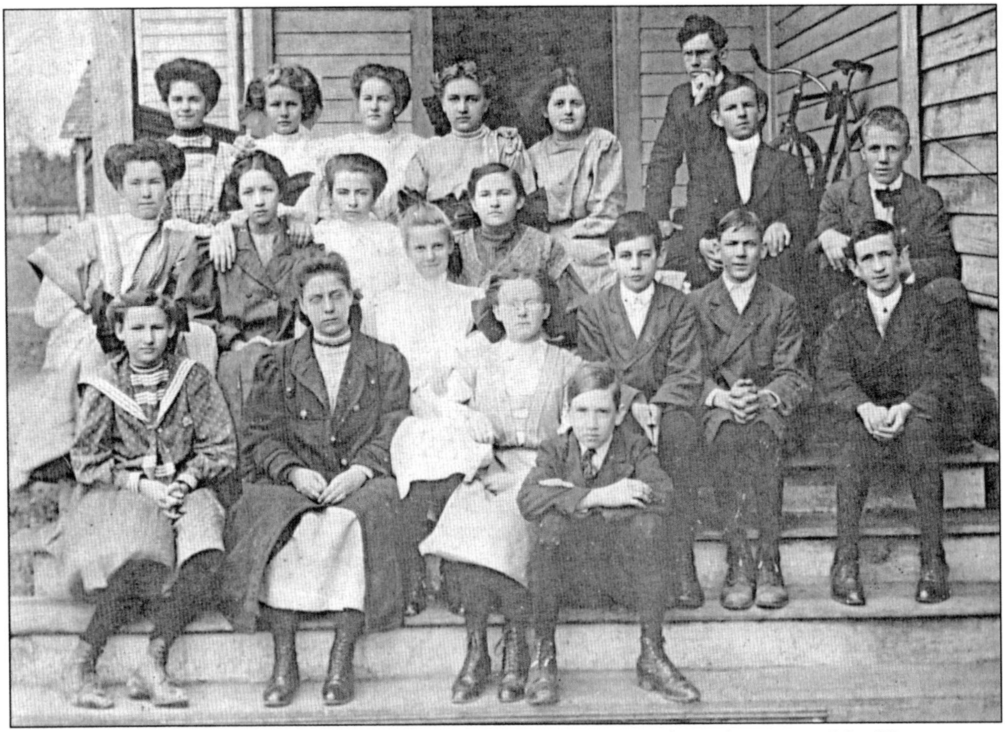

Pictured on the steps of St. Elmo in Uniontown are a group of students. They seem to be dressed for school pictures. This picture probably dates from the period of 1915 to 1923, since this building was taken down around 1923 to make room for a new one. (Courtesy of the author.)

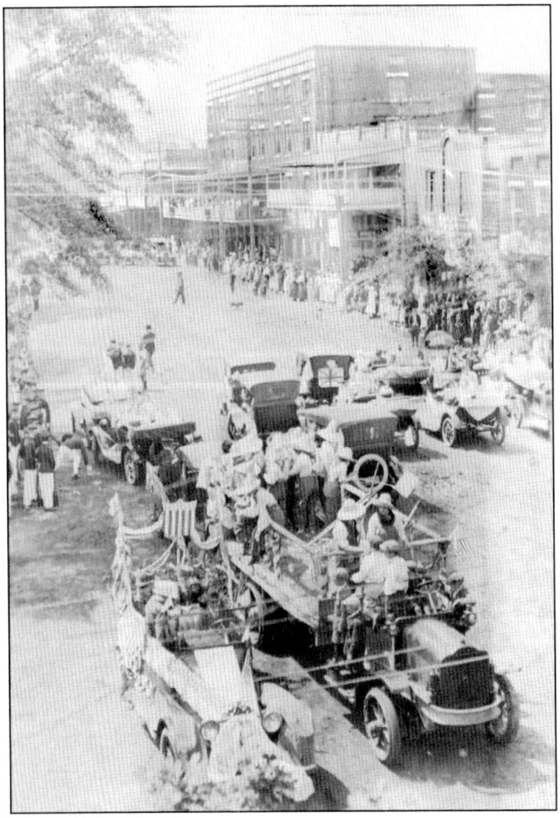

This picture seems to depict some type of celebration held in Marion. From the looks of things, it was most likely a Fourth of July celebration. Note the fire engine in the forefront of the photograph. The scene is on Washington Street. The streets have been blocked off. A close look reveals the presence of band members. The old open-topped cars are interesting. (PCHPS.)

This is another scene of the same celebration. This scene is in front of the courthouse, with a very large group of people on hand for the celebration. The flag is a large one hanging across the front of the building. Barely visible through the trees is the front of the old Marion Bank and Trust Company Building. (PCHPS.)

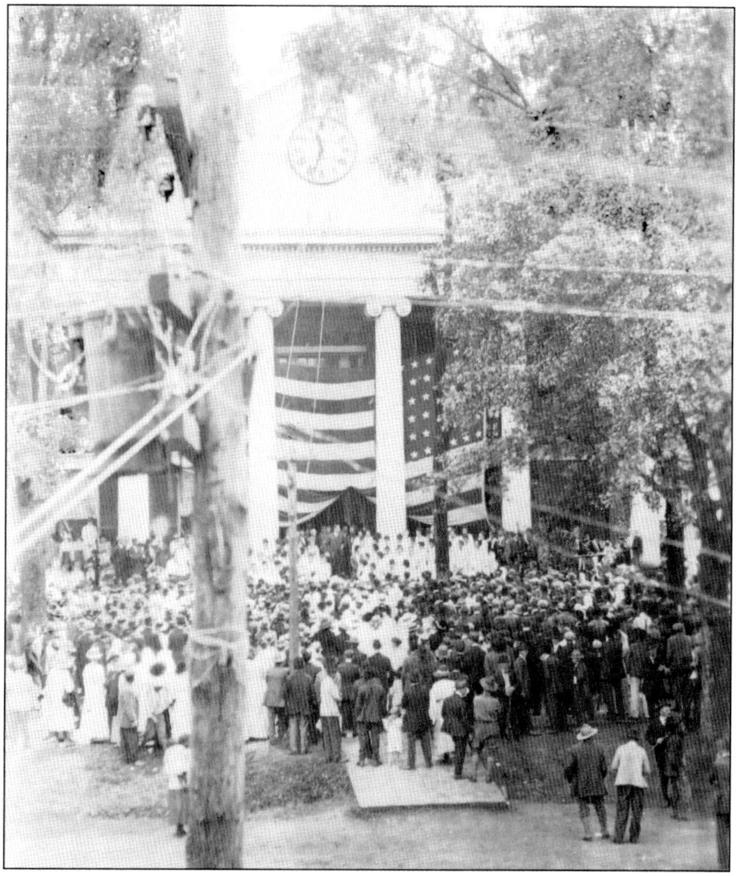

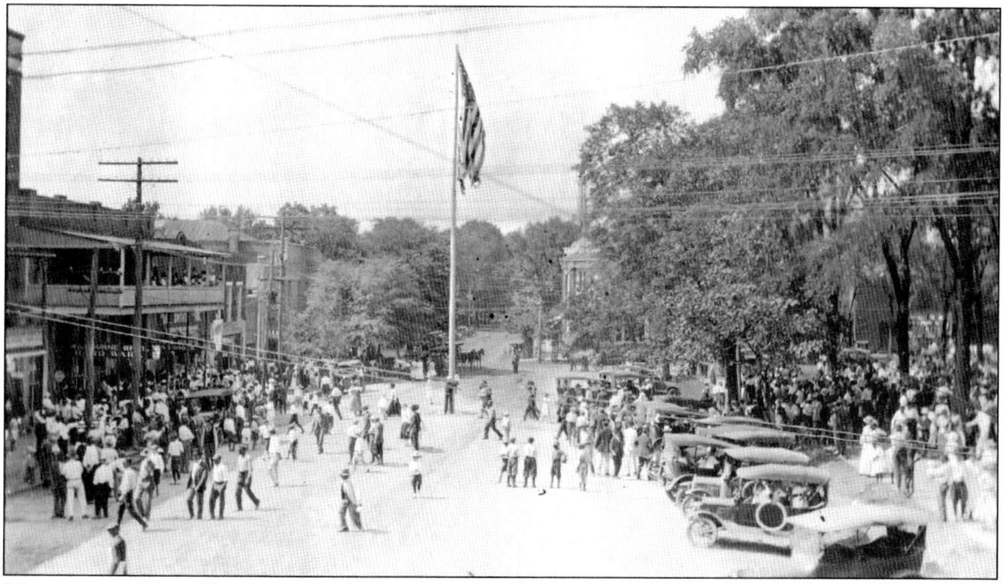

This scene of the celebration looks north up Washington Street. A flag pole has been placed in the middle of the street. Note the large crowd in attendance. Again, the old Marion Bank and Trust Company building is visible through the trees. (PCHPS.)

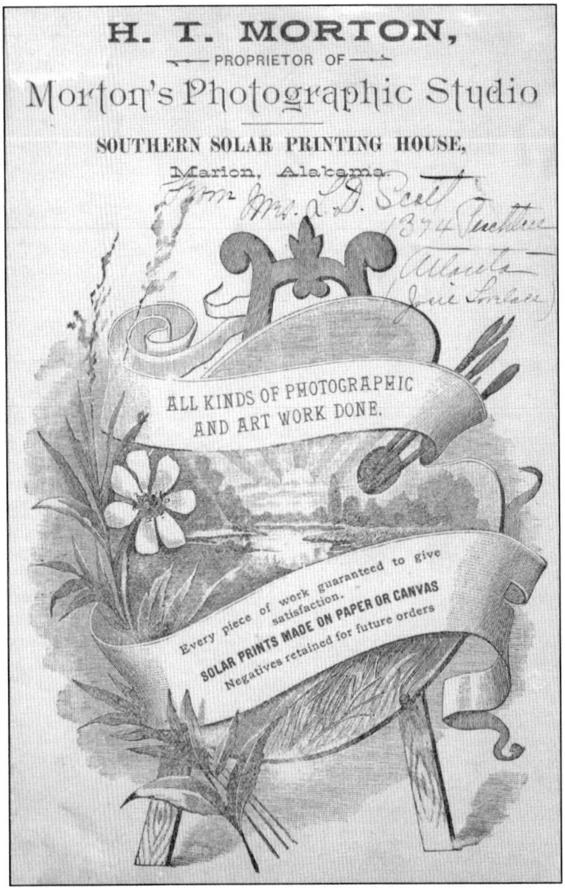

Pictured is a postcard that advertised "H. T. Morton, Southern Solar Printing House" of Marion. Morton later moved to Birmingham and became a noted photographer there. It seems that solar photography did not remain as popular as the photographer did. The 1872 photographs used here are his work. (SU.)

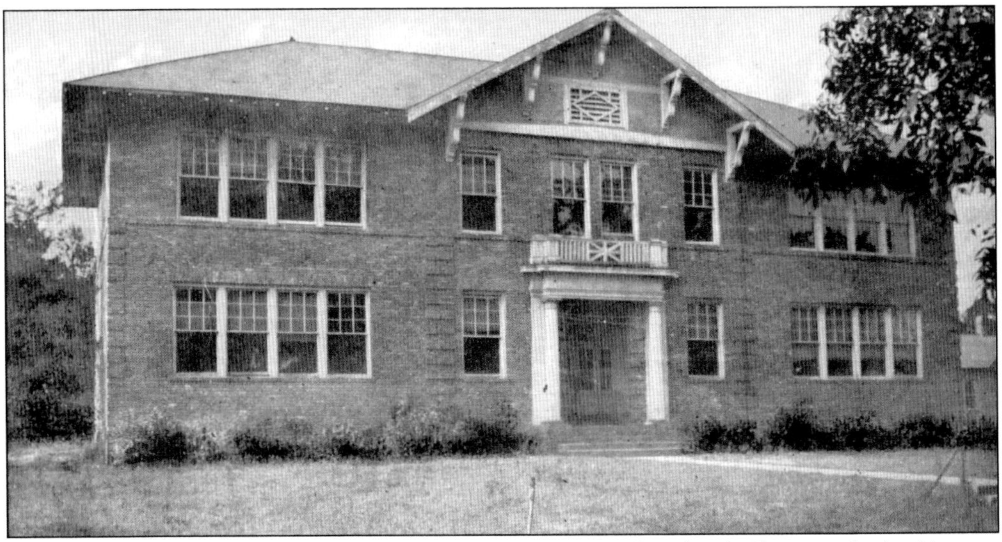

This postcard and similar ones are labeled Perry County High School. This was the building in use by the citizens of Marion prior to the old Marion Female Seminary being used for a public school. It was located on a hill near the seminary building. Several older citizens were asked about the building, but none remembered it. (PCHPS.)

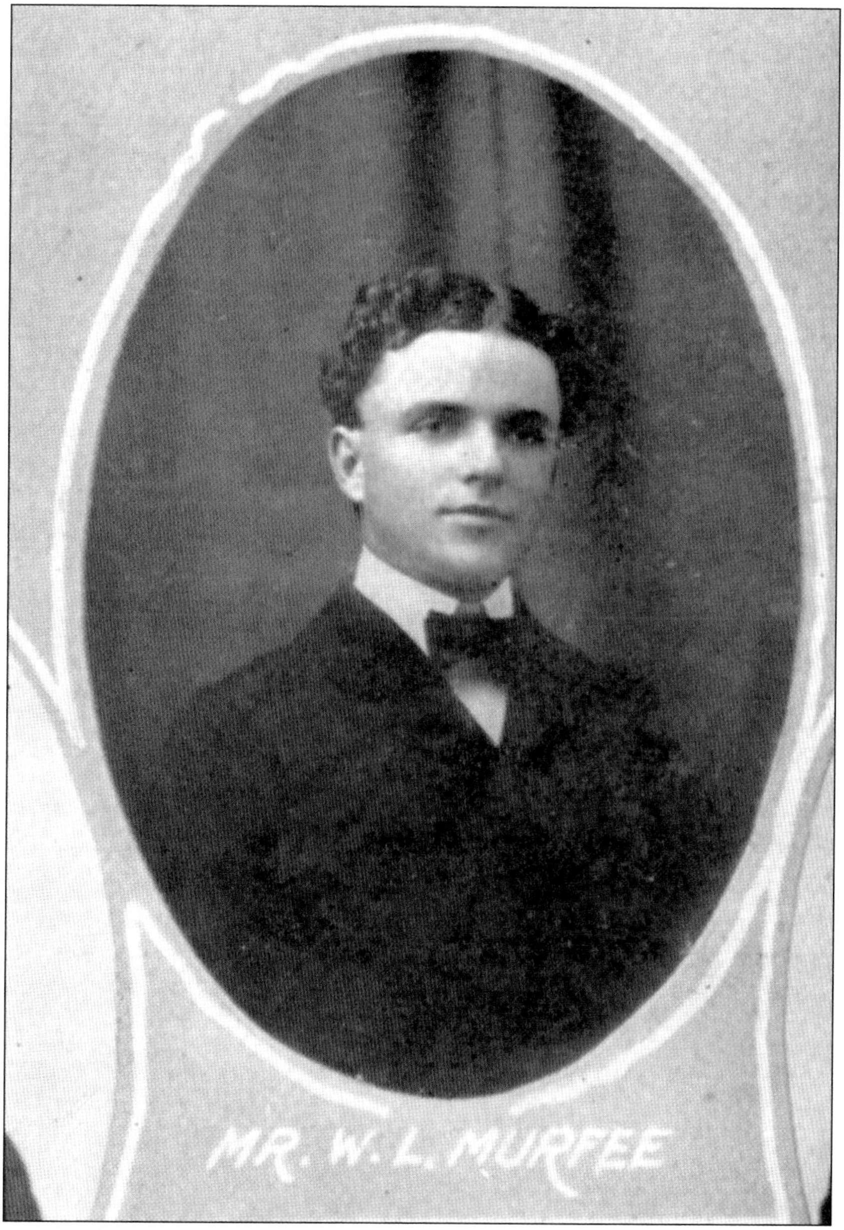

Walter Lee Murfee was the son of J. T. Murfee and the brother of H. O. Murfee, the first and second presidents of Marion Military Institute. He received his education at Marion Military Institute, the University of Virginia, and the University of Chicago. Murfee returned to teach at Marion Military Institute, and in 1906, he served as comptroller and superintendent. In 1917, he succeeded his brother, H. O., as president, thus, being the third Murfee member to serve in that position. He was very active in war efforts during World War I, especially in campaigns for the Red Cross, liberty loans, and others. He and his brother made unique contributions to education in the South. During their presidencies, they brought some of the best educators to the state. During the administration of Murfee and his brother, Marion Military Institute received national recognition, and the school had students from every state and territory, as well as from foreign countries. (MMIFA.)

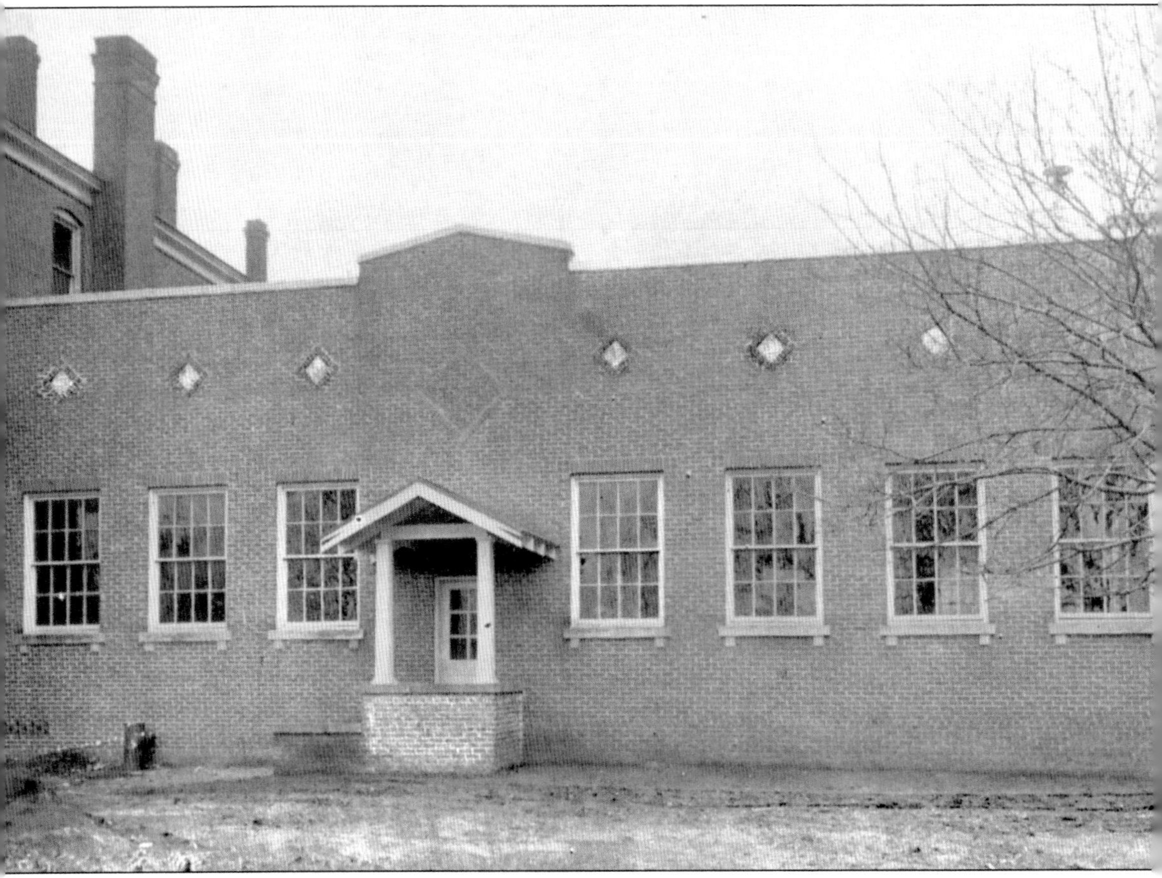

A new gymnasium was erected on the campus of Judson College about 1917. It was to the rear of Alumnae Auditorium and the music annex. Among the facilities provided were an indoor tile swimming pool and basketball court. Courses were offered in swimming, tennis, track, horseback riding, basketball, tether, tennis, volleyball, indoor baseball, captain ball, and archery. The students in 1918 had to purchase a uniform of crimson jersey; black Galatea-pleated bloomers; heavy, black, canvas, rubber-soled shoes; full-length cotton tights; white canvas hat; and a crimson torque with a black border. Swimming suits were regulation natural gray. A solarium was added to the roof of the gymnasium during the presidency of Dr. Leroy G. Cleverdon. After a new and modern facility, Riddle Gymnasium, was constructed, the pool was covered and the area used as a practice area for the Judson Choir and for other activities, as needed. Later the building was torn down and replaced with the Marian Acree Tucker Music Hall. (JCA.)

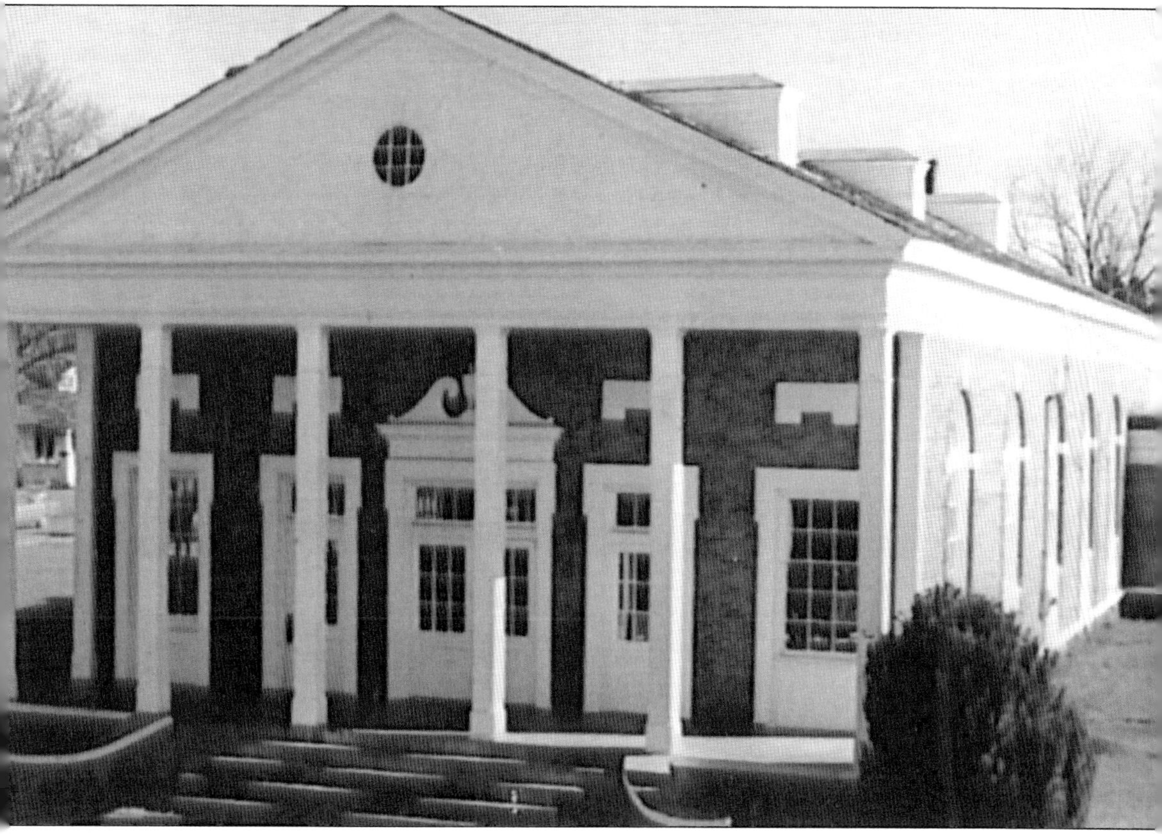

The 1867 incorporation papers call this "The Lincoln School of Marion." In 1868, the local founders sought the aid of the American Missionary Association, an auxiliary of the Congregationalist Church. The agreement between the local founders and the American Missionary Association specified that the school be "used in such a manner as to afford the means of education to the largest practicable number of applicants, preference being given to those preparing to teach." The school was constituted, at first, of a primary and normal department. The normal department moved in 1887 and became what is Alabama State University in Montgomery. Mary Elizabeth Phillips came to the school as principal in 1896 and found it in a very rundown condition. Lincoln School at one time had a very large campus in Marion. Students attended not only from the local and surrounding areas of Alabama but also from adjoining states. Under the leadership of Phillips, the school grew. After her death in 1927, the Phillips Memorial Auditorium was erected in 1939. This is the only building of the original campus remaining. (LM.)

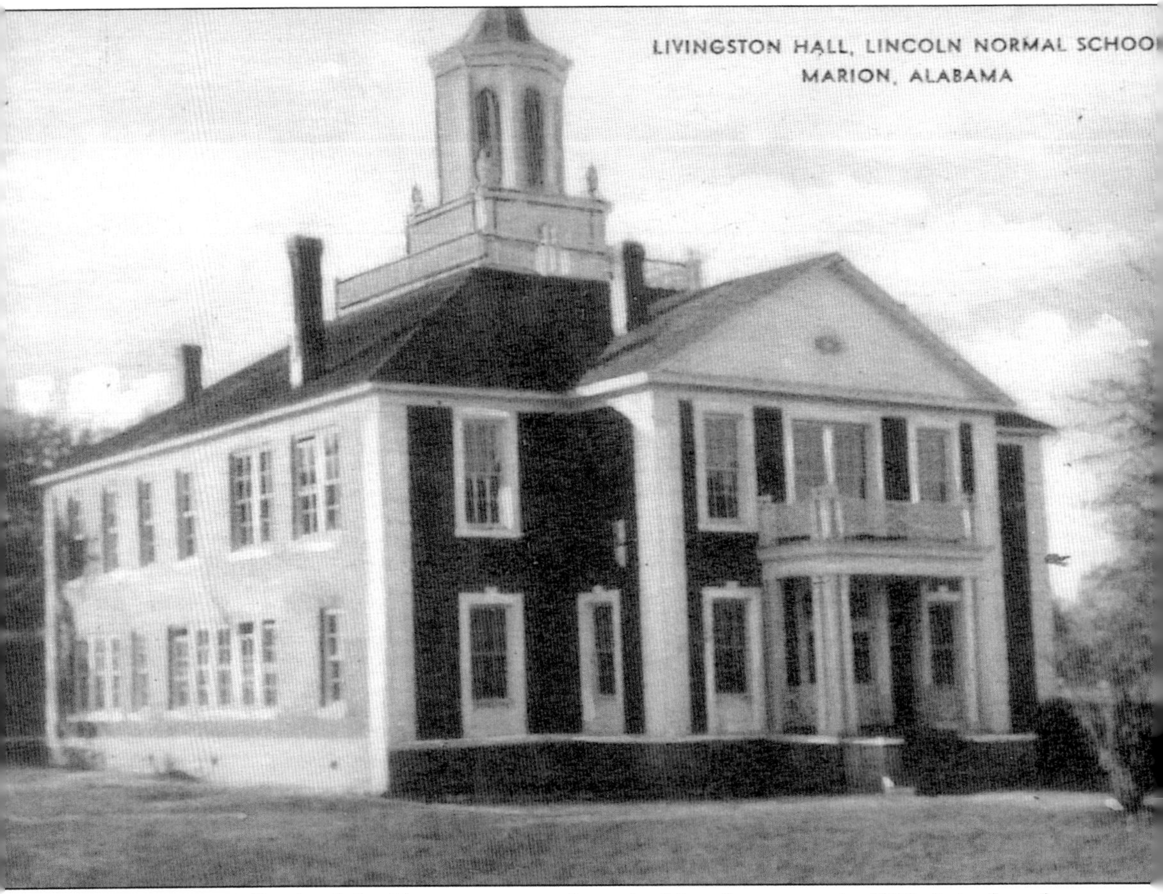

Livingston Hall, a brick building, was erected on the Lincoln campus in 1902. It is thought to be one of the finest buildings that graced the campus. Note its cupola and belvedere. Mary E. Phillips had raised some of the money and was promised matching funds, so the go-ahead was given to begin construction. The story is told that when less than half finished, the workmen went on strike because they wanted more money. Phillips was gone for a few days, and when she returned, she called the students together and explained, "Our new building is less than half finished, but we have no workers. In the last few days I have learned to lay bricks. If you will help, we can learn our lessons while mixing cement and handling the trowel. I will be your teacher if you will construct your own building." (LM.)

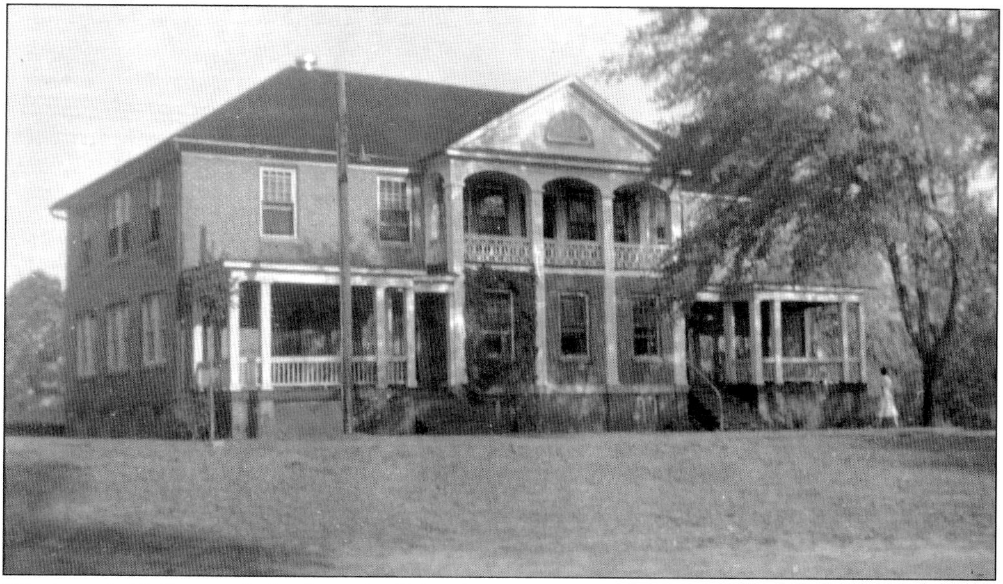

Woolworth Hall served the Lincoln School as a science and home economics building, with quarters for teachers. Mary Phillips was ever vigilant in getting the most for her money. She had raised $4,000 at a Lincoln's Day Chapel service in 1922 and sent it to headquarters to be matched. Reverend and Mrs. Woolworth gave $1,000, so the school was named in their honor. (LM.)

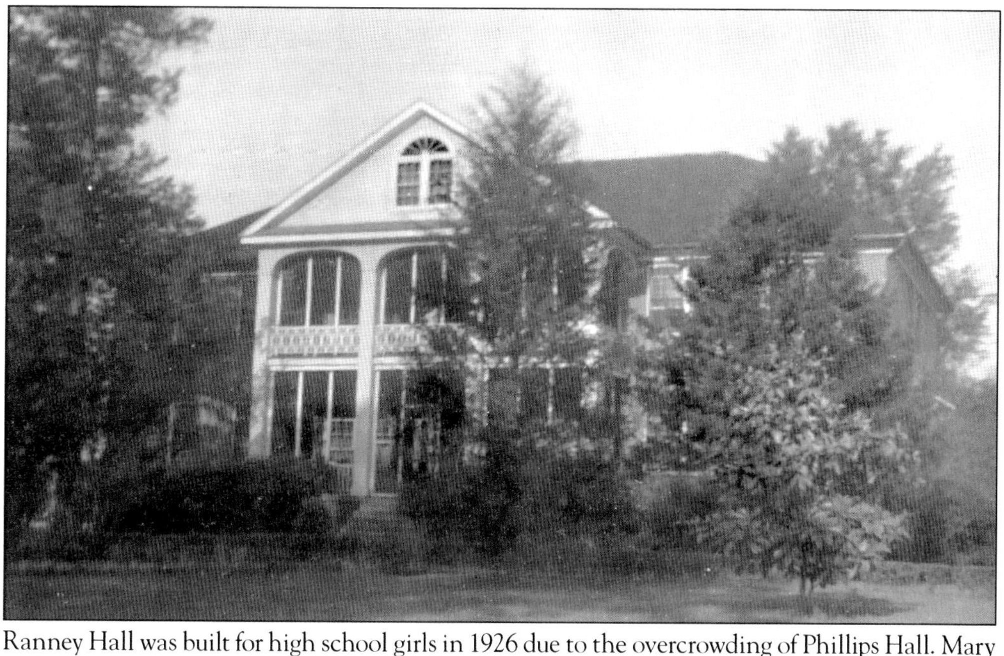

Ranney Hall was built for high school girls in 1926 due to the overcrowding of Phillips Hall. Mary E. Phillips was so pleased she commented that her next project would be to landscape the campus. Before she could do that, she became ill and died in 1927. Others followed her as principal, but none matched her accomplishments. (LM.)

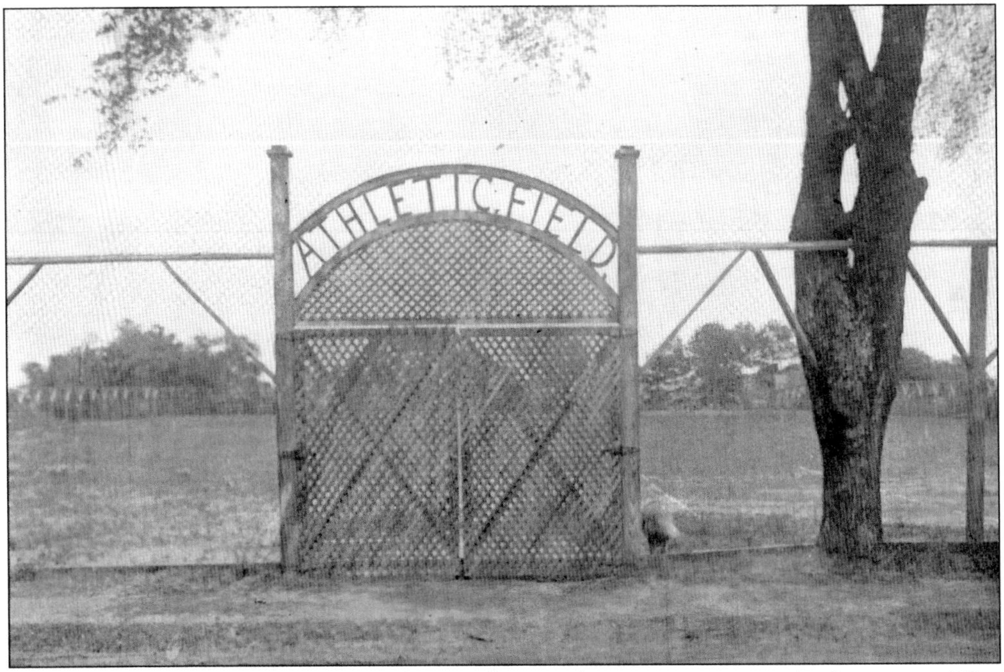

It is obvious by the yearbook that Judson College students were very involved in sports. This picture appeared in the 1919 *Conversationalist* and is labeled "Gate to Athletic Field." The field was located behind the president's home and to the north of Elmcrest. Again, the school seems to have been ahead of the times with its emphasis on physical fitness. (JCA.)

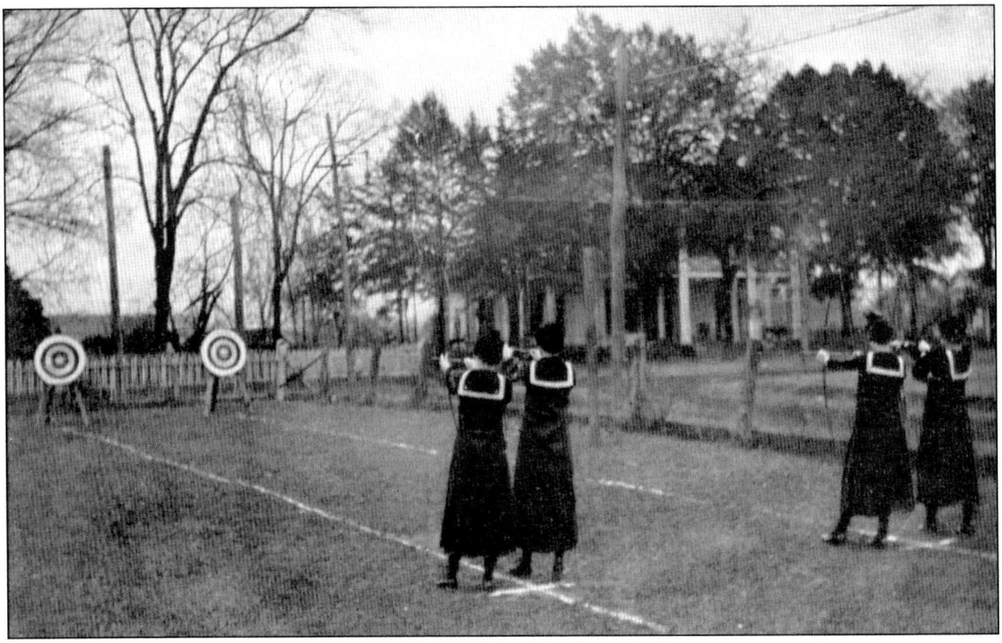

There are many pictures of the physical activities of Judson College students. This one portrays an archery class in process. The dress seems to be a standard sailor-type design. In the background are Elmcrest and the Goree home. Following tradition, archery is still offered by Judson College. (JCA.)

Among other sports were softball, tennis, track, and basketball. In this scene is a group of basketball players dressed in dark uniforms with sailor collars. Each has a turban-like hat to hold her hair out of her eyes. The hats seem to be tied in different styles. The practice and/or game field was outdoors. (JCA.)

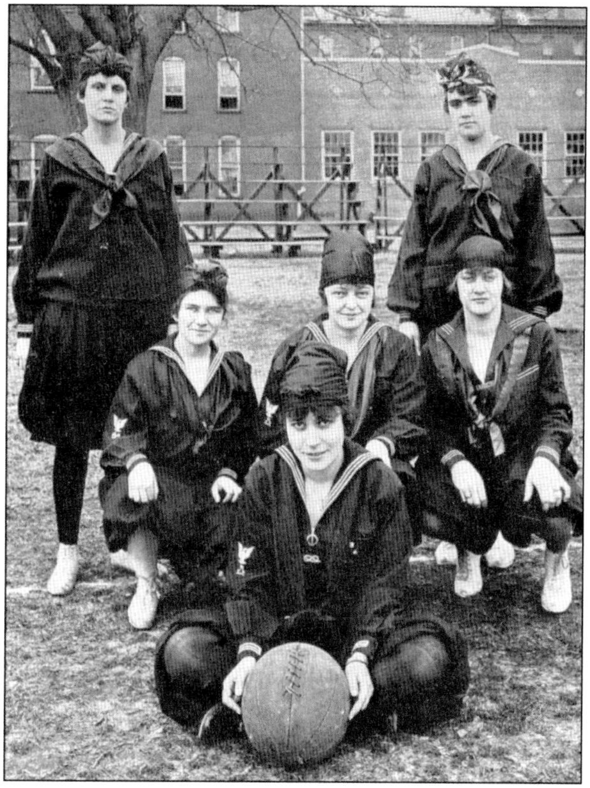

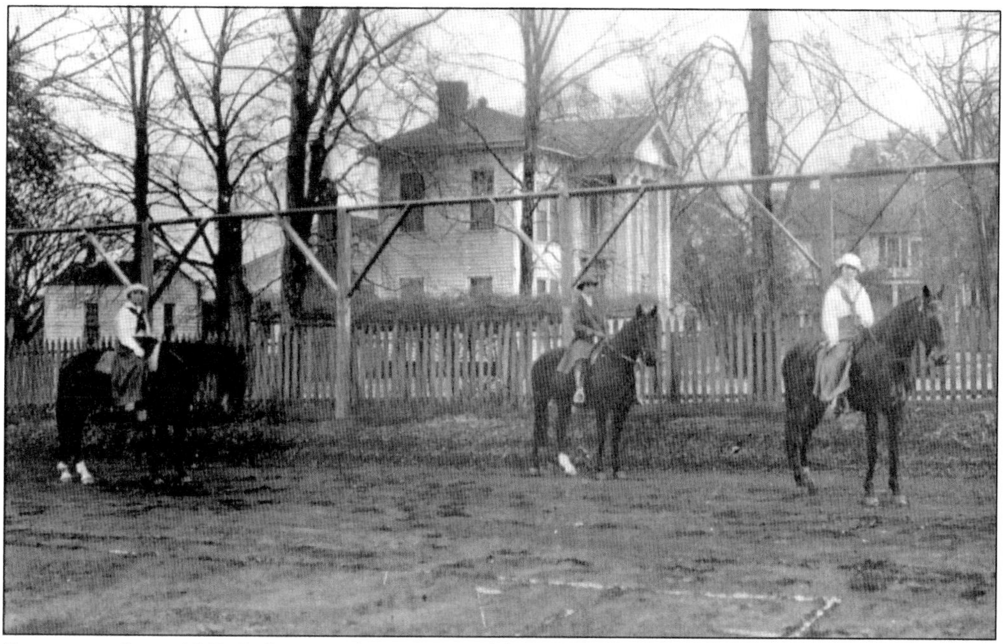

Even as early as 1919, Judson students enjoyed horseback riding. Here three students are seen as they ride on campus. In the background is Elmcrest, and further to the rear is the Langston Goree home, built about 1834. The house was constructed with wooden pegs and nails. Goree was one of the early trustees of the school. (JCA.)

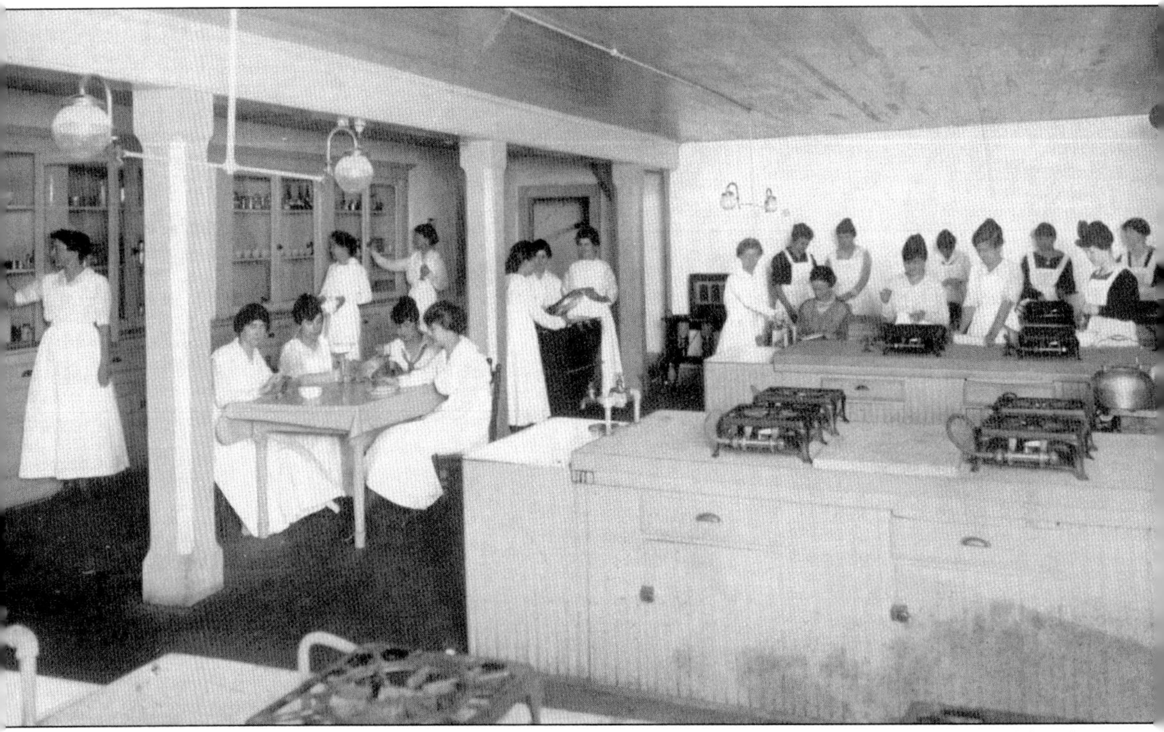

In 1919, Elmcrest, the Judge John Moore home on the Judson College campus, was used by the home economics department of the school. Pictured above is the interior of the building, depicting a kitchen scene with students working on assignments. Notice the double hot plates that are on the counters. The School of Home Economics offered four courses in cooking. Two of the courses were designed so that the students learned the principles of cooking certain foods along with the study of utensils and equipment. They also learned to plan and serve meals at home. The other two courses included one whose aim was to teach efficiency and management in the preparation of meals, cooking, and serving a meal and one that taught food conservation and cooking for the invalid. Each of the classes had a recitation and a laboratory segment. (JCA.)

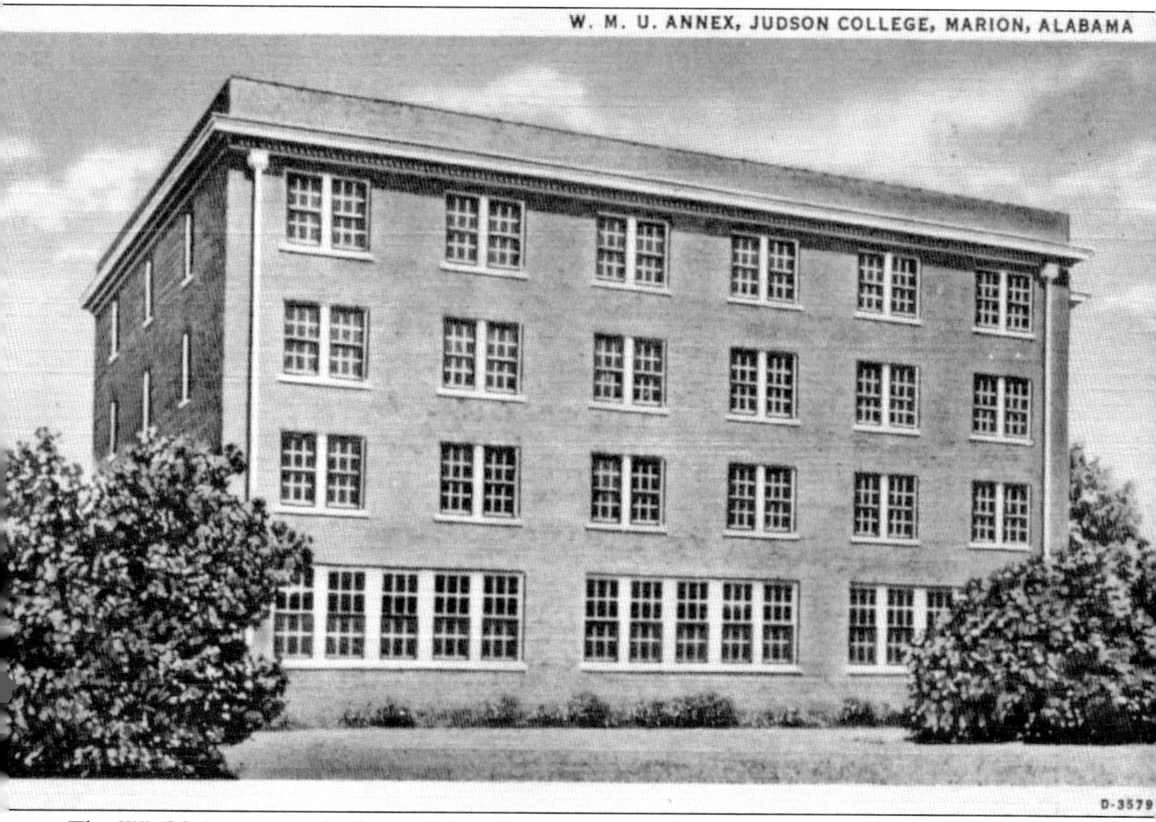

The WMU Annex was built in 1925 as dormitory space for students on the campus of Judson College. The Alabama Woman's Missionary Union (WMU) pledged $50,000 from the first gifts made by Alabama WMU members to the cooperative program. Ground was broken for the building in April 1925. When complete, that building and its furnishings came to a total cost of $76,000. Originally, the first floor of the building contained classrooms, and the upper floors were the dormitory rooms. There was a covered walkway that connected it to Jewett. The 1925–1926 Judson College Catalog states that "the architecture is simple in style, designed to meet the needs and purposes of modern college students." In 1957, a wing that joins the older building at a right angle and runs parallel to Lafayette Street was added. It provided additional classrooms, dormitory rooms, an office, and a parlor. The building serves as dormitory space for current Judson College students. (JCA.)

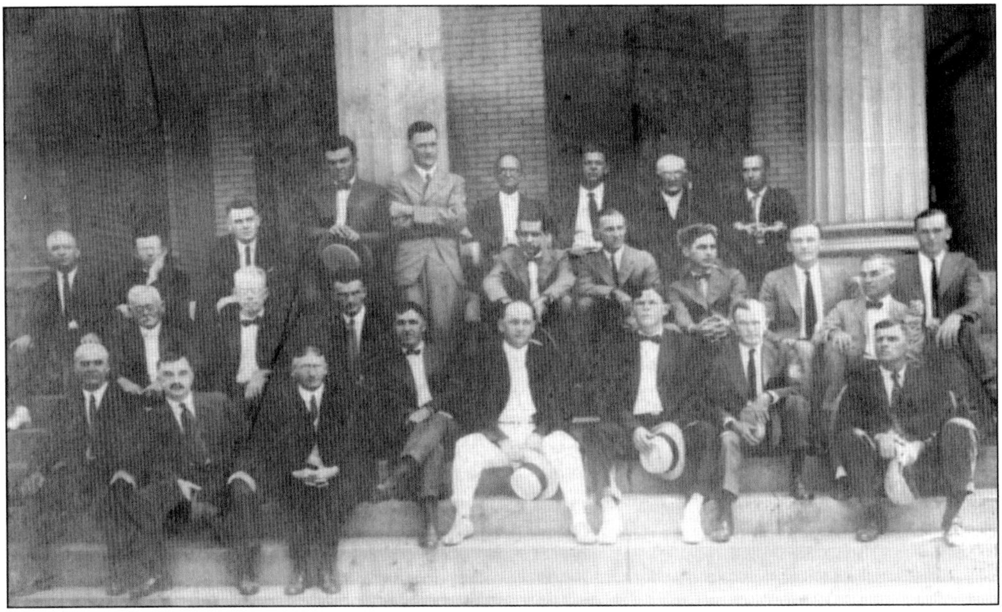

Seated on the steps of the Uniontown Presbyterian Church are the male members of the church in this undated photograph. From left to right are (first row) Walter J. White, L. A. Ward, Rev. R. L. Ben (minister), Stanley White, E. E. White, Will Buck, Welch Morrisette, and unidentified; (second row) Tom Hudson, H. T. Bledsoe, James Long, Henry McCorkle, Edward White, John G. White, Coleman Long, Will J. Munford, and Robert Long; (third row) Hardie Bradford, Haywood Craighead, H. G. Baylor, Carl C. Morgan, T. Ralston Long, Bob Hart, W. J. Hearn, John West, and Jim Anderson. This is probably a 1930s or 1940s photograph. (Courtesy of Kitty Grey Long.)

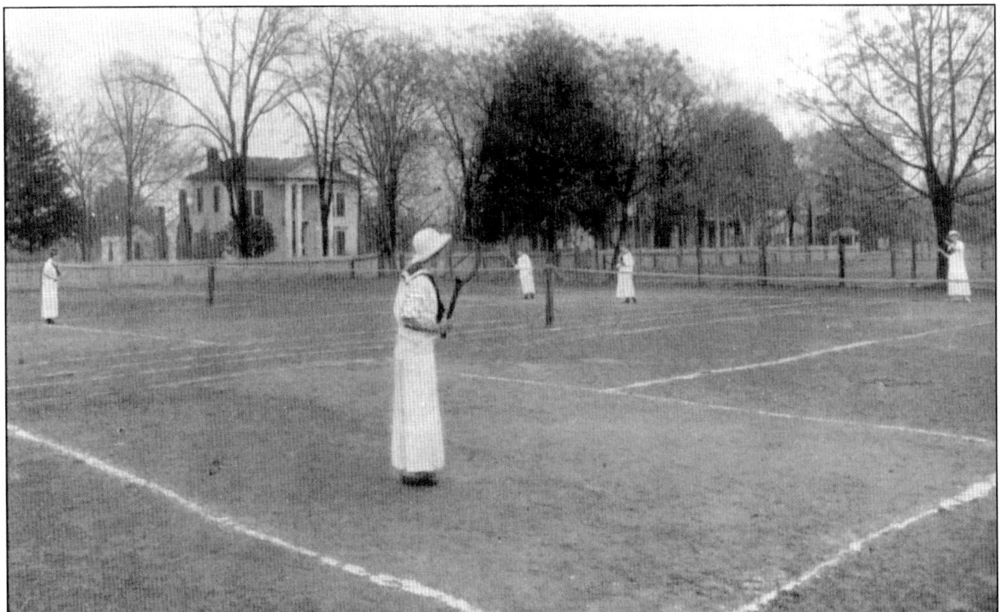

In all the sports activities, the dress seems to be a dark color, except for tennis. Here it is white with dark sailor collars and ties. The players also wore hats. The list of required physical education dress items does not include a dress for tennis. (JCA.)

Five

War and More Change

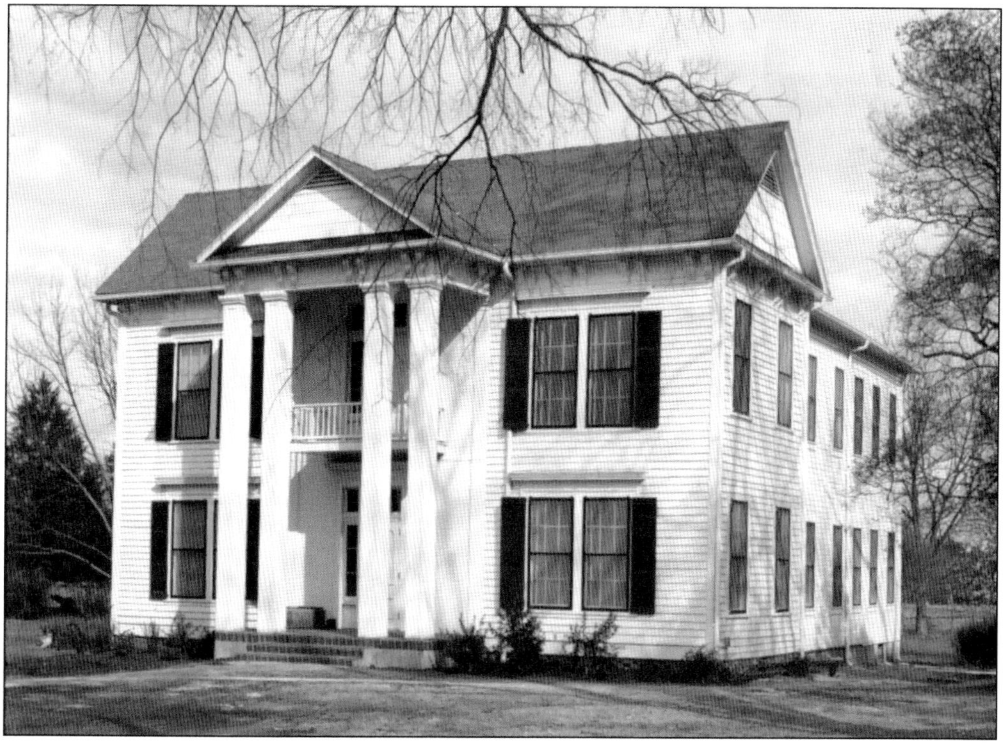

Elmcrest suffered a fire in 1947. The building was renovated, and the front looks much as it did in an earlier time; however, additions were made to the rear of the building. On the right side, an addition of at least two to three rooms deep is seen. The building has been used for dormitory space, faculty housing, and other needs. (JCA.)

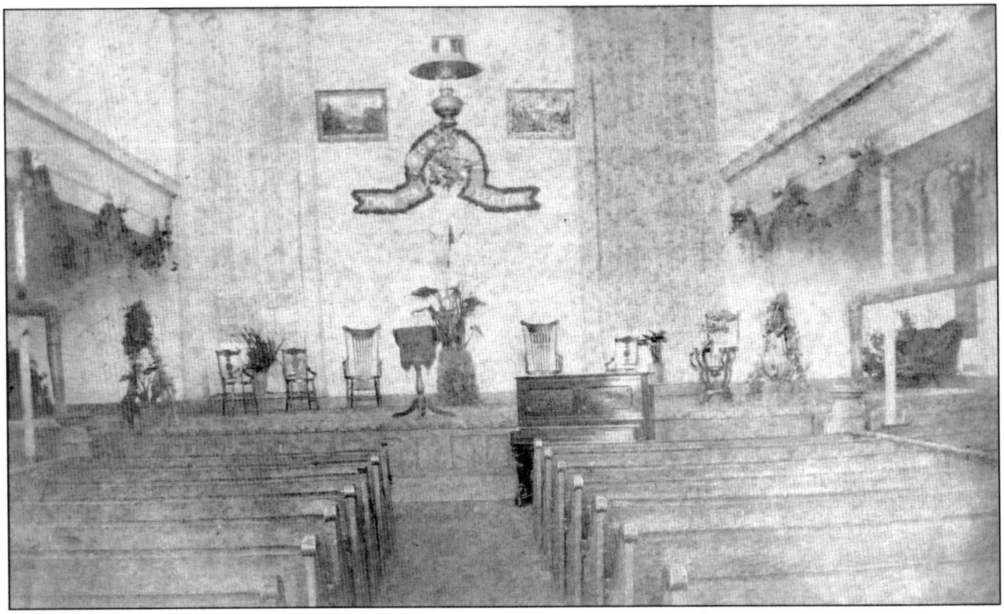

The interior of the Marion Military Institute chapel in the 1930s shows the balconies on either side; there are no windows in the rear of the building. The balconies seem to be supported by wooden posts. There is a military-type crest on the back wall. The stage furnishings are mixed, and there is an old upright piano on the floor. (MMIFA.)

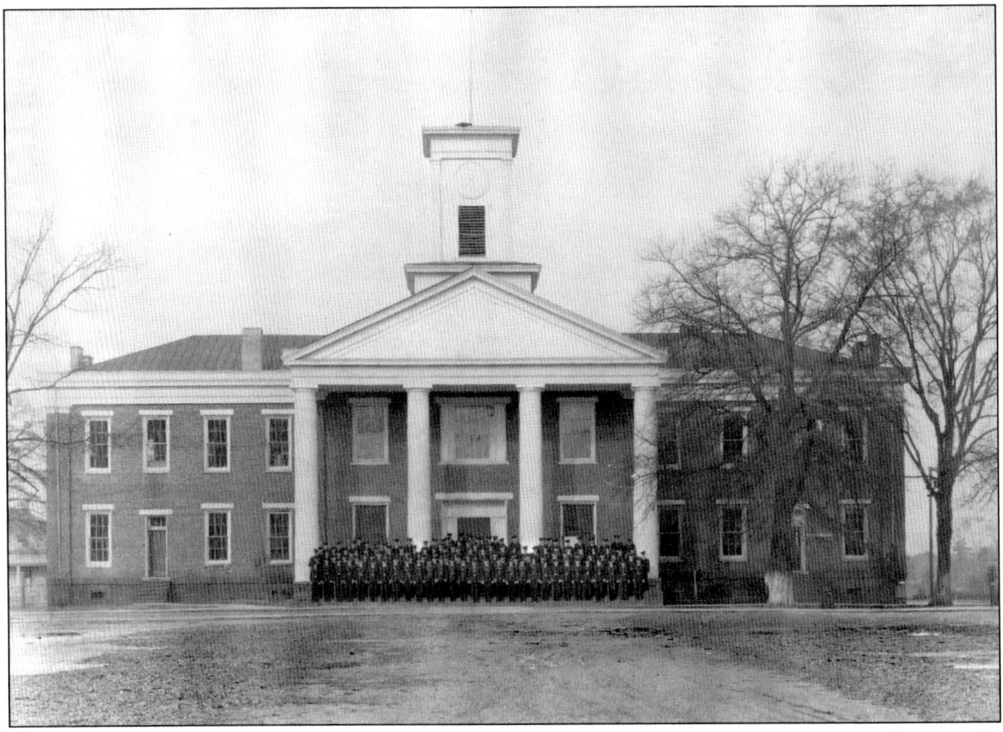

The corps of cadets is standing on the steps of the chapel for a group picture in this 1930 photograph. The picture was taken before the wings were added to either side of the chapel. This was also made before the parking area was added in front of the chapel. (MMIFA.)

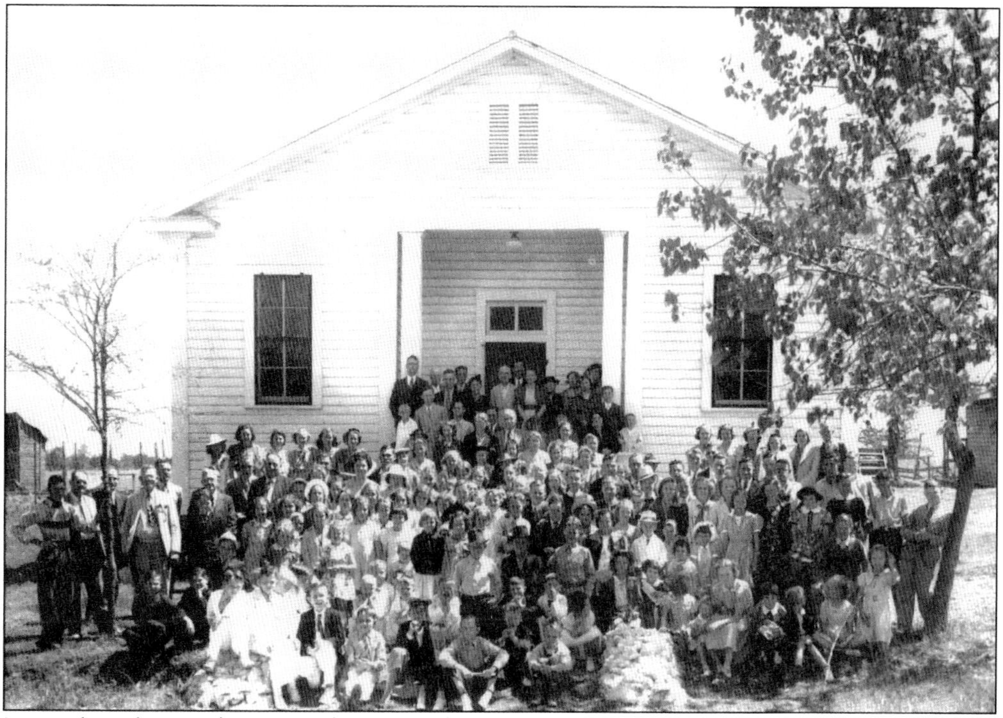

Located in what was known as the Mill Village (Uniontown), this church served as a community church for the village. After the Baptists bought property and built their own building, it became the property of individual denominations. Gathered in front of building are members of the community who worshipped there. Today it serves as the church building for the Church of God. (Courtesy of Linda and Roy Calhoun.)

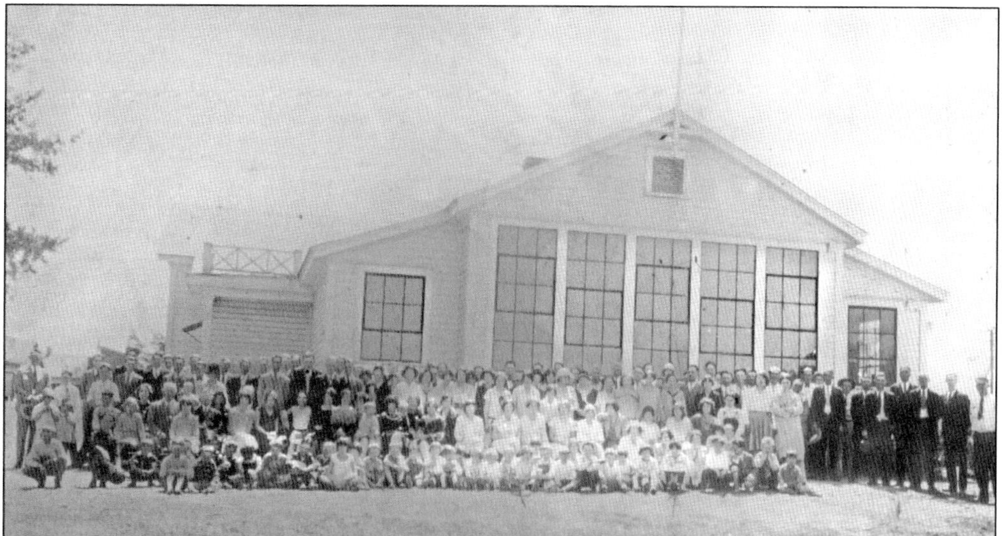

Up until the 1950s, a school for grades one through six operated at Mill Village (Uniontown). Pictured here are a group of students during the 1940s. When it closed, students attended Uniontown High School. The building was ignored and finally rotted away. (Courtesy of Linda and Roy Calhoun.)

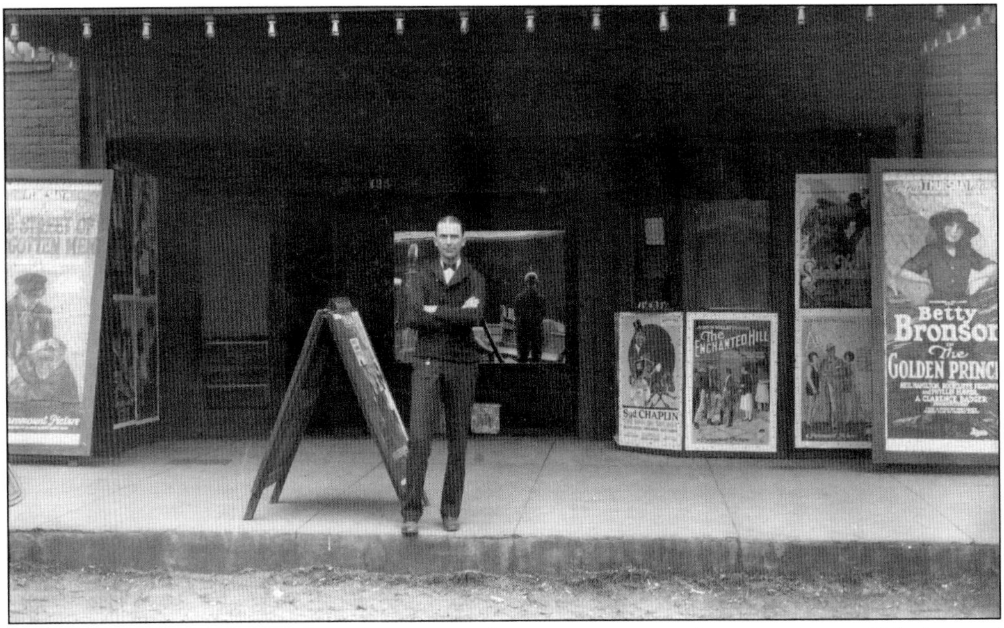

Over the years, a moving picture theater served as entertainment for generations of Marion and area residents. Above is the outside of the Bonita Theatre with its owner at the time, Malcolm Moore. Handbills abound advertising current and upcoming attractions. Its location was on the northeast corner of Washington and Lafayette Streets. (PCHPS.)

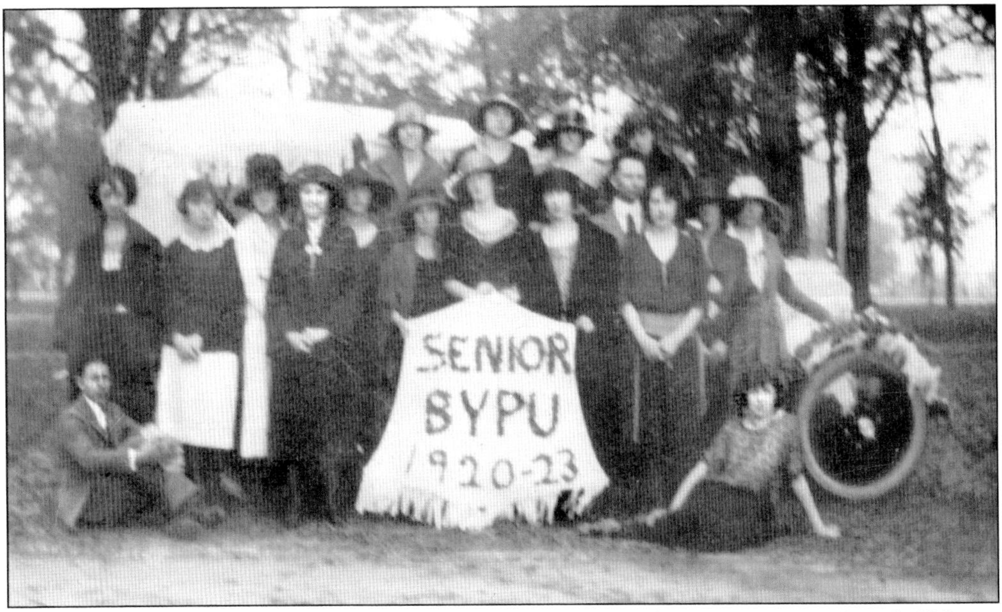

This picture depicts the members of the Siloam Baptist Church's Baptist Young Peoples' Union (BYPU) at a convention, site unknown. The group was organized in 1920, and by 1923, it had won the state efficiency banner. There seems to be some type of parade in progress to celebrate the event. (Courtesy of Siloam Baptist Church.)

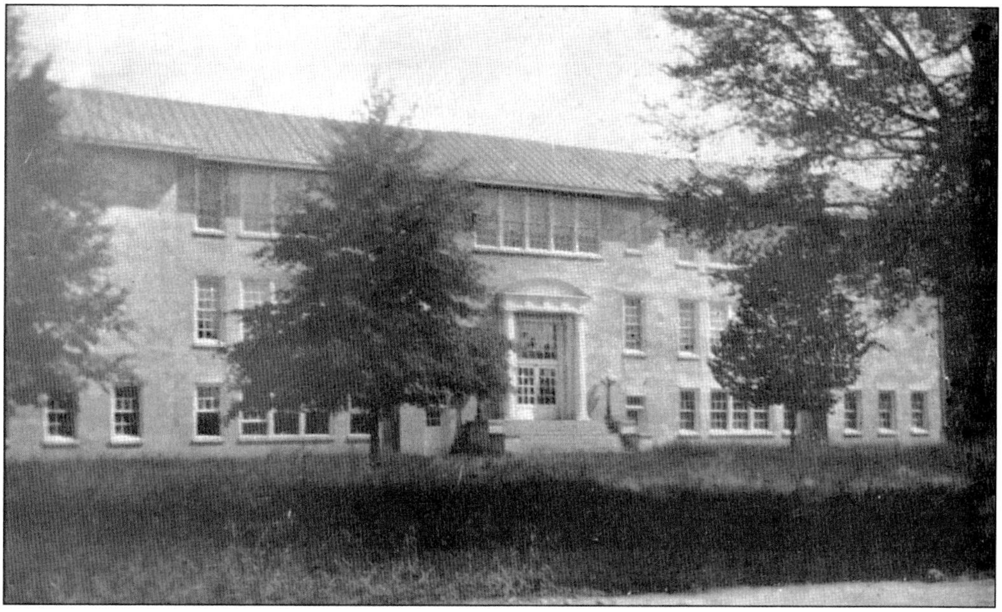

Built in 1924, Uniontown High School served white children in grades 1 through 12 until the 1960s. Integration came, and for a while, it served as the Uniontown Middle School. It was closed and remained empty for a number of years. The insides burned in late 2009, leaving only the outer walls standing. (Courtesy of the author.)

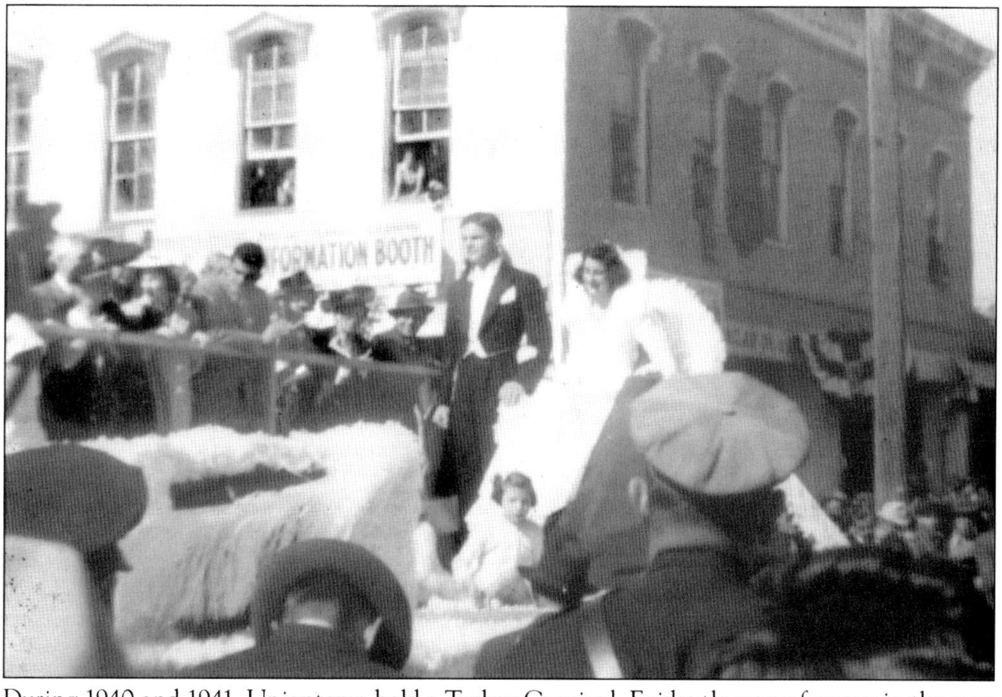

During 1940 and 1941, Uniontown held a Turkey Carnival. Evidently many farmers in the area raised turkeys, and this was a way of promoting their sale. Pictured in the convertible are a king and queen of the activities. The building may have stood on the northeast corner of U. S. Highway 80 and Water Street. The building is no longer standing. (Courtesy of the author.)

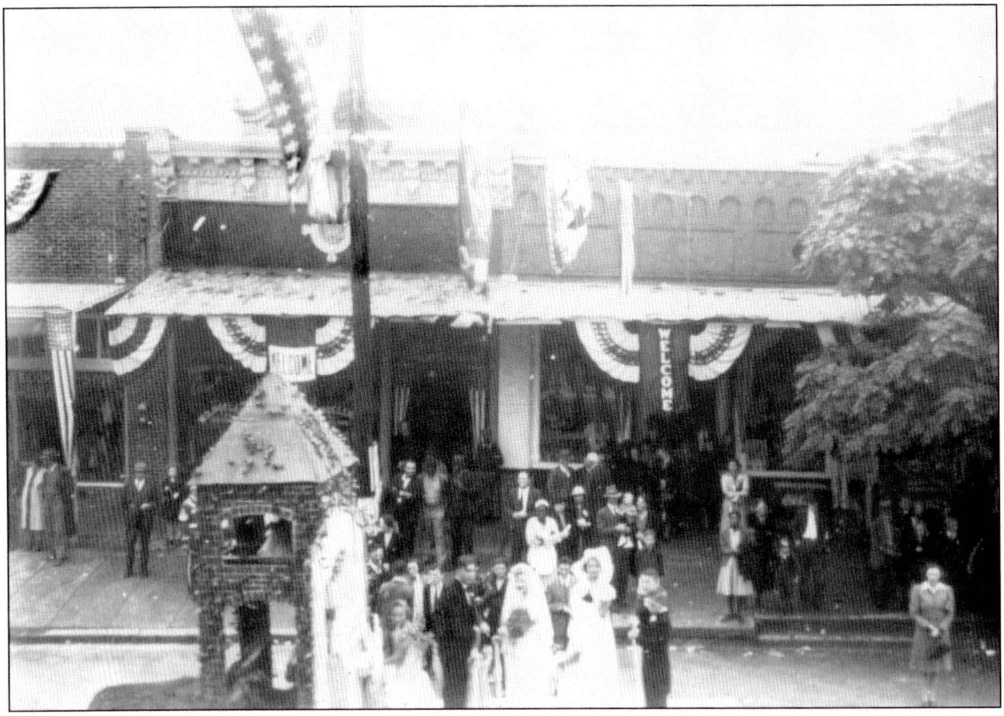

A street scene from one of the Turkey Carnivals is featured here. The stores are believed to be on the west side of Water Street. Building facades have changed, so it is impossible to determine the exact location. Stands have been placed for various activities along the street. Also, the sidewalks were wooden planks. (Courtesy of the author.)

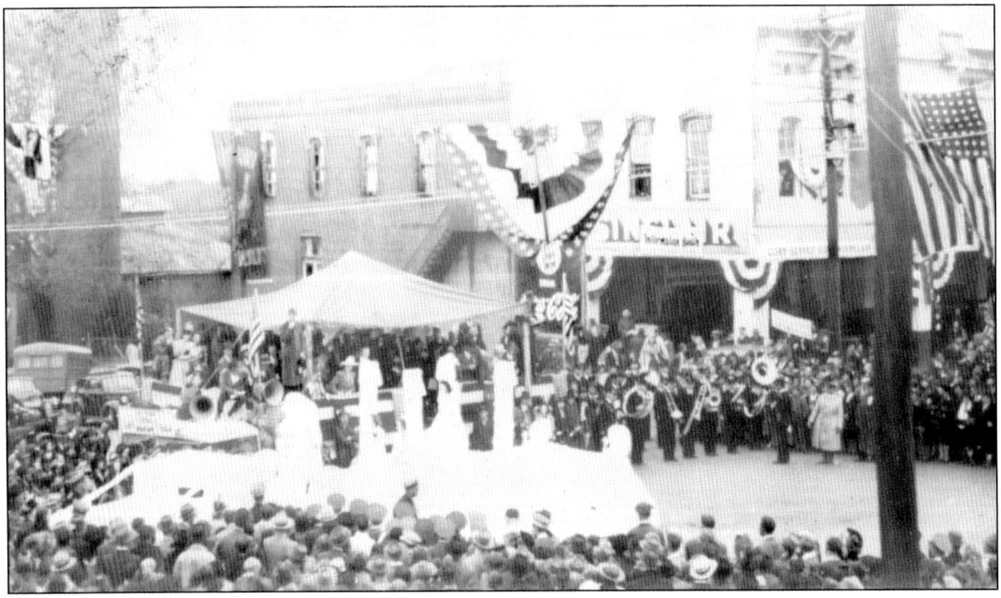

This is another street scene from one of the Turkey Carnivals. The two buildings seem to border on Front Street as it goes down the hill to city hall. The buildings are no longer there, but the city water tower seems to be at the bottom of the hill. This seems to be the speaker's stand. Also note the band to the right. (Courtesy of the author.)

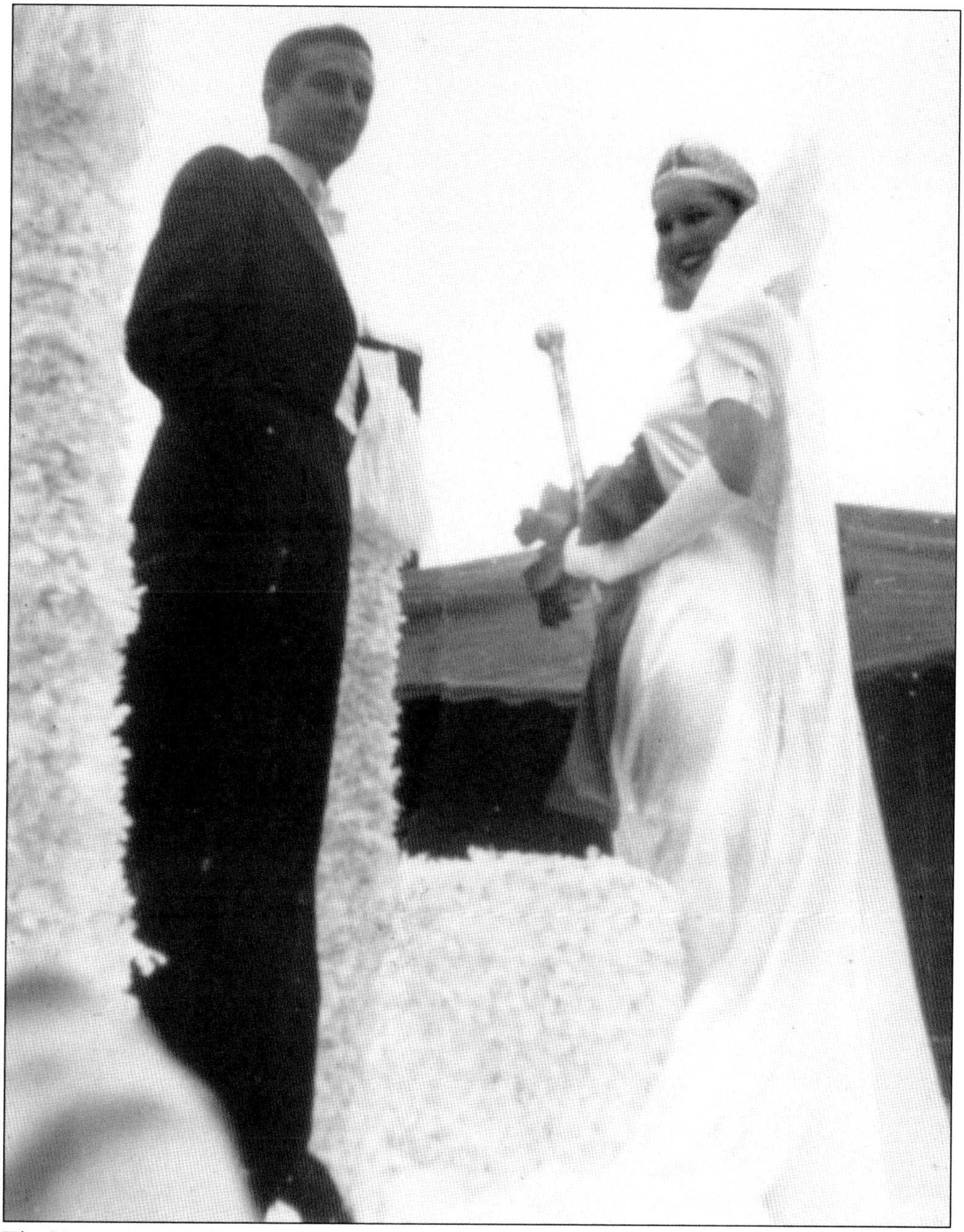

The Uniontown Exchange Club sponsored these carnivals and did an excellent job advertising them statewide. Attendance for the 1940 Turkey Carnival was estimated to be 12,000. Pictured are the king and queen of the Turkey Carnival for 1940. The queen was Martha Brown, and the king was Ralston Long. Gov. Frank Dixon and his wife were in attendance, and he gave the keynote address. Other activities during the day included band concerts, parades, a football game, horse racing, and novelty events. Each carnival ended with a grand ball. The band in 1940 was Jan Garber. The prize turkey was sent to Pres. Franklin Delano Roosevelt. Many thousands of turkeys were sold as a result of the carnival. Because of World War II, the carnival was not held during the war years, and then it was never revived. (Courtesy of the author.)

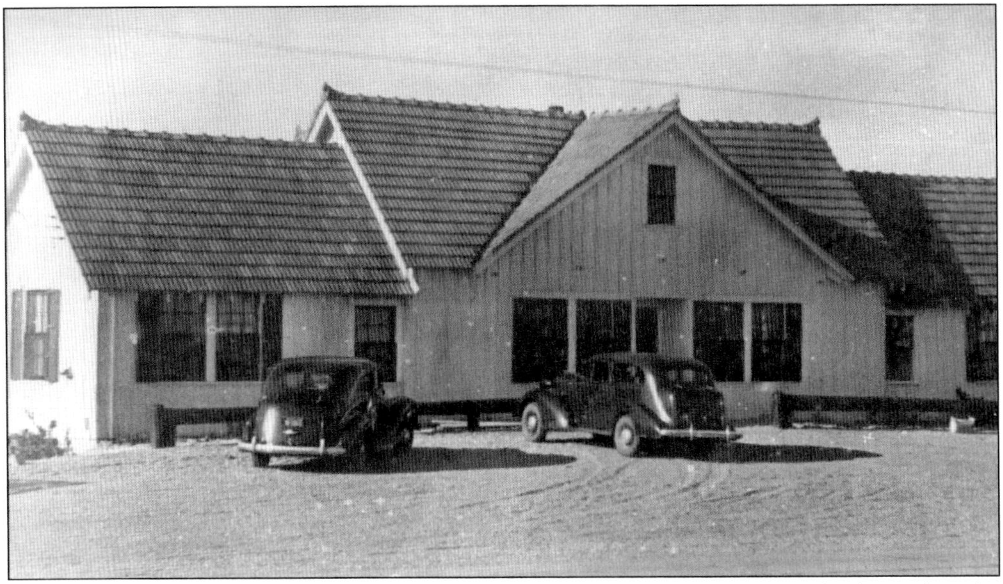

Begun in the 1930s, Green Gables operated as a nightclub in Uniontown until it burned in the early 1980s. For many years, Uniontown teenagers were assured of a safe place to go because of the oversight of the manager. Their parents also enjoyed it for a night out on the town. Many people from all over the state have fond memories of meals at Green Gables. (PCHPS.)

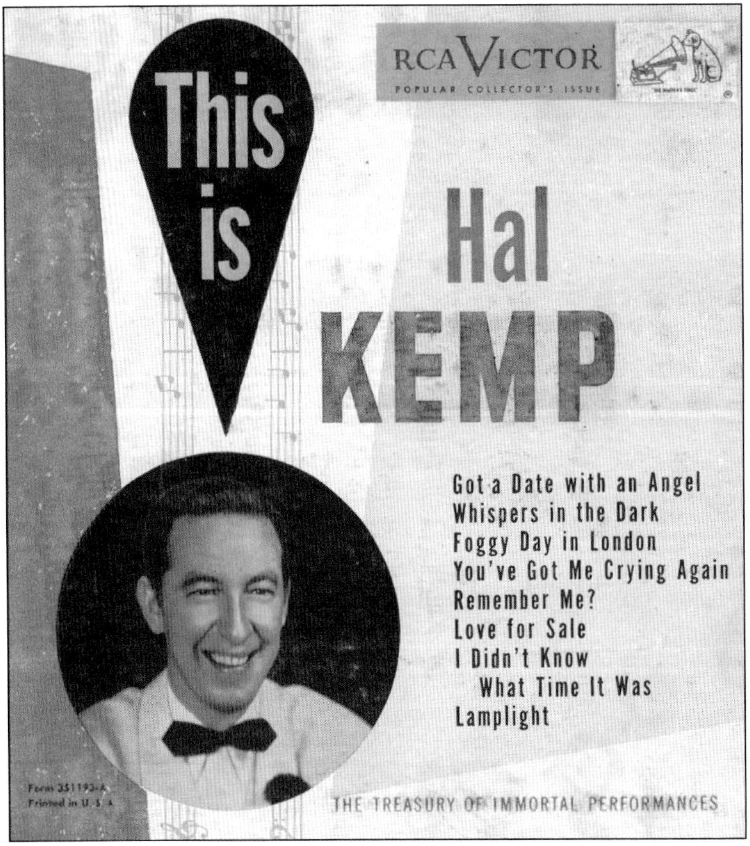

Hal Kemp was born in Marion. His father established the Marion Light and Power Company and brought the first electricity to Marion. He probably received his early musical training from teachers at Marion Military Institute. He became a band leader during the Big Band era and was killed in an automobile accident in 1940. (PCHPS.)

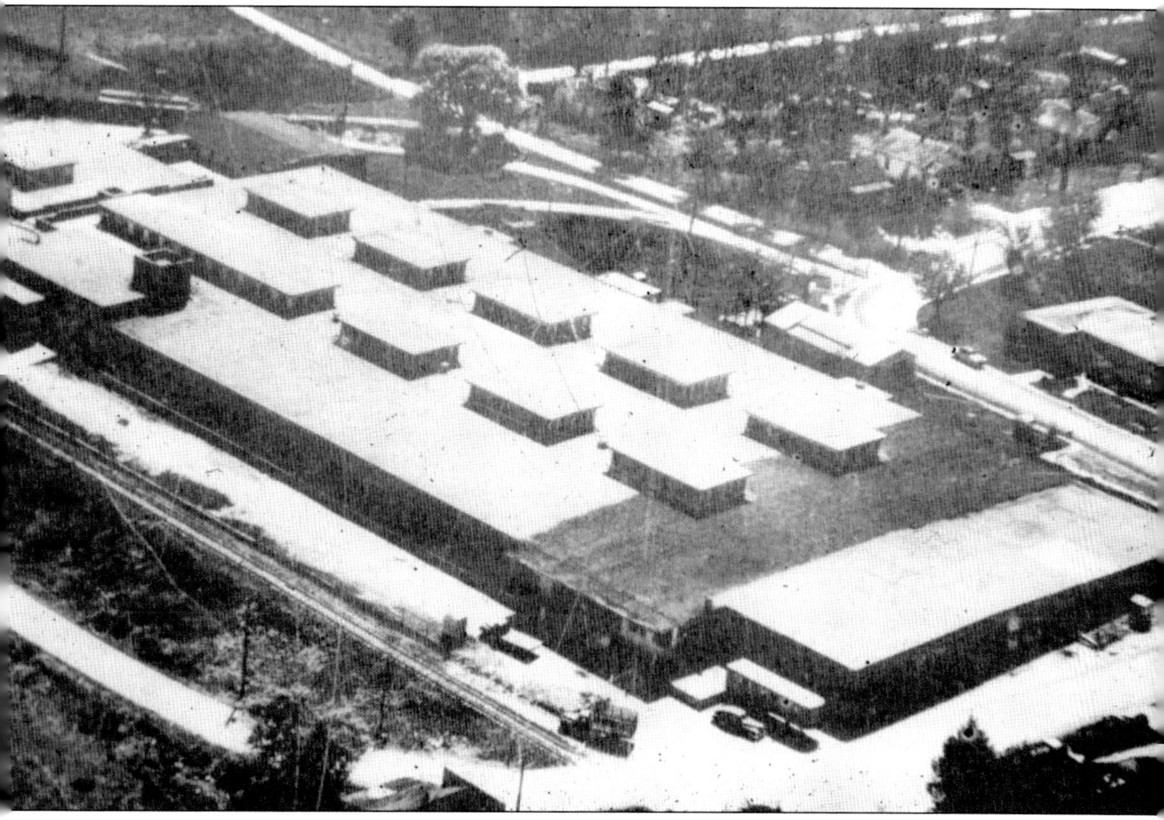

This picture shows how large the cotton industry had become in Uniontown. The aerial view of the cotton mill shows a much larger building than that of 1899. In the background, the homes of Ella White Mill Village are visible. The population of the mill village during the height of the cotton mill was probably more than the town. The railroad is seen to the left, and the building to the rear was the office building for California Cotton Mills. In 1954, this all disappeared when the cotton mill moved. For a period of time, a shoe plant and then a garment plant operated in the building. Many of the homes are still there and are occupied by descendants of employees of the cotton mill. The only evidence of the cotton mill is a very long slab of concrete. (Courtesy of the author.)

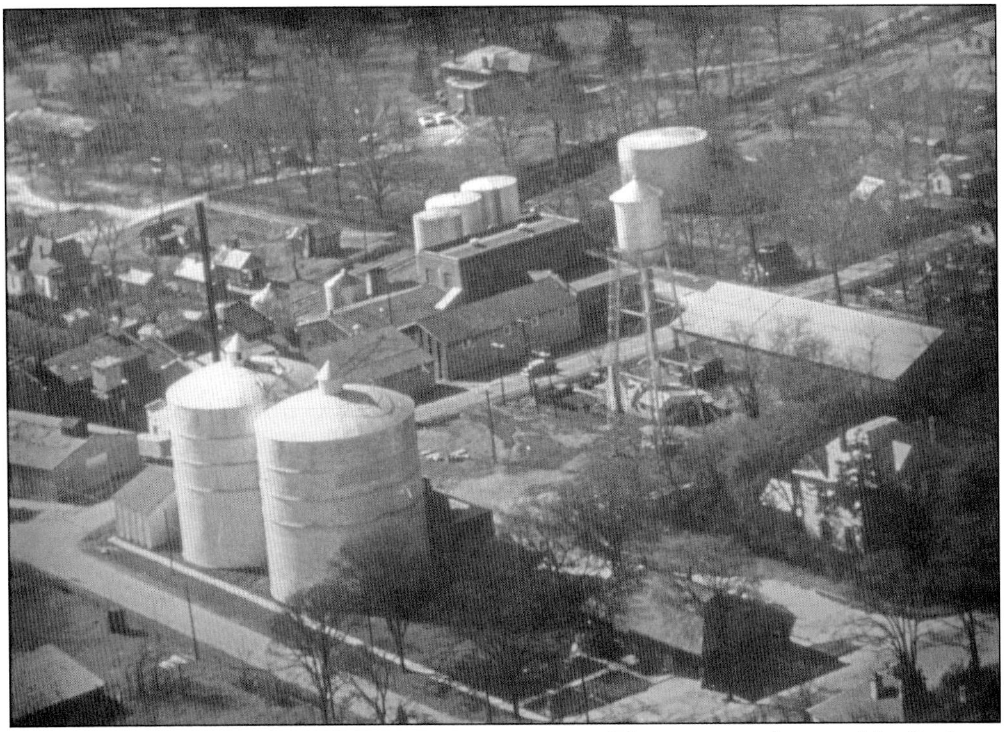

This is an aerial view of the Buckeye Oil Mill. It was located south of U.S. Highway 80. It was supported by the by-products of the cotton mill. When the cotton mill closed, the oil mill lost its supplier, and it closed also. There is no evidence today of this large complex of tanks and buildings. (Courtesy of the author.)

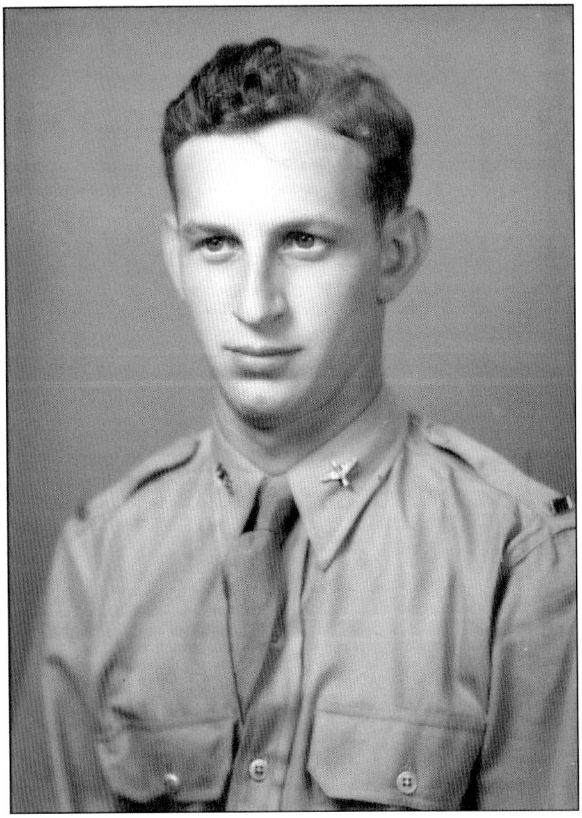

Edwin Robinson Glass of Uniontown was a captain and army pilot during World War II, flying missions over the "Hump." At an undisclosed airstrip, he recognized Gen. and Madam Chiang Kai Shek. He spoke to the general and then, very much the southern gentleman, bowed and kissed the hand of Madam Chiang Kai Shek. He died in 1944 flying the "Hump." (Courtesy of Emma Glass Beasley.)

Flora Proskauer Marx was one of the last Jewish residents of Uniontown. Her husband owned a large dry goods store. At the end of the 19th century, there was a very large Jewish population in the town. In fact, there is a Jewish section in Rosemont Cemetery. The music room in the new addition to Uniontown High School was named for her. (Courtesy of Emma Glass Beasley.)

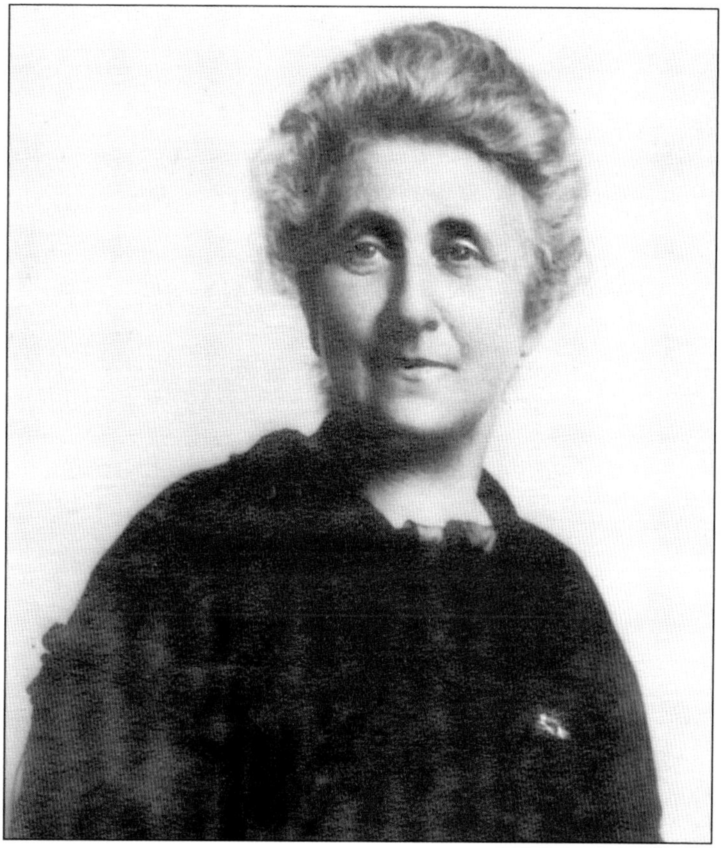

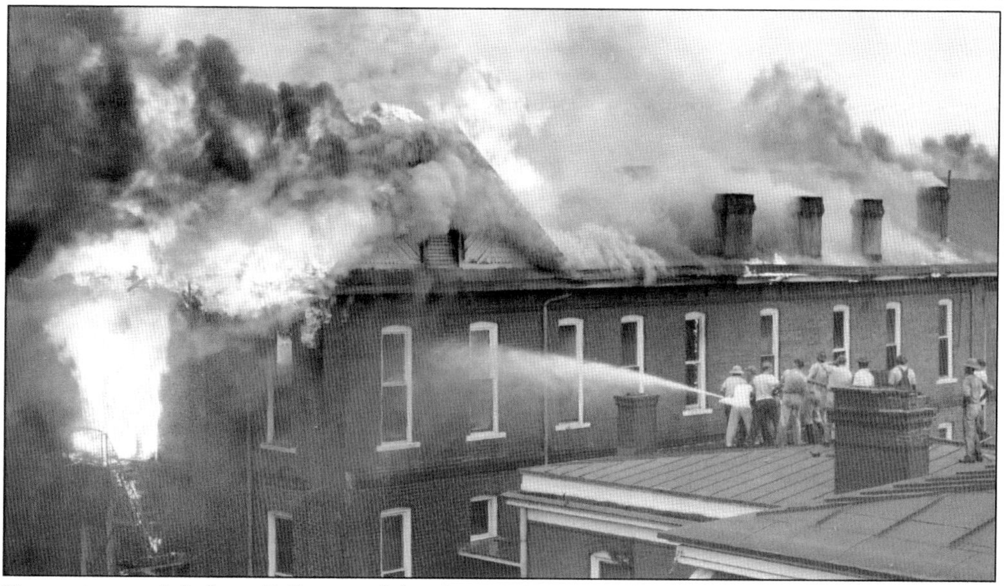

Fire again struck Judson College on July 15, 1947. During a thunderstorm, the dome atop Jewett was struck by lightning. Firemen from Marion and surrounding towns tried to save the building, but to no avail. In this view, firemen are seen on the roof of a building to the rear, with hoses aimed at Jewett. By the valiant efforts of the firemen, nearby buildings were saved. (JCA.)

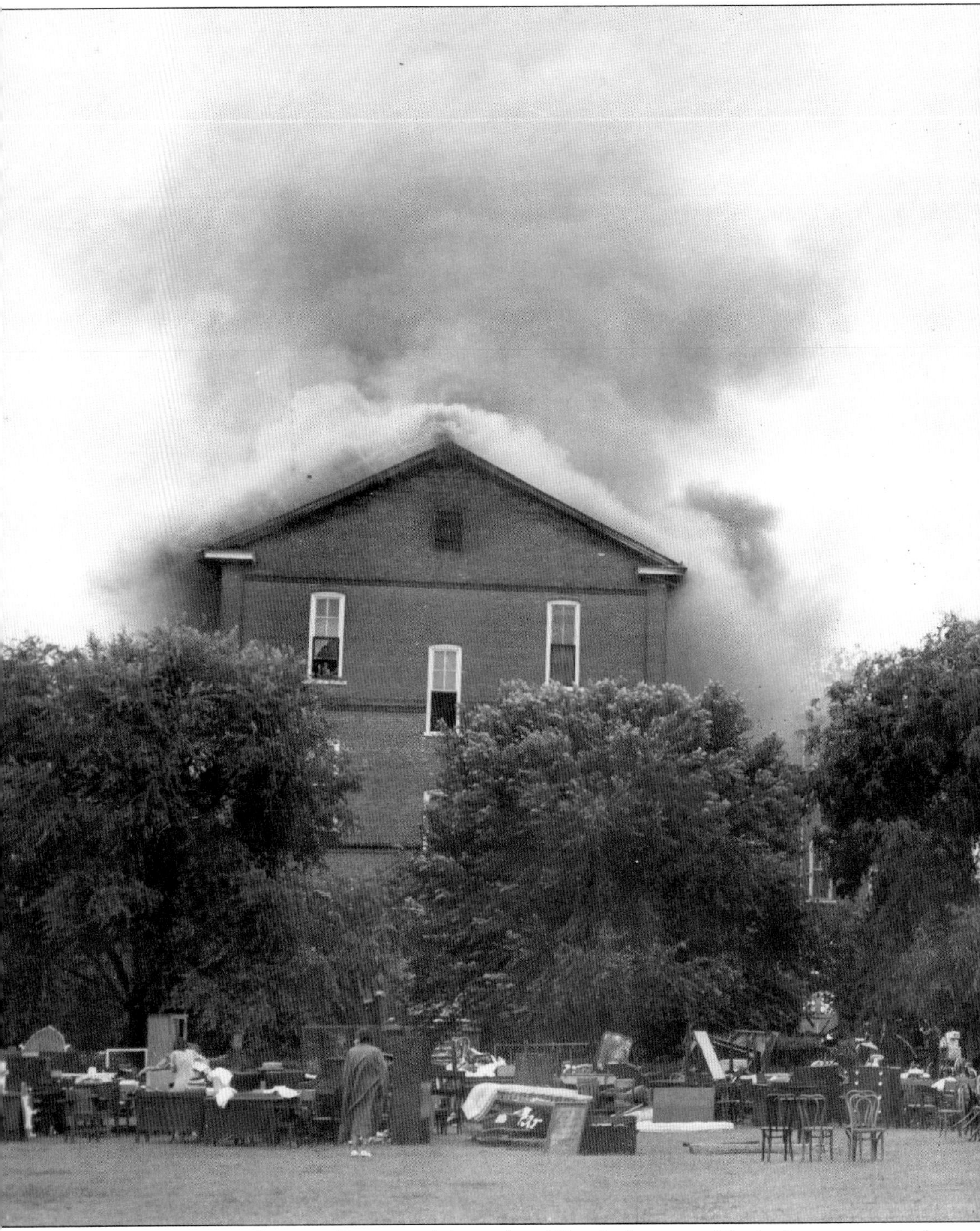

This scene is from the rear of Jewett and shows the old brick chimney of the boiler system, which is still standing. Across the rear of the building are scattered items rescued from the fire. In this scene, it looks as if the central section and the section to the right are completely engulfed in flames, and the section to the left is just beginning to burn. Everyone who was there tried to

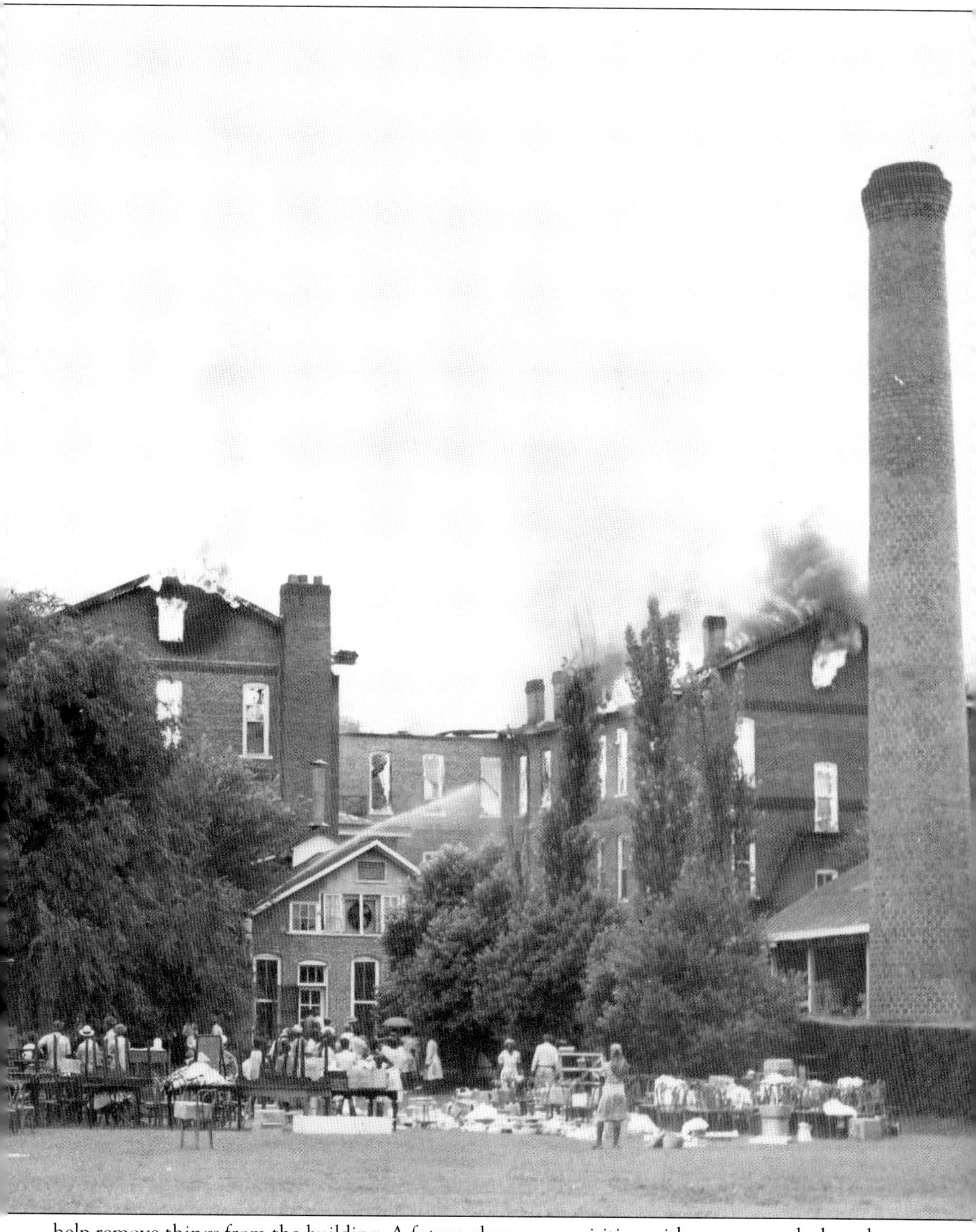

help remove things from the building. A future alumna was visiting with a group, and when she heard the word "fire," she picked up a bag containing hockey sticks and got it outside the building. Afterwards, she was not able to pick up even one side of the bag. (JCA.)

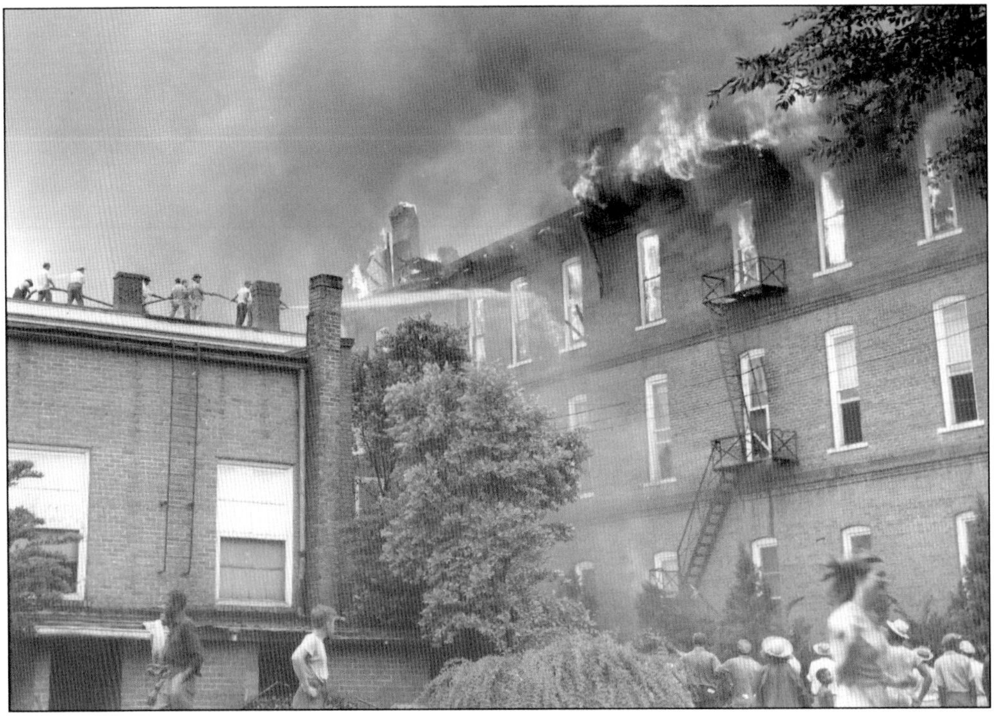

This scene is from the south side of Jewett. The firefighters are standing on the roof of the old gymnasium. Notice the flames as they shoot out from Jewett's roof. What is so interesting about these pictures is that the building burned in the daytime and there is a record of the burning. (JCA.)

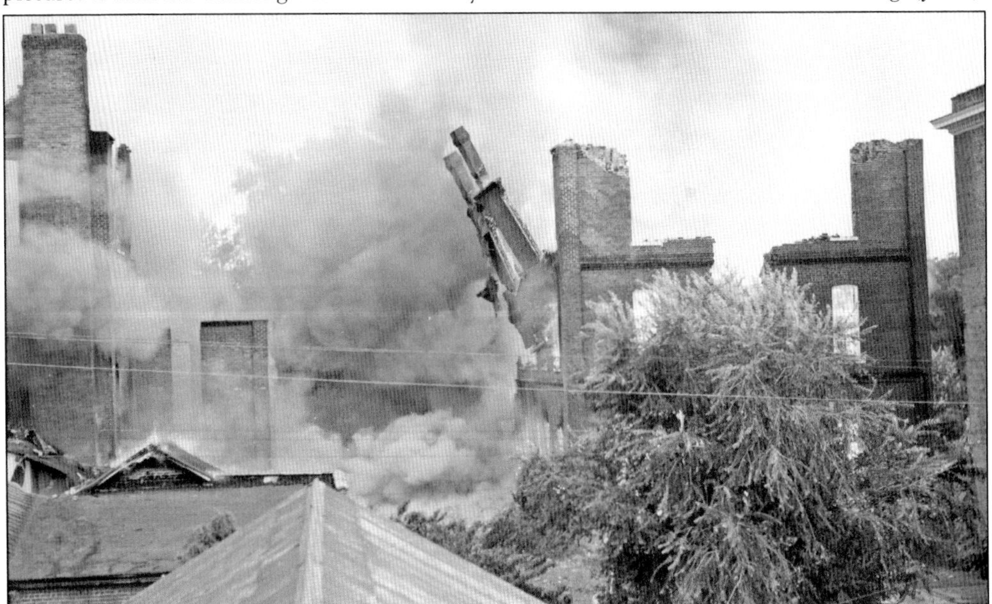

Sections of the wall are beginning to fall. After the fire was finally extinguished, most of the walls had fallen, with only columns from the loggia remaining to remind students, faculty, staff, and friends of the building that once stood there. It is interesting to see what details the pictures reveal about the flames and the falling building. (JCA.)

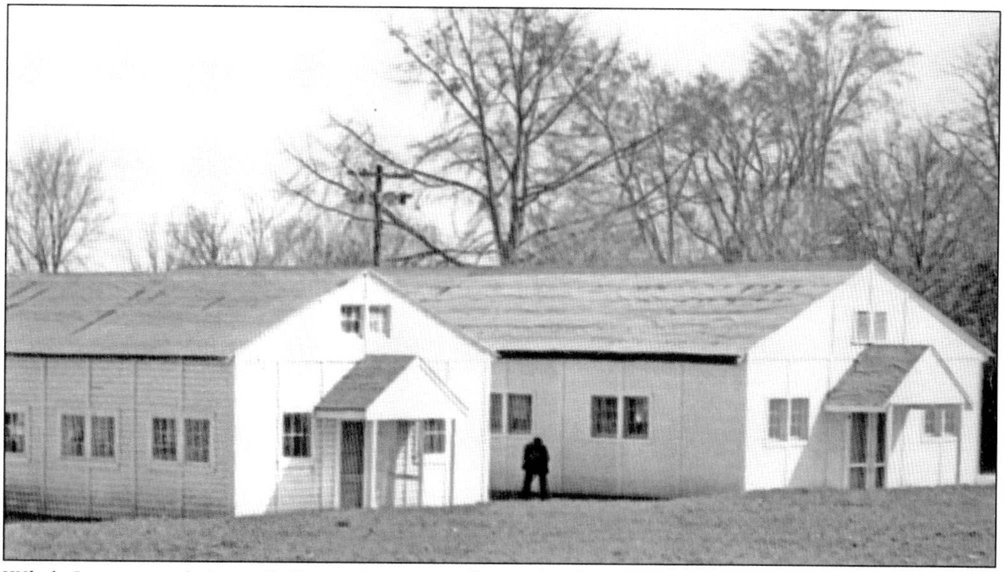

While Jewett was being rebuilt, students once housed in Jewett would need a place to live. Tom C. King, descendant of Edwin D. King, an Anniston businessman, and a trustee ordered prefabricated buildings to provide emergency accommodations. The buildings used for student housing were called Jewett Village. (JCA.)

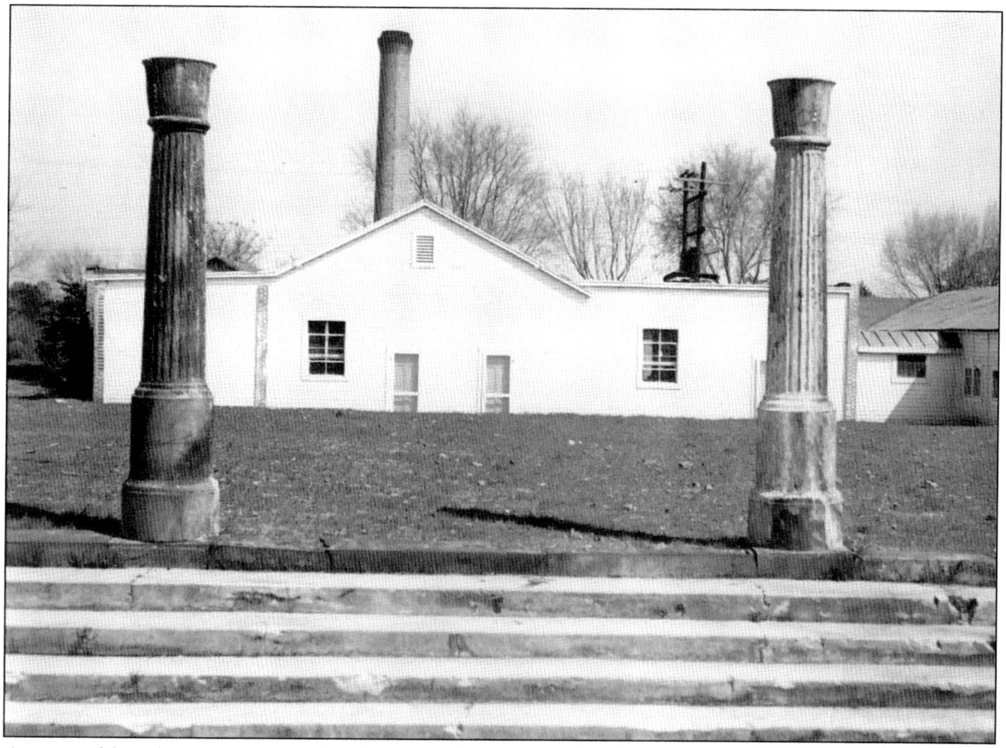

A ground-breaking ceremony for the third Jewett was held on April 25, 1949. In this view, the concrete flooring from the burned building has been cleaned in preparation for the ceremony. Some of the remaining columns from the loggia of the burned building perfectly frame several of the prefabricated buildings in use. (JCA.)

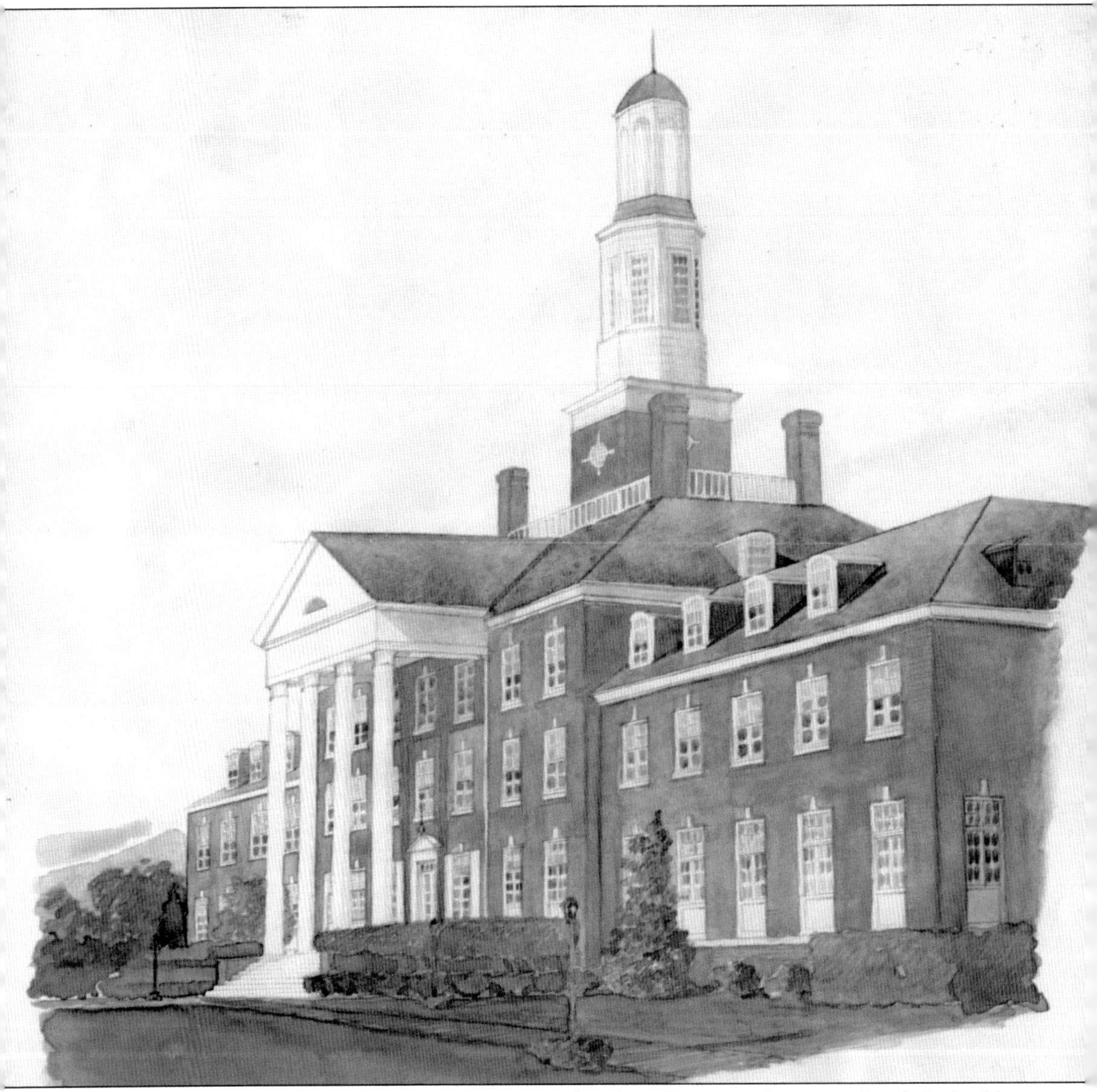

The administration, board of trustees, alumnae, and students began to plan immediately for building a new Jewett on the same site. The incoming senior class president said "Will live in pup tents, if necessary, until a new Jewett is built right where the old one stood." The plan selected was for an academic revival building with a dominant tower, a full height entrance portico with classical columns, and dormer windows. The building was ready to receive students by the beginning of the fall 1951 term. The building contained dormitory, office, and classroom spaces. A dining room and chapel were later added to the rear of the building. Today it contains classrooms and office space. (JCA.)

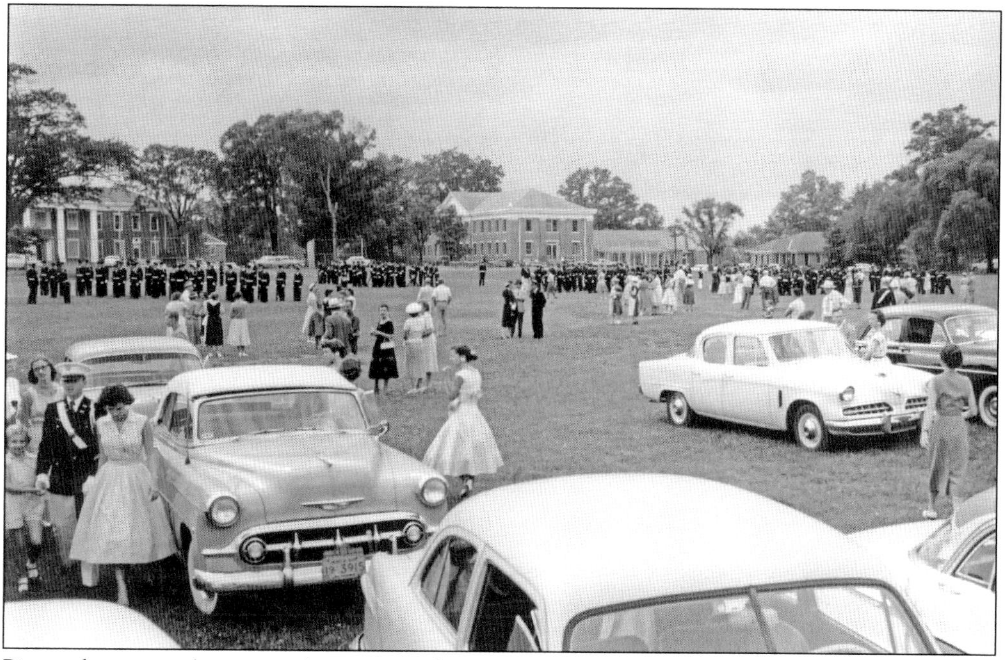

Pictured is a special event on the campus of Marion Military Institute about 1955. It was most likely a homecoming football game. Note the cars and the dress of not only the cadets but also the girls. In the background on the left, a company of cadets are lined up in march formation. (MMIFA.)

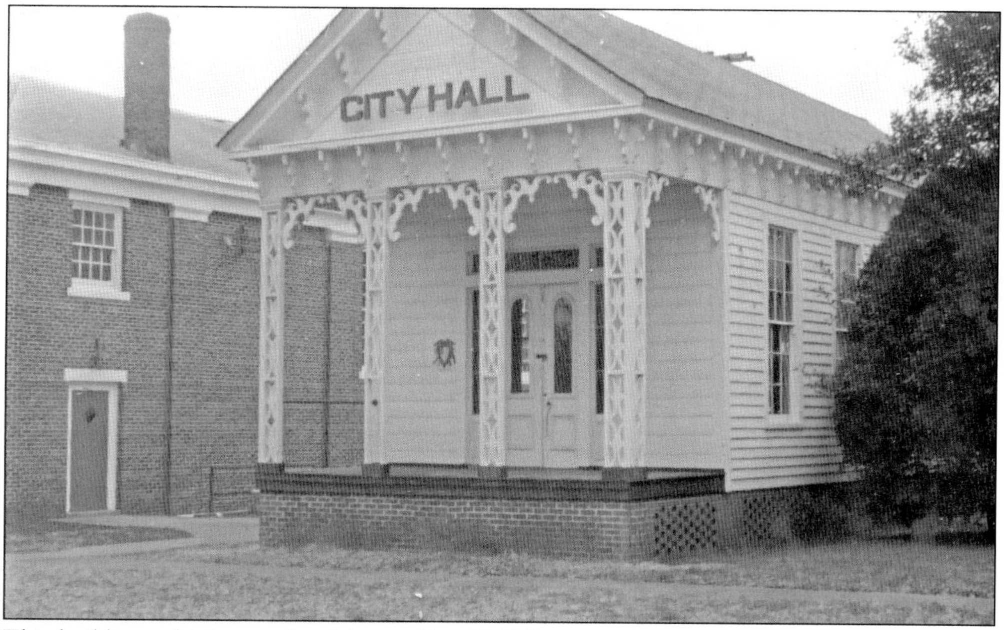

This building, which served as Marion City Hall for many years, is seen in its new spot on the Marion Military Institute campus. The outside has been restored so that, to old-timers, it is recognizable as the old city hall, but the inside has been renovated to house the Alabama Military Hall of Honor. (Courtesy of Kitty Grey Long.)

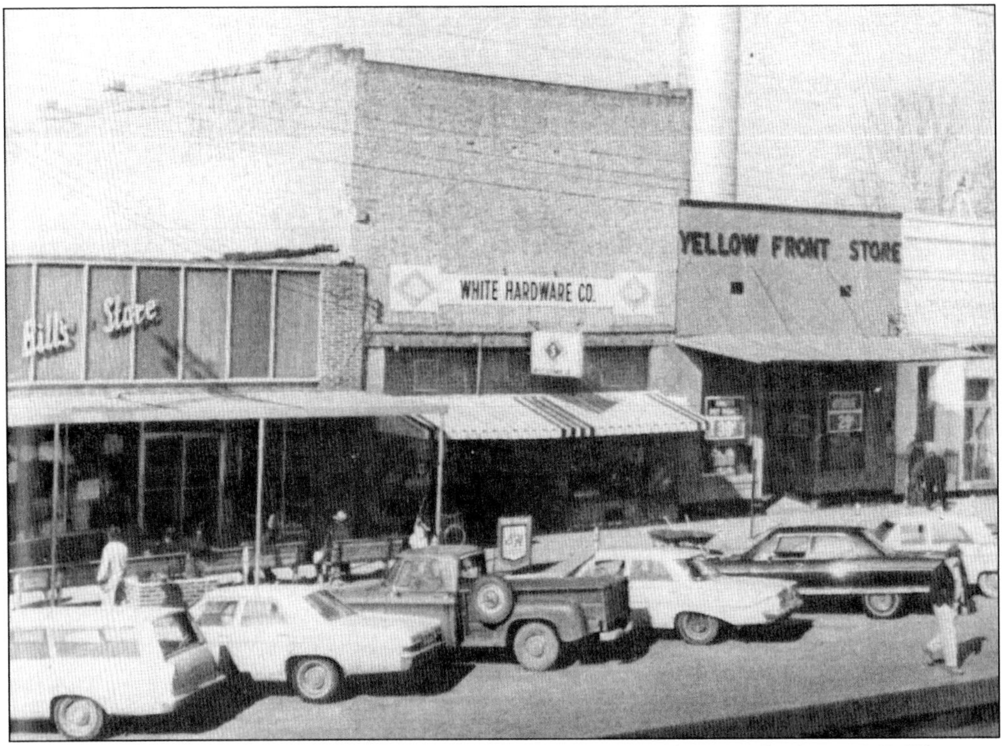

This Uniontown street scene is looking west from Water Street and was made about 1968. The two-story building was the old Nonemacher Hotel and, later, White Hardware. When the Nonemachers operated a hotel in the building, there were no stairs inside, and the only access to the upstairs rooms was by a stairway on the outside at the front. (Courtesy of Linda and Roy Calhoun.)

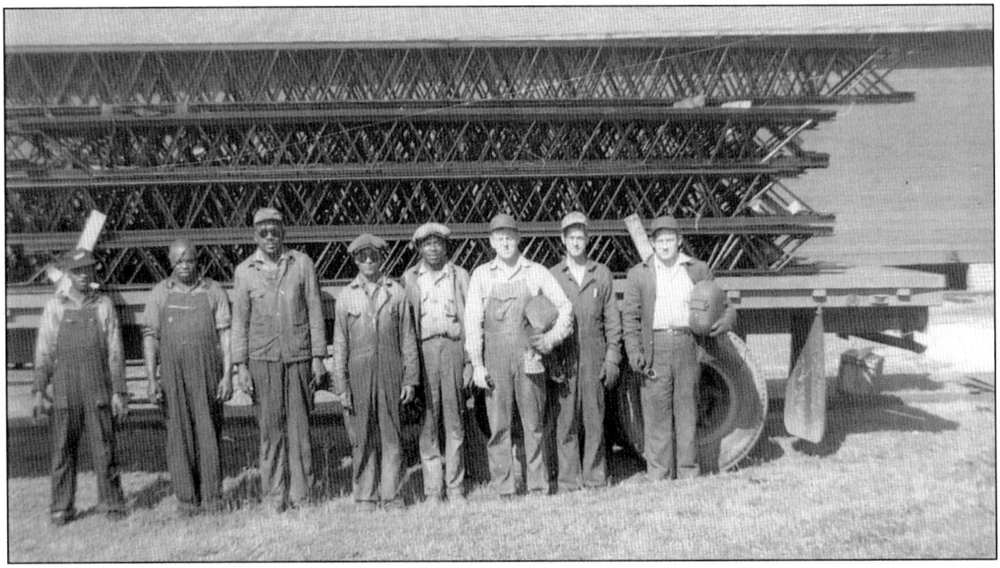

Cahaba Steel operated in Uniontown for some 15 to 20 years. A native son, Franklin Glass, and his partner, Lewis Spaw, of Houston, Texas, established a steel joist fabrication plant to help the economy after the cotton mill left in the 1950s. Recorded on the back of the photograph are the words "First Load of Joists Shipped from Cahaba Steel." (Courtesy of Linda and Roy Calhoun.)

At some point the Bonita Theater became the Neely Theater. The name change reflected the name of the new owners. The location was the same, the northeast corner of Washington and Lafayette Streets. This is the theater that most people of today remember. It closed in the early 1970s. (PCHPS.)

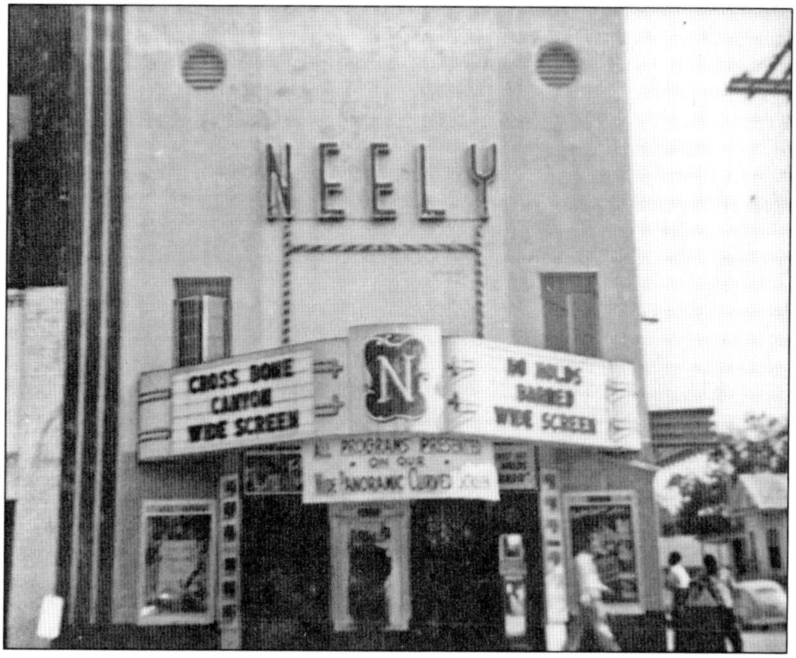

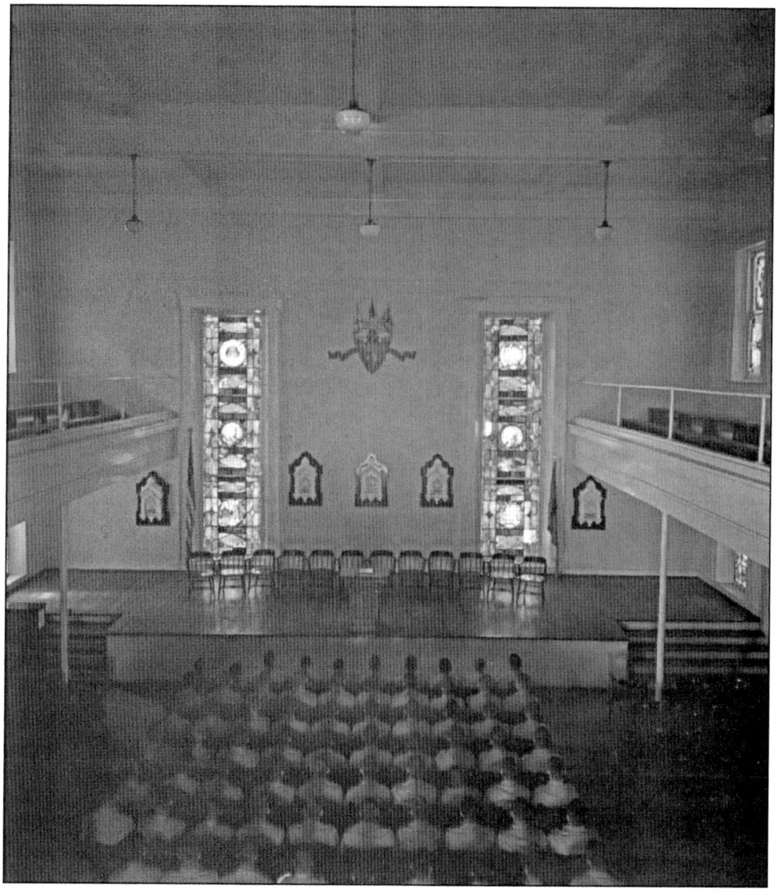

This is the inside of the chapel at Marion Military Institute before a 1972 fire. Note the balconies on both sides that ran the length of the chapel from front to back and across the rear. The balcony was supported by slender fluted columns of cast iron. The chapel was completely remodeled after the fire. (MMIFA.)

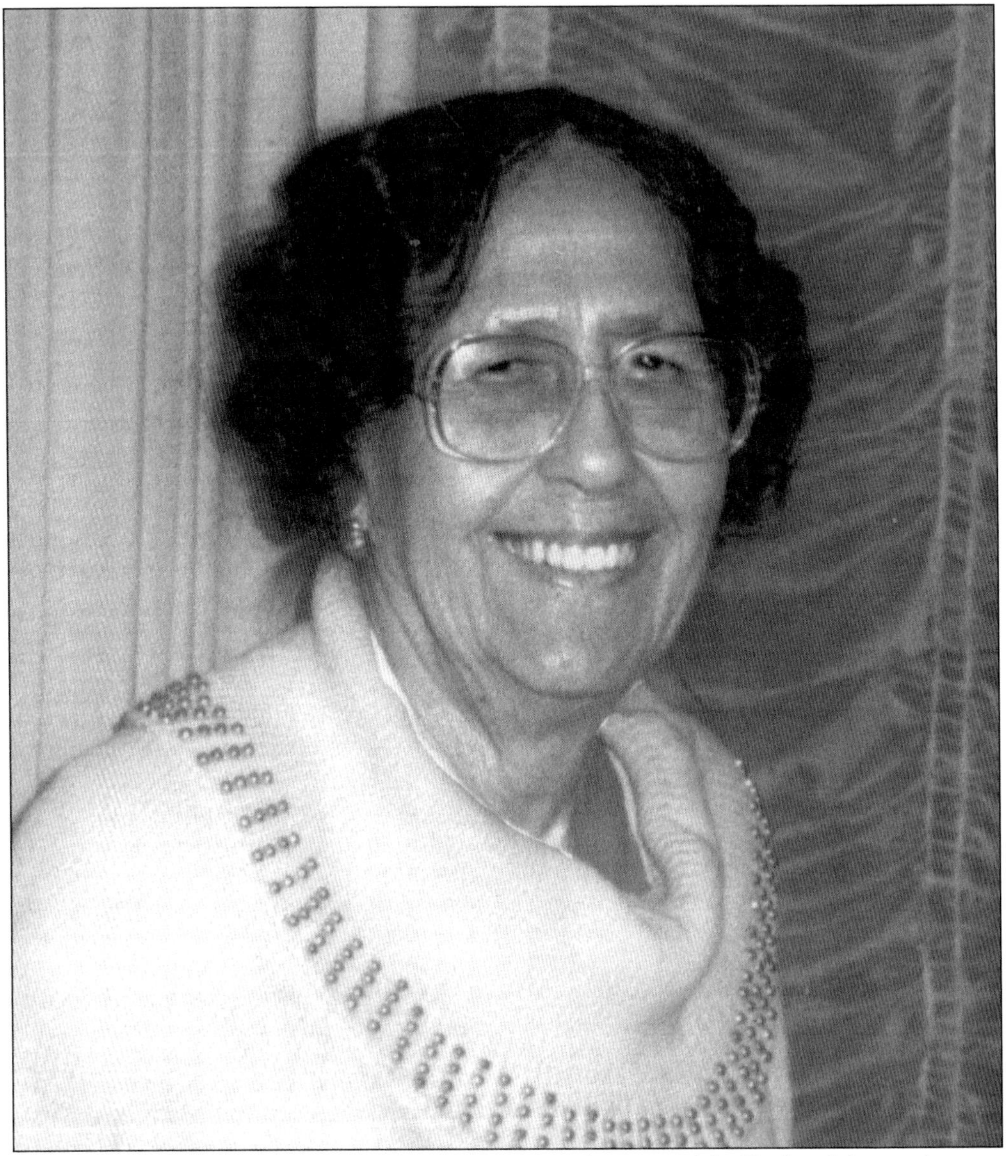

Idella Jones Childs was born and lived in Perry County her entire life. She lived during the time that social and political change brought an end to legal racial discrimination. She wanted equal treatment under the law for all people. She taught biology, algebra, history, and social studies in the segregated school system of Perry County for 35 years. Childs was a member of the Alabama Historical Commission and a founding member of the Black Heritage Council. In 1872, she was the founder and first chairperson of the Perry County Arts and Humanities Council. Childs was the first black woman to serve on the Marion City Council. She was the recipient of many awards at national, state, and local levels. Her life was a model of integrity and concern for others. After her death in 1998, she was placed in the Alabama Women's Hall of Fame. (AWHOF.)

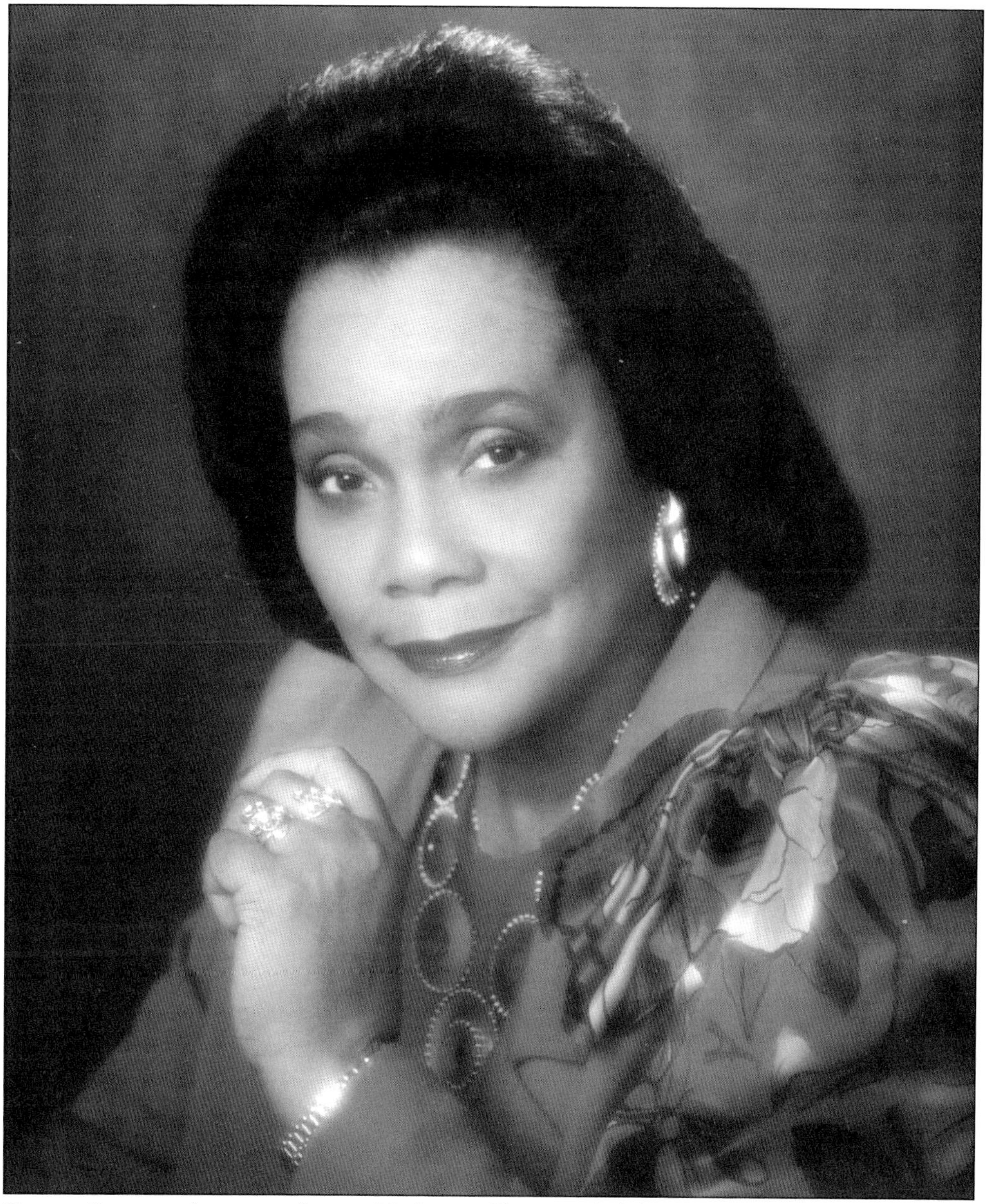

Coretta Scott was born on a farm in Heiberger. She attended the Crossroad School, a one-room school, for some time and then entered Lincoln School in Marion. She was the valedictorian of her high school graduating class in 1945. She excelled in her studies and was very interested in music. She attended Antioch College in Ohio, where she earned a bachelor of arts degree in music and education. She received a scholarship to the New England Conservatory of Music. In Boston, she met Martin Luther King Jr. They were married at her home church in Perry County. After graduating from the conservatory, she and Reverend King moved to Montgomery. She aided her husband in his work with the civil rights movement, and after his death, she continued to serve the cause of justice and human rights. After her death in 2006, she was placed in the Alabama Women's Hall of Fame. (AWHOF.)